⊖LIFEPLAN⊕

THE SUNDAY TIMES
LIFEPLAN

Edited by Richard Girling
Psychology Consultant: John Nicholson

COLLINS
8 GRAFTON STREET, LONDON W1

First published 1987 by
William Collins Sons & Co Ltd
London · Glasgow · Sydney
Auckland · Johannesburg

© Times Newspapers Ltd 1987

First published in *The Sunday Times* in March-June 1987
This expanded edition first published in September 1987
Edited and designed by Sackville Design Group Ltd

British Library Cataloguing in Publication Data

Sunday Times Lifeplan.
1. Self-actualization   2. Self-culture
I. Girling, Richard
158'.1   BF637.S4

ISBN 0 00 412304 2

Designed and produced by Sackville Design Group Ltd
and Bookworm Typesetting Ltd, Manchester
Printed and bound in Great Britain
by Jarrolds, Norwich

CONTENTS

CONTRIBUTORS

Richard Girling is Lifestyle Editor of *The Sunday Times.*

John Nicholson is a psychology lecturer and management consultant who has advised many organizations on change. These include Jaguar Cars, IBM, Gillette and the Mercantile Credit Company. Author of *Men and Women, How Different Are They?,* he is currently writing a book about how companies should deal with their customers.

Ted Polhemus is an anthropologist specializing in studies of body decoration and popular culture. He is author of *Fashion and Anti Fashion, Social Aspects of the Human Body* and *Pop Style.*

Glenn Wilson is a senior lecturer in psychology at the University of London, and co-author with H.J. Eysenck of *The Psychology of Sex.*

Tom McNab is a leading athletics coach and a novelist.

Joy Melville is a freelance writer. She was an assistant editor of *New Society* from 1971 to 1982 and is the author of many books, including *Phobias and Obsessions* (1977), *First Aid in Mental Health* (1980) and *The Tranquilliser Trap* (1984).

Norman Harris is a *Sunday Times* sports journalist with a particular interest in sports and fitness. He is Director of *The Sunday Times.* National Fun Run, Britain's biggest running event, and is a former winner of a national orienteering title.

Madeleine Kingsley is a freelance journalist and book reviewer. She writes for a number of national newspapers and contributes regular features on social style to *Company* magazine. She was text editor of the BBC Domesday project in 1986.

Kevin Durkin is a lecturer in social psychology and author of *Television, Sex Roles and Children.*

Caroline McGhie is property correspondent of *The Sunday Times.*

Norman Lebrecht is a writer on music and the arts who has made a special study of Gustav Mahler and turn-of-century Vienna.

Eric Dymock is motoring correspondent of *The Sunday Times.*

Frederic Raphael is a television playwright, novelist and bibliophile.

Graham Rose is gardening correspondent of *The Sunday Times.*

David Wickers is a freelance journalist, travel writer and author of several travel guides to Britain and France.

Dr Denis Craddock is author of *The BMA Slimmers' Guide.*

Diana Wright is personal finance editor of *The Sunday Times.*

Tony Osman is systems editor of *The Sunday Times.*

Dr Hugh Bethell is a coronary rehabilitation specialist.

Dr Alan Maryon Davis is senior medical adviser of the Health Education Authority.

Additional research by Suzanne O'Farrell.

INTRODUCTION TO LIFEPLAN

Lifeplan offers a challenge and an invitation. The challenge is to take a realistic view of yourself, and of your life, and identify areas in which you might improve. The invitation is to let us guide you towards that improvement.

This does not mean we are addressing ourselves only to people with 'problems'. No life is so perfect that it cannot be made better. The successful executive who thinks he has no time to relax will find as much benefit in this book as, say, someone who wants to overcome claustrophobia or give up smoking.

The core of the Lifeplan programme is its questionnaires. They occur in four broadly-themed groups spread throughout the book, containing more than 300 questions in all. With a number of obvious exceptions (the questions on physical fitness, for example, will not be useful to people with severe physical handicap), they are designed to be applicable to all respondents. Your scores in each category will be meaningless unless you answer *all* the questions. If there is no option which precisely matches your opinion, then you should choose the one that approximates most closely to it.

With very few exceptions, the questionnaires do not reflect matters of right and wrong. Their usefulness is to give you a means of quantifying aspects of your life which you might not have realized were measurable – happiness and anxiety, for example. We do offer guidance, but in the end it is for you alone to judge whether your scores are satisfactory, and whether you should take any steps to improve them.

The questionnaires allow space for two tests to be completed (you can do more by using separate sheets of paper). We recommend you complete Test 1 immediately, then – if you identify any problem areas and resolve to improve them – use the second column of squares to re-test yourself at a later date and check your progress.

All the questionnaires have been prepared and carefully tested by psychologists and other specialists who are leading authorities in their fields. Used sensibly and honestly (you cheat no-one but yourself if you answer falsely) they will enable you to pinpoint with remarkable accuracy the aspects in which you are falling short of your potential, and help you set your own reachable targets for improvement.

You might simply want to look better and feel healthier; come to terms with advancing age; make more creative use of your leisure time; overcome shyness and make more friends; repair a troubled family relationship; feel more secure where you live; learn to stop worrying and sleep more peacefully at night. It is the purpose of the Lifeplan project to demonstrate that all this, and more, is possible. All it takes is realization that change is desirable, coupled with realistic expectations and sensible planning.

THE SIX STAGES OF CHANGE

Anybody can change. You can become more assertive, conquer a phobia, crack a bad habit. All it takes is realization that change is desirable, coupled with realistic expectations and a degree of sensible planning

Self-analysis is one of the most distinctly human activities. It includes being able to recognize that you are not perfect and that you could be different.

Some people are more interested in change than others, but I doubt whether anyone can honestly say he or she has never thought: I'd be much happier/more successful/richer if only... If only what? What are the things about yourself that it makes sense to try to change?

When people analyse the parts of their lives they feel least comfortable with, and try to work out what they are doing wrong, three things stand out. The first is the failure to accept that *other people are different*. They do not always want the same things as you do, and they do not necessarily share your view of the world. Perhaps the most useful change that most of us could make would be to stop using other people simply as points of comparison. Instead, we should be trying to develop the knack of thinking ourselves inside another person's head.

Making the same mistakes?
A second candidate for change derives from the realization that *other people are not telepathic*. The fact that they are different does not mean other people have *nothing* in common with you. They almost certainly share your wish to rub along with the people they have to deal with. But you cannot expect them to change themselves to accommodate you unless you tell them what you would like to happen, and what effect their behaviour is having on you. Most of us could benefit from spending a little more time identifying our own requirements and communicating them to those we work and live with, asking them to respect our legitimate rights without seeking to deny them theirs.

Finally, you can transform your life by realizing that *you do not have to keep on making the same mistakes*. You need to get into the habit of interrogating your problems. When something goes wrong, do not be content with fire-fighting. When the crisis is over, work out why it happened and what needs to be changed to stop it happening again. If you log problems as they occur, you will find that very few are unfamiliar and none insoluble – if approached in the right frame of mind. You should make it your business to see that a problem always pays for the inconvenience it has caused by teaching you something useful.

Wanting to be different is a basic feature of humanity. It is also a personality trait, closely linked with self-esteem and contentment. It is not just a 20th-century whim. Self-betterment is a theme which has run through literature since classical times. It is also a feature of most religions. However, universal education and mass culture – both recent phenomena – have certainly made us more aware of lifestyles different from our own. Social mobility has increased as traditional values and class allegiances have crumbled. At the same time, economic boom conditions have made it possible for everyone to entertain a vision of a different life and a new personality to match it.

Fortunately, human beings are designed to change as their environment changes. This does not mean the process is easy, but it does suggest that we have the mechanisms with which to accomplish it – provided we select the right things to change and choose the right ways of changing them.

There is an element of psychological conservatism in all of us – just as well,

1 The honeymoon 'This is what I always dreamed of – a brilliant new job, fantastic salary, expense account and company car.'

since it is not only cats who are killed by excessive curiosity and the urge to explore. We are conservative not just on our own behalf, but about other people too. Most of us try to cocoon ourselves in a web of cosy familiarity in which the key people in our lives play vital roles. We feel threatened if they rebel against the roles in which we have cast them, which is why partners, friends and colleagues all have to be let into the secret if you are proposing to change yourself.

Concentration and stamina
What sparks off the process? Most of us use only a fraction of our potential. It is this that makes self-improvement and real change more than mere wishful thinking. For example, almost everybody could improve their memory or their ability to get on with other people. Concentration and stamina can be increased too, and most destructive habits can be unlearned, whatever your age – provided you really want to change, and plan the process sensibly.

Before setting a programme of self-change in motion, you must check that it is really *you* that you want to change, rather than some aspect of your lifestyle. You also need to make sure you under-

2 The identity crisis 'What am I doing here? Everything is so different and unfamiliar. Can this really be me?'

3 Incompetence 'The harder I try, the worse it seems to get. I was a fool to think that I could get away with this.'

4 Tough questioning 'Where's the support? Who is supposed to make the decisions? What do you mean, I am?'

5 The trough 'I've really had enough. This is the end. I really can't see how I can go on ... and yet there doesn't seem to be any way out of it. I can't see how I can go back, either.'

6 Back from the dead 'I know the salary and car have to be earned. I must do it, and I can do it. This is the real me.'

stand yourself properly. No two people are the same. We all have different needs, and it is up to each individual to establish his or her own requirements. You should avoid being in a situation where you are merely pandering to someone else's wishes: for example, trying to do a job or function in a relationship by following guidelines designed for someone else – usually your predecessor.

At work, many problems arise from just this situation. Since only you know exactly what is involved in your job, you have to work out how you can do it most effectively and find the workstyle which suits you best. Exactly the same applies to relationships, subject to the proviso that the solution you come up with needs to be acceptable to anyone else involved. It is important not to underestimate yourself or your capacity to change. Do not passively accept other people's estimates. How can they know what you are capable of? You do not know yourself, and they can only guess at your determination to improve.

When people are asked what they would most like to change about themselves, the two most frequent responses are: losing weight and giving up smoking. At first glance, both seem daunting enterprises. Researchers have found that 97 per cent of people who try to lose weight still weigh as much, if not more, a year later. This does not mean that it is impossible to lose weight. Most people who go on a diet do not need to. They are not medically overweight and are often unrealistic in the targets they set themselves. More important, severe dieting is a very inefficient way to lose weight in anything more than the short term. So most dieters have chosen the wrong thing to change, and the wrong way to change it. As for smoking, a recent survey of ex-smokers reveals that only six per cent felt bad-tempered, or put on weight, as a result of giving up tobacco. More than half of those questioned claimed they had been surprised by how easy the process had been.

None of this means that we have *carte blanche* to change ourselves. It is easier to change your behaviour or your attitudes than it is to alter your essential personality. Fortunately, most of us would be perfectly satisfied to alter what we do or how we feel. For example, a very shy person will cheerfully accept this aspect of himself or herself so long

as it does not prevent him or her from chatting easily to a stranger, or reduce the person to abject terror when he or she has to make a speech. As a matter of fact, public speaking is a knack quite easily taught. Very shy people may still feel anxious, but provided they lose their inhibition about speaking, and are able to disguise their anxiety, their essential shyness will no longer hold them back. In time, their anxiety about speaking in public is likely to be substantially reduced, if not eliminated altogether.

You can learn to become less anxious, just as you can learn to relax or to stand up for your rights, by well-tried and painless psychological techniques. Often, what makes change possible is a chance meeting. You discover that someone else in the same boat as yourself has managed to bail out effectively, or even abandon the ship altogether. New techniques can be learned: for example, deep breathing before speaking in public, or a simple formula to be repeated silently which can see you through the first moments of a social encounter you have been dreading. Techniques can be behavioural or to do with the way you think about things. Something as simple as making a list of what actually needs to be done can be a remarkably effective way of liberating a very busy person from the feeling that there is so much to do there is no point in starting to do it.

Focusing on specifics often alleviates free-floating or generalized anxiety. You can also identify aspects of your personality that are currently a source of weakness, and either neutralize them by close examination or turn them into positive virtues by re-directing them constructively. These are the sorts of change we are all capable of making with little outside assistance. Often, simply understanding why you do something gives you the power to control it.

The mechanism of change
The best sort of change is self-generated and self-motivated. Next best is to be given a thorough explanation of why you are being asked to change and a substantial say in how the change is to be accomplished. Experts can help by suggesting techniques, or by sharing their knowledge about how other people have tackled change. Individual change, however, can be initiated only by

individuals.

How is it brought about? There is no simple formula that works for everyone and all types of change. But one technique that many people find effective is to treat change as a three-stage operation.

Stage 1: imagine what life will be like when you have changed.
For example, many overweight people find it difficult to lose weight because they do not anticipate what it will be like to be thinner. At first, all goes well, but halfway through their planned weight reduction programme they panic. The problem is that they suddenly notice people are treating them differently. The realization that they are about to lose the court-jester's licence that goes with being fat, and the discovery that they are being taken seriously, stops them in their tracks. Often it undoes all the good work. Similarly, if you want to give up smoking it is vital to prepare yourself for life without tobacco by imagining yourself without a cigarette in the situations where you smoke most. How will you respond to the astonishment – and scepticism – of the people you are with? Without this preparation, it is easy to convince yourself that change is impossibly difficult.

Stage 2: behave as if you already are the person you would like to be.
This is a role-playing exercise, appropriate to all new situations. Of course, you are not really the person you are pretending to be, but you can get the feel of the part by adopting the trappings. You can see this process in operation when someone gets a new job. They ape the mannerisms of bosses they have had in the past or actors they have seen playing executives on TV. Similarly, young people going to college for the first time find it difficult to know how to behave. So they ask themselves: what do students do differently from schoolchildren? Quick answer: they wear college scarves and (if they are male) shave less often. Hence the disguise adopted by many first-year students to see them through one of life's more difficult *rites de passage*.

Stage 3: make role-playing become a reality.
The transition is usually gradual, a matter of losing self-consciousness and no longer asking whether this person

refusing a cigarette, arguing with the lecturer, or insisting on his rights being respected, is really you. If the process of change is all about selling an idea, then the first customer has to be yourself. Because if *you* do not believe in the new you, what chance have you got of convincing anyone else?

The process of change
What happens when we set out to change ourselves? Most research on the actual course of change is based on people who have been given new jobs, but the six stages identified in this work seem to apply to change generally. The first phase has been called *The Honeymoon*. This is a period of euphoria, when you concentrate on the positive aspects of the change and forget that there may be a price to be paid. It is followed by an *Identity Crisis*, a period of self-doubt when you ask yourself disturbing questions. What was wrong with the old way of doing things? Am I really up to this? Why did no one tell me it was going to be so difficult? Next comes a period of *Incompetence*. This may be a protracted stage and one that can happen alongside the fourth period – *Tough Questioning*. Why is nobody telling me what to do? Where is the support? Who is supposed to be making decisions? What do you mean, I am?

This realization leads to the fifth stage – *The Trough*. There are only two ways out of this. You can give up, and go back to the old way of doing things – which may not be possible if personal change is part of more general changes in an organization, or if you embarked on it with a partner. Or you can press on with renewed determination to succeed. If the change *is* successful, you will reach the sixth stage, known as *Complete Integration*, or sometimes *Back from the Dead*, as it describes the moment when, after assessing your strengths and weaknesses, and taking the necessary remedial action, you become comfortable with your new persona or competent in a new position.

Why do so many attempts to change peter out long before the final stage? The two major enemies of change are ignorance and over-optimism. If you have misjudged yourself, or have not really decided what it is you want to change, then you have very little chance of success. You must be realistic both in what and how you try to change.

Significant change never happens overnight, and progress is rarely smooth. Stopping too soon is one of the major reasons for failure. Another is being deterred by temporary setbacks. You have to anticipate resistance to change, from yourself as well as from other people. Where there is no resistance, there is usually no change.

Given realistic targets and appropriate techniques, success hinges on having the right attitude. You need to be on guard against pessimism and excuses. Perhaps the most common of these is the argument that we cannot really expect to change ourselves because we are simply the products of our genes. It is true that genes do affect personality, but behaviour and attitudes cannot be inherited. What we *do* inherit is a nervous system predisposed to develop in certain directions, depending upon the circumstances in which we lead our lives. Genes may set boundaries beyond which we cannot expand. Sadly, however, most of us never even approach the limits of our potential.

The age of change
Studies of how individuals develop over a lifetime show that many important personality traits remain fluid up to the age of 30. It is, however, impossible to make useful generalizations about when we become our adult selves because changeability is itself an aspect of individual personality. Some people develop in a very consistent fashion, others much less predictably. Most of us find change difficult as well as threatening, and some fail to adapt when it would be better to do so. It is never the case that we *cannot* change, simply that we *do* not.

We know that change is possible because it occurs without any conscious effort on our part, merely with the passage of time. Parents of teenagers who get into trouble can take heart from the fact that although more than half the male population commits a criminal offence during adolescence, only a handful continue to do so beyond their early 20s. And while progress through the adult years is marked by a moderate physical decline, most of us also experience personality change for the better.

Specifically, researchers find that we gain in self-confidence, happiness, security and emotional stability between the ages of 30 and 60. These are only general trends, because individual mis-

fortune can produce a very different picture but they do make the point that deliberately trying to change yourself does not necessarily involve any conflict with nature. It may just be a matter of accelerating or boosting changes that would have occurred anyway.

Despite our capacity to change, few of us realize our potential. There are many reasons for this, but the most important must be lack of motivation. It is a truism that weak-willed people find it most difficult to alter their behaviour. Other people are also a powerful deterrent to self-generated change. The less confident you are, and the more you rely on the approval of your peers and partners, the less likely it is that you will manage to change yourself.

We become more set in our ways as we get older, and of course change requires not just learning but unlearning. So anything that makes us less flexible makes change less probable. However, it is never literally impossible to change your life, or even to plan it better, given sufficient determination and provided that you stick to the following guide:

Checklist for change
● Commit yourself to the idea that change is possible.
● Explore all your reasons for wanting to change.
● Check how well you know yourself.
● Decide exactly what it is that needs to be changed. Is it you or just some aspect of your lifestyle?
● Make sure that you understand and are prepared for the likely consequences of change.
● Make specific resolutions.
● Set yourself a series of modest, short-term goals rather than going for the jackpot from the beginning.
● Make sure the change is something you start on right now. The *mañana* spirit is fatal.
● Avoid negative thinking. Do not talk yourself into failure, and avoid both unrealistic strategies and people who are unlikely to help you to succeed. Do not be discouraged by other people's responses and do not make too much of temporary setbacks.
● Keep a constant check on how well you are doing. Reward yourself for successes – either by allowing yourself an indulgence or, better, by simple self-congratulation. Get other people who are sympathetic to help, too.

YOU

1 Happiness

YES NO YES NO

1 Do you seem to have more than your share of bad luck?

2 Do you often feel depressed when you wake up in the morning?

3 In general, would you say you are satisfied with your life?

4 Do you ever feel 'just miserable' for no good reason?

5 Do you think you are contributing to the world and leading a useful life?

6 Would you agree that it is hardly fair to bring a child into the world the way things look now?

7 Does it seem to you that you get a fair share of the breaks?

8 Do you often suffer from loneliness?

9 Do you see your future as quite bright?

10 Is there at least one person in the world who really loves you?

2 Self-esteem

TRUE FALSE TRUE FALSE

1 I reckon I can do things as well as most people.

2 It's not easy being me.

3 If I had to make a speech, I'd be terrified of making a fool of myself.

4 It's not often that I think of myself as a failure.

5 There are lots of things about myself I'd change if I could.

6 Other people's criticism doesn't often bother me.

7 Other people tend to be better-liked than I am.

8 If I have something to say, I usually go ahead and say it.

9 I rarely feel ashamed of anything I have done.

10 When people say nice things about me, I find it hard to believe they really mean it.

3 Aggressiveness

YES NO YES NO

1 If someone does you a bad turn do you usually manage to ignore it?

2 Do you often grind your teeth consciously or unconsciously?

3 Do you sometimes get so annoyed that you break crockery or throw things around the house?

4 Can you usually manage to be patient, even with fools?

5 Do you like to play at ducking people when you're having a swim?

6 Would you rather say you agree with somebody than start an argument?

7 Have you ever felt you would really like to kill someone?

8 Do you think that if someone is rude to you it is best to let it pass?

9 Do you just laugh when you read the stupid things some politicians say in the newspaper?

10 Do you often make sarcastic remarks about other people?

4 Assertiveness

YES NO YES NO

1 Do you find it difficult to say no to any kind of demand on you?

2 If someone went to the front of the queue would you do something about it?

3 Do you usually put yourself second in family matters?

4 Do you believe that it is necessary to fight for your rights, otherwise you risk losing them altogether?

5 Do you make a point of complaining if you are sold shoddy goods?

6 Do you have great difficulty in leaving situations when you have had enough?

7 Do you find it difficult to get rid of a salesman who is persistent and wasting your time?

8 Do you hesitate about asking a stranger for directions in the street?

9 If you were working on a committee would you tend to take charge of things?

10 If you have been given poor service in a restaurant or hotel, do you always make a fuss?

5 Sensation-seeking

YES NO YES NO

1 Do you get restless if you are not involved in several different activities?

2 Do you dislike sharp and witty people who sometimes cause offence?

3 Do you often have difficulty finishing off what you have started?

4 Have you sometimes spoiled a good relationship by having too much going on at once?

5 Are you nervous about exploring a new city, because there's a chance of getting lost?

6 Do you find that people become boring when you can predict what they're going to say?

7 In a restaurant, are you very unwilling to order dishes you've never had before?

8 Are you turned off by people who say shocking things just to get a reaction?

So who do you think you are? Is your own view of yourself likely to be shared by others? Before you can realistically embark on any programme of change, you have to know as much as possible about the way you are now. You must confront the reality of ideas and attitudes which may have become as rigid as your unused muscles. Are you really as fair-minded and flexible as you suppose? Have you spent enough (or any) time questioning *why* you think the way you do? And do you even know what you *look* like? Are your trousers, your shoes, your hair, telling tales behind your back? And what does your house say about you? And the car you drive? All these things make statements about the person you think you are. Are they legal, decent, truthful and honest? If not, now is the time to own up and take a new look at yourself.

See page 51 for interpretation of your answers

9 Do you like a good deal of variety and change in life?

10 Do you think you'd be nervous about trying scuba-diving?

6 Anxiety

YES · NO · YES · NO

1 Do you blush more often than most people?

2 Would you say you don't often lose sleep over problems?

3 Are you usually a calm person who is not easily upset?

4 As a child, were you more afraid of the dark than most other children?

5 If you've made an awkward social gaffe, do you usually get over it quite soon?

6 Do you find it difficult to sit still without fidgeting?

7 Do you usually manage to keep your cool when things don't go according to plan?

8 Can you relax easily when sitting or lying down?

9 Do you often wake up sweating after having had a nightmare?

10 Have you *ever* felt the need to take tranquillisers (eg Valium)?

7 Adaptability

TRUE · FALSE · TRUE · FALSE

1 I often wish people would be more definite about things.

2 It's not always necessary to make sure that your work is carefully planned.

3 I do sympathise with people who can't make up their minds about what they really believe.

4 I think a well-ordered pattern of life with regular hours suits me best.

5 We'd be lost without words like 'probably', 'approximately' and 'perhaps'.

6 The trouble with many people is that they take things too seriously.

7 People who seem unsure or uncertain about the world make me feel uncomfortable.

8 I try to keep an open mind about things.

9 I always finish what I start.

10 I like to have a place for everything and everything in its place.

8 Do you care what you look like?

YES · NO · YES · NO

1 Do you ever come out of a clothing store with more than you went in for?

2 It is your birthday. For a present, would you prefer to receive something for the home or car rather than clothing or cosmetics?

3 Does it usually take you more than half an hour to get ready to go to a party?

4 Does it make your day if someone compliments you on your appearance?

5 You are going out to dinner. In your wardrobe is a garment which would look perfect for the occasion, but is either a little too warm or not quite warm enough. Do you wear it anyway?

6 Are there any items of clothing for which you enjoy shopping?

7 Are there any items of clothing for which you do not enjoy shopping?

8 Do you consider getting your hair cut a chore rather than a pleasure?

9 Do you buy new clothes only when your old ones wear out?

10 Do you get dressed up only when it is absolutely necessary?

11 Walking past a mirror, are you likely to sneak a glance at yourself?

12 Have you ever got dressed to go out, then changed your mind and put on a completely different outfit?

13 A relative gives you a present of a tie or scarf which you don't like. Do you wear it?

14 On holiday, do you make a point of 'working on your tan'?

15 If you're choosing a new swimsuit, are you guided more by style than by price and practicality?

16 Do you have a 'best side', or a particular expression or posture, which you make a point of displaying in photographs?

17 Do you care what your underwear looks like so long as it's clean?

18 Whether you admit it or not, do you ever enjoy (or enjoy thinking about) going to a fancy dress party in an outfit which leaves all the other guests speechless?

19 Is there any part of your body which you worry about being ugly?

20 If you were to go on a diet, would the reason be health rather than appearance?

CANUTE MEETS THE OSTRICH

Does your blood-pressure rise every time you open a newspaper? Are you tempted to send angry letters to the editor? Are you the only one in step? Would others think of you, perhaps, as just a little too inflexible for your own good?

A politician on the radio has just said that there is only one party for which a good Christian can vote. Next on is an Anglican priest. He believes the policies of that party are diabolically inspired. Both speak calmly, but with absolute certainty. They talk the same language, share at least two important interests, and seem to belong to the same age group and social class. Yet probably there are few listeners curling up in anticipation of a good debate. The interviewer certainly is not. Recognizing the futility of bringing an irresistible force into contact with an immovable object, he swiftly closes the item – wise man. He would be better employed refereeing a fight between a fish and a bicycle.

How we love our convictions – and the whole screen of beliefs, opinions, gut-feelings and prejudices through which we view the world. Psychologists define conservatism (with a small 'c') as anxiety in the face of uncertainty, which is confusing, because the way that psychological conservatism expresses itself is anything but uncertain. The characteristic stance of conservative people is dogmatic and unbending, their tone confident, even hectoring. They are not much interested in facts (Do not try to blind me with science), reasons (I know what I like), or pros and cons (Just tell me: is he one of us?). Ambiguity and complexity are anathema to the conservative mind; 'progress' is a very dirty word indeed. And the response of the dyed-in-the-wool conservative to all three is identical: behave as if they do not exist and keep on doing things the way you always have.

The tendency to fall back on traditional certainties is clearest whenever and wherever the pressure of change is most intensely felt. For example, it was surely no coincidence that California's emergence in the 1970s as the centre of the American high-tech industry was accompanied by a dramatic increase of support in the state for fundamentalist religious and political ideas.

Psychological conservatism colours our interpretation of everything we do or experience. You see it most clearly in people's attitudes. Not just about politics, for there are psychological conservatives at both extremes of the

---

Me Tarzan, you Jane: Is it true?

1 Parents usually maintain stricter control over daughters than they do over sons, and rightly so.

2 For the most part, it is better to be a man than it is to be a woman.

3 Competing and winning are basically masculine traits.

4 Few couples can cope with a situation in which the woman works and the man stays at home to look after house and children.

5 Not many of us would be happy if we were part of a couple in which the man was considerably shorter than the woman.

6 No matter what people say, women really like dominant men.

7 It is more important for a man to be successful in his career than it is for a woman.

8 Most people are more comfortable with a male boss than with a female boss.

9 Men feel uncomfortable with women who are more intelligent than they are.

10 A competitive woman is harder to get along with than a competitive man.

Each statement reflects a traditionalist view of sexual stereotypes. The more of them you agree with, the more conservative your view about the roles of men and women. All these precepts are commonly believed; none of them stands up to scientific testing.

---

political continuum, but also, for example, about sex. Research shows that psychological conservatives are less adventurous in their sex lives. In fact, in all areas of life, conservative people are not interested in novelty or in considering alternatives. They prefer to act according to instinct and habit.

The problem with this is that they become increasingly out of touch with reality and out of place in their changing environment. Neither is it a recipe for long-term prosperity or good health. Being a square peg in a round hole increases their chance of being struck down by a stress-related illness, while denial is one of the least effective ways of coping with any anxiety that arises from the things that are actually happening.

Of course, there are situations in which it is an advantage to present a resolute, uncompromising face to the world. The British Empire was built on such 'masculine' qualities, and even today politicians try to rekindle the Bulldog Spirit when the going gets tough. In everyday life, however, No Deal is rarely an effective negotiating stance. You have a better chance of getting your way if you present yourself as co-operative, sympathetic and responsive to other people's suggestions. These qualities are still generally regarded as 'feminine'. Yet they are at least as effective in men as they are in women. This holds true both in the home, where power is now balanced more evenly between partners than at any other time in history, and at work, where the Great Man style of leadership has been largely superseded by team management.

Masculine and feminine traits
The notion that behaviour can be divided into masculine traits (aggressive, independent, dominant, analytical) and feminine traits (emotional, expressive, nurturant, intuitive) still has widespread support. Until recently, mental health professionals used to urge parents to encourage in their children only those forms of behaviour that come 'naturally' to their sex. This approach to child-rearing appeals to parents of a conservative disposition because it reduces complexity – for parent and child – and tends to produce conservative, traditionally sex-typed adults.

In a society where the roles of the two sexes are defined and distinct, such people flourish. They are applauded for their decisiveness or admired for their tranquillity, depending on their sex. But in today's world they are at a disadvantage, because there is substantial overlap between how men and women are expected to behave. Both must be able to assert themselves when their rights are threatened; either may be called upon to offer consolation to a distraught friend. With one British wife in seven now earning more than her husband, it is hardly surprising that going Dutch is the rule. Domestic bill-sharing, too, is commonplace in households where both partners are working.

Nothing is more restricting in a relationship than too rigid a delineation of who is supposed to do what. If only *you* cook and only *I* know how to fix the boiler, then what happens when one of us has to spend a week away? And the children are not likely to be convinced by Daddy's protest that of course he wants to know how they are getting on at school if Mummy is the only one who ever comes to meet the teacher.

Is tenderness unmanly?

Women have always had the ability to mend fuses, just as men have not needed to develop any new muscles to push prams. It is only *attitudes* that have got to change to make standard practice of behaviour that only a generation ago would have seemed eccentric. For example, nowadays women not only go out to work, but are allowed to 'get on'. At home, men routinely carry out tasks that their fathers would not have dreamt of undertaking, for example, sharing cooking, housework and childcare with their wives.

Even more important, the distinction between the world of home (a woman's domain) and the office world (man's territory) has become blurred. It is bound to be eroded further by advances in telecommunications which will allow more of us to work at home. The rise of the home-office can only increase men's involvement in family life, and with it the need to feel at ease displaying such 'unmanly' qualities as tenderness, tact and unselfishness.

In tomorrow's world, success will belong to people of both sexes who have sufficient emotional versatility to be comfortable with both 'masculine' and 'feminine' behaviour. You can discover

where you stand on this aspect of personality by taking the Emotional Versatility test, in the Lifeplan Scorechart (see page 14). Alternatively, how do you respond to the picture of the woman body-builder holding a baby. Does your gorge rise at the thought of a woman pumping iron?

If you score well on the emotional versatility test, you will be pleased to learn that people like you are less likely to become mentally ill and are better also at handling problems in their relationships. They have more self-confidence than people with a more limited behavioural repertoire, and they tend to be more sensitive and more ambitious – a telling combination.

Confounding the stereotype: Carolyn Cheshire, the former British bodybuilding champion, proves that muscle development – a supposedly 'masculine' trait – in no way conflicts with her femininity.

To be really effective, however, emotional versatility needs to be accompanied by intellectual flexibility – and the courage to rethink your attitudes. In the long term, the point-blank refusal to question your convictions must leave you looking like a cross between an ostrich and King Canute. This posture is not wholly compatible with successful life-planning.

THE CHAIN OF ENVY

No life is so perfect that it cannot gain by example from others; none so desperate that there is nothing in it to be admired. The possessor of an apparently enviable life – David Botschinsky, lay practitioner in homeopathy and herbal therapy – was invited to nominate the person whose lifestyle he most admired. The choice fell on Peter Blake, the painter. Blake himself nominated the master of masked Japanese wrestling, Kendo Nagasaki, who in his turn named entrepreneur Richard Branson. And so the chain continued, until it reached the opera singer Donald McIntyre – who said he would like to be a doctor of holistic medicine. Just like David Botschinsky

THE DOCTOR WHO WANTS TO BE A PAINTER

David Botschinsky, *homeopathic doctor*. My life may seem enviable, but the problem is having to tell people what they might not want to hear. It can be hard. And any doctor has to be very disciplined, very careful. You cannot always tell people in a straightforward way what you think. At the same time you are dealing with human emotions and stress, yet you are unable to express emotion yourself. That can be difficult. It is why many doctors become musicians. I started to learn the piano once, but got no further. And I have written a children's story with my mother. More than anything else I like the idea of being a painter. It is creative, and you can be fully creative in the way you want to be – you do not have to adjust to what others want or expect. You are self-sufficient.

THE PAINTER WHO WANTS TO BE A MASKED WRESTLER

Peter Blake, *painter*. My interest as a painter is humanity, but at the edges of humanity – especially the twilight parts of the entertainment world. I have always loved professional wrestling. Good versus Bad. Black versus White. And especially the mystique of the masked wrestler. Who is he? In my fantasy world I see myself as a Kendo Nagasaki. He is the best and the most professional. He comes out in an extraordinary Kendo outfit, and takes off a black mask to reveal red eyes. It is incredibly intriguing, I do not know how he makes his eyes so red. And although he is English, his head is completely shaven but for a tuft at the back like a horse's mane.

THE WRESTLER WHO WANTS TO BE AN ENTREPRENEUR

Kendo Nagasaki, *masked wrestler*. I do not do anything to make my eyes appear red. It is just a *look*!

Richard Branson is the person I would like to be. His is a remarkable career. He started from a phone box and built an empire. A real entrepreneur in the old sense. He lives his life on the edge, up front, taking risks. He is not one of these faceless magnates who hides behind the frosted windows of a chauffered limousine and travels to the States by Concorde or on the QE2. He goes over in a speedboat or a hot-air balloon. And you feel that he is accessible, that he is a person of the people. If I met him I think I would want to ask him how he manages to keep the pace up, how he finds the energy and incentive to go on.

THE ENTREPRENEUR WHO WANTS TO BE A REPORTER

Richard Branson, *entrepreneur*. It goes back to a yearning for learning. I see life as one long university course. I love the challenge. For instance, when I took my pilot's licence to fly a hot-air balloon I learned about all sorts of new things, including navigation and meteorology – and I realized that for the previous 15 years I had watched the weather on television and never understood it. There would be a question of motivation if I was doing the same thing all the time, and I do wonder about people who carry on making money but lead a dull life.

If I had to do something else I would be a journalist. It has a similar appeal – meeting interesting people and being in areas one does not know about. I would not mind editing, which I once did, but I daresay it would be more interesting to be out and about. It would also improve my writing skills.

THE REPORTER WHO WANTS TO BE A JOCKEY

Jane Chilton, *reporter*. It is true, you do meet a lot of different people, but the great thing about journalism is that each day is totally different. You know roughly what is likely to happen, but it is unpredictable and I like that. I would hate to be in a routine job – I worked in a shop for a bit and although I liked the people I found the job stifling.

In my fantasy world I would like to be a jockey. It is one of the few sports where there is scope for women to be on a par with the men. I was brought up in the country, I love horses, and it would be very pleasant to be working with them every day. I think I would also enjoy the competitive side of it. There is no better feeling than to be on a flat-out gallop across a large open space with the wind in your face.

I know that there is an element of danger involved and I think I would thrive on that. I enjoyed once being on a raft, shooting rapids in North Carolina, where you really did not know what was going to happen next. I should think steeplechase-riding is a bit like that. The nearest I have come to riding in public is when I rode a camel at Darlington Show – as part of an assignment. I was also looking forward to doing a parachute jump, before it was called off. The other thing I would quite like to be is a fighter pilot.

THE JOCKEY WHO WANTS TO BE A NURSERY TEACHER

Lorna Vincent, *National Hunt jockey*. It is very enjoyable. There is a big thrill in going flat out and jumping fences and from the fact that it is dangerous. That is what I thrive on. It is an amazing feeling. You have to be brave to do it. But women will never dominate racing, so I have to make the most of a limited opportunity. If I could not ride I would be a nursery teacher. I already do some work as a nanny – which started when I came to Lambourne, and began living in the nearby village. I love to see very small children doing something for the first time – walking, or reading a word – but older children seem a bit obnoxious. I do not think I could stand a nine-to-five job. I *have* to be with horses, they are my life. I think nursery teaching is the only thing I could do, if I couldn't work with horses.

THE NURSERY TEACHER WHO WANTS TO BE AN INTERIOR DESIGNER

Jean Clegg, *nursery teacher*. We have been running Brompton Bryan Nursery School for 25 years. It is a lovely age group of children, they absorb information like sponges.

My husband and I started the school in the house, then added a large wooden hut. The house is an old vicarage with huge, well-proportioned rooms, which means the furniture can be arranged in various ways. I like a room in which you can move things around. I get a lot of pleasure out of that. One thing I learned early on was that it was a mistake to bring cottage ideas to a house of this size, and I continue to learn through experimentation. I enjoy looking at other people's houses and thinking what I would do if I had a choice. It would be great fun to be an interior designer.

THE INTERIOR DESIGNER WHO WANTS TO BE AN OPERA SINGER

David Roos, *interior designer*. It can also be political! I used to be a stage designer, but now I work as an interior designer, mainly on grand houses. There is a big psychological element. When to step back, when to step forward. And when you do step forward you have to do it with a vengeance. Getting the design up is the creative part – the easy, enjoyable part. Winning the client over and carrying it through is the difficult part.

An opera singer's job is almost the reverse of mine. There may be difficulties in the preparation period, dealing with people and resolving problems. But when you come to the performance the adrenaline focuses your mind and energy. The curtain goes up and there is no way out. You just have to get on with it. And no one can stop you. You cannot say, 'It is not working, let's come back to it tomorrow.' It is over to you and all you can do is give it your *all*. It makes opera singing a most enviable occupation.

THE OPERA SINGER WHO WANTS TO BE A DOCTOR...AND SO BACK TO THE BEGINNING

Donald McIntyre, *operatic bass-baritone.* Being absorbed without any distractions is what I like about my job. But no job can be like that all the time. I suppose I spend about half the job doing what I like. The other half is spent in planes, taxis, hotels.

If I had to be something else I would like to be a doctor of holistic medicine, treating the whole person. I should think you would have to be an all-rounder, a bit like a singer. You have to know about physiology, psychology, diet, and be a priest into the bargain. Assuming that one had built up some sort of reputation, it would be quite satisfying to be able to give people what *you* know was right and wanted to give them, rather than what they expected. Again, a bit like singing. And it might not be what they wanted to hear, of course.

YOUR ATTITUDES

Questions of attitude – social, political and spiritual – form crucial parts of our personalities. When does attitude become prejudice? When does prejudice turn to bigotry?

The legendary Kerryman's reply to the visitor who asked for directions to a local landmark – "Well, sorr, to begin with, I wouldn't start from here" – has special piquancy for people trying to bring about change in their lives. Like the bemused tourist, aspiring Lifeplanners *have* to set off from where they are, just as they can work only on the material they have.

This raises an interesting question: how are we supposed to get a fix on our present position? It obviously involves understanding our basic personality because that affects everything we do. But it also means focusing on the jumble of opinions, prejudices and views which colour our interpretation of everything that other people do – in other words, *our attitudes.*

Attitudes are related to personality. Sometimes they spring directly from it: for example, having an authoritarian personality certainly inclines a person towards prejudiced attitudes. Attitudes also support aspects of personality and reassure us that we understand what sort of people we are. Aggressive people require target groups for their spleen, just as philanthropists need to have their altruism stirred by charity appeals. These elicit the giving behaviour on which their view of themselves rests.

Attitudes can also function as an insurance policy. A positive attitude towards religion, for example, can reduce the fear of death, just as a strong belief in a particular political creed provides a handy guide-book for forming instant opinions.

However, attitudes are less global than personality. For example, the man in the New Yorker cartoon who said that he hated *everyone* regardless of race, creed or colour, was revealing his personality rather than his attitudes. To hold prejudiced attitudes, you need to be more discriminating than this, though not to the point of confining your feelings about people to individual cases. Individuals suffer as a result of other

What are your politics?

Answer true or false.
1 As a nation, we rely too much on the state to bail us out of trouble.
2 Nationalizing industries spreads the nation's wealth evenly among the people.
3 People should be free to choose which type of school they send their children to.
4 The National Health Service is being undermined by people using private health-care plans.
5 The right to strike should be protected at all cost.
6 Maintaining law and order is one of the most important issues facing the country today.
7 You should always support your country.
8 Big businesses care more about profits than they do about people.
9 High earners should pay more taxes.
10 Defence should always be one of the government's highest priorities.

Interpretation

For questions 1, 3, 6, 7 and 10, score two points for each True answer; zero for every False. For questions 2, 4, 5, 8 and 9, score two points for each False answer; zero for every True.

The higher your score, the more Conservative your political attitudes. Sixteen or more makes you a dyed-in-the-wool reactionary; six or less indicates a Socialist of the old school. Floating voters and Alliance supporters will probably fall between the two factions.

How religious are you?

Answer true or false
1 There is no survival of any kind after death.
2 The churches should try to increase their influence on the life of the nation.
3 The universe was created by God.
4 Most religious people are hypocrites.
5 There are no such things as 'supernatural powers'.
6 The great religious leaders were quite different from ordinary beings.
7 The idea of God is an invention of the human mind.
8 Organized religion is our best defence against the evil trends in modern society.
9 Religious beliefs of all kinds are just superstition.
10 The average person cannot live a decent life without religion of some sort.

Interpretation

For questions 2, 3, 6, 8 and 10, score two points for every True answer; zero for each False. For questions 1, 4, 5, 7 and 9, score two points for each False; zero for every True.

A high score (14 or more) indicates that you have a respectful attitude towards religion and attach importance to the spiritual dimension. Low scorers (less than 6) will probably want to substitute the words 'superstition' and 'supernatural' for 'religion' and 'spiritual' in the previous sentence. They will tend to be atheist or agnostic and will have little respect for the churches or any other institutions of organized religion.

people's prejudices, but they do so only because they are seen as belonging to a disliked group – immigrants, the unemployed, 'yuppies' (young upwardly mobile people), or whatever.

If you are in any doubt about the importance of attitudes, ask a couple of football supporters – one from London, the other from Buenos Aires – to give you their views of the first 'goal' Diego Maradona scored against England in last year's World Cup. Alternatively, contrast a devout Roman Catholic's opinion of the Pope's view of contraception with that of a humanist. And if you are uncertain as to the *durability* of attitudes, see if you can persuade any of the four to shift their ground.

What are attitudes?

Attitudes are opinions which are evaluative and emotional. We need them because life is too complicated to manage without them. In an ideal world we would judge every situation on its merits. We would identify and evaluate all the relevant elements, weigh up the pros and cons of each possible course of action and then make and implement rational decisions.

In the real world things are totally different. We have neither the time nor the cognitive apparatus to absorb all the evidence available to our senses, let alone to process it. What we take in is drastically reduced as the result of an unconscious censorship operation. We actually 'best-guess' what we should be concentrating on and prejudge both people and situations on the basis of previous experience and the attitudes we hold.

As a result we tend to see what we expect to see and to filter out events which contradict our expectations or challenge our attitudes. Parents, for example, believe their teenage children are impossibly contrary because they notice only the arguments they have with them. They are hypersensitive to any sign of trouble because this is what the experts have led them to expect. And they are astonished – though often delighted – when a neutral observer points out the vast area of shared opinion which exists between most adolescents and their parents.

What this means is not that we are all bigots – bigotry consists of systematically ignoring evidence which challenges our view of people or situations – but that we would be swamped by the sheer volume of what is going on around us if we did not habitually make prejudgements. Attitudes and stereotypes are part of this process, *prejudice* merely the word used to describe a preliminary evaluation that is unfavourable.

Psychologists tend to treat attitudes as a necessary evil. Necessary they certainly are, but they become harmful only when they operate as blinkers instead of filters.

To prevent this happening, you should do two things. First, you need to appreciate how prejudgements ought to be used. They should be treated like an opening bid at bridge, or the first offer in an industrial negotiation – i.e. as a means of setting a process in motion, rather than something to be engraved on tablets of stone. Second, you must become aware of your own collection of attitudes and prejudices so that you can check that they are not restricting you.

In a business context, you frequently come across otherwise competent sales people whose effectiveness is seriously reduced by their attitudes towards women, black people, young people, people with red hair or beards – the list is endless, since it seems that any characteristic that is perceptible to another person (and some that are discernible only by intuition) can become the basis of their prejudgement of you. It may also dictate the treatment you receive at their hands, via the influence of their attitudes. This is why the salesman who believes that a white male wearing a suit is the only person who could afford to buy an expensive item is an expensive liability to his employer.

How we acquire attitudes
We have attitudes about everything we consider significant. Attitudes are picked up, starting at an early age, from all the important figures under whose influence we fall – parents, teachers, friends, media pundits, cultural idols and the rest. The impact of personal experience should not be underestimated in the formation of attitudes.

However, the fact that our attitudes are acquired rather than inherited does not mean that they are easy to ditch or even to modify. Consider some of your own: how do you respond, say, to people with noticeable accents, posh or regional; or to those who rest their elbows on the table when they eat; or those who never/always wear a tie; or to Volvo (or, alternatively, Capri) drivers, or those who name their children after film stars? Is there any logic in any of this? Intellectually you know there is none, yet to change would be somehow to go against the grain. You soon discover that it is not easy.

In some areas – politics, for example – the question of generation (and hence fashion) is important. In the 1960s, for example, university students from all social backgrounds wanted to save the world through the politics of the left, so much so that it then seemed almost perverse to have anything good to say about capitalism. Today, the attitudes have been reversed. Students from all social backgrounds now have 'yuppiedom' fixed firmly in their sights, and are set on a course of self-advancement. They cannot understand anyone who would enter a polling booth to vote against their personal self-interest.

Some of our most firmly-held attitudes are based on a very shaky knowledge of the facts. Law and order is a good case in point. It comes high on most people's list of issues on which they hold strong views. But how much do you *really* know about crime and criminals? Check with the questionnaire.

Attitudes – consistent or contradictory?
Do our attitudes need to be consistent? Psychologists used to believe that we devoted an enormous amount of intellectual energy to making sure that the various attitudes we held did not contradict each other. In this view we are not so much rational as *rationalizing* creatures, for whom the belief that we are right is more important than actually *being* right.

More recent evidence suggests that we do not after all demand internal consistency and logic. Support for a particular political party often has nothing to do with the policies of that party. For example, research reveals that many Labour supporters have very strong Conservative beliefs and that a surprisingly large number of younger voters say they support the Social Democratic party because they want a strong, authoritarian kind of government. We also seem quite happy to say one thing to one person and the opposite to someone else or even to the same person in a different situation.

Changing our attitudes
The fact that we can hold contradictory attitudes and produce opinions on demand belies the notion that we are slaves to our attitudes. Should you nevertheless find yourself wanting to change an attitude – in yourself or in someone else – there are one or two principles worth bearing in mind.

Assuming the target is intelligent, both sides of the argument must be presented. Psychological studies show that arguments *for* the desired outcome must come first and you should keep in mind what professional persuaders know only too well – that people are always more able to be persuaded when they are in a state of anxiety. Aim, therefore, to make the listener feel anxious about what you might be going to say and then present him or her with a specific action plan.

Suppose, for example, that you want to convince a group of politicians to rethink their attitudes to higher social security benefits. You might begin by pointing out the short-term medical and long-term social consequences of bringing up children on inadequate diets. But you would then have to explain how the extra money could be found without either increasing taxes or making cuts in other programmes that the politicians support.

The person doing the persuading must appear authoritative, trustworthy and likeable. The stronger the initial resistance to the message, the more positive the pitch needs to be. If the circum-

---

How altruistic are you?

When did you last:
1 Give directions to a stranger?
2 Donate money to a charity?
3 Give blood?
4 Stop a lift and hold the door open for a stranger?
5 Allow a neighbour you did not know very well to borrow an object of some value to you?
6 Buy charity greetings cards not because you needed them but because you knew it was a good cause?
7 Offer your seat on a bus or train to a stranger who was standing?
8 Volunteer to look after a neighbour's pets or children without being paid for it?
9 Offer to help a handicapped or elderly stranger across the street?
10 Donate goods or clothes to a charity?

Interpretation
Score two points for each action you have carried out in the last month; score one point for each action you carried out more than a month ago but within the last year; score zero for all other answers.

A score of more than 11 indicates you have an unusually generous attitude; a score of four or less suggests that helping other people does not come high on your list of priorities.

Many of your attitudes may be the result of programming – rather like a robot!

stances are such as to justify really Machiavellian tactics, try to arrange a diversion during the presentation, to make it difficult for counter-arguments to be marshalled.

Attitudes are not changed easily, as many marketing directors have discovered to their cost. They *do* change, though, often simply as a result of time passing. Youthful certainties fade in the face of experience and newly-discovered abilities – perhaps on the golf course or with a user-friendly word-processor – can dispel in a moment attitudes which have lasted for half a century!

Following the Lifeplan formula of clearer understanding, specific goals and a realistic plan of action, you should be able to neutralize even those unhelpful attitudes that cannot be jettisoned.

What do you know about crime?

Answer true or false
1 The elderly run the greatest risk of being attacked.
2 Psychopaths are typically withdrawn and controlled.
3 Most victims of rape know their attackers.
4 Your chances of being robbed are lower than your chances of being admitted to hospital as a mental patient.
5 Most rapists are armed.
6 The typical householder must expect to be burgled every couple of years.
7 Young offenders under 17 in Britain are responsible for less than 20 per cent of all crime.
8 Most crimes are not reported.
9 Anti-shoplifting signs increase the level of shoplifting.
10 Once married, a man is likely to turn his back on crime.

Interpretation
These questions all concern matters of objective fact. The correct answers are: 1 false, 2 false, 3 true, 4 true, 5 false, 6 false 7 false, 8 true, 9 true, 10 both true and false. Getting married reduces criminality among men in their 20s, but those who do carry on offending after marriage actually commit more crimes than before.

If you answered the majority of the questions incorrectly, perhaps there is a case for revising your attitudes on this emotionally-charged subject.

BEING YOUR AGE

For something that happens almost imperceptibly slowly, the process of growing older casts a peculiarly dark pall over the imaginations of the young. But adulthood, middle-age and old-age in their turn are all less wearisome, and more rewarding, than they seem in prospect. All it takes to live in peace with your age is a little flexibility, and the realization that wisdom is as desirable as strength and beauty

There are two very different ways to think about your age. The first is sometimes called the Shakespearean tradition after the Seven Ages of Man speech in *As You Like It*. This suggests that life falls into distinct phases and that adulthood contains a series of predictable crises which occur automatically – not because of what is going on in your life but as the result of a universal life-cycle stretching from cradle to grave. One depressing feature of this alleged cycle is that you must expect things to get worse and life to get harder as you get older.

The second distinct approach to ageing is summed up in the saying, 'You are as old as you feel'. Writing in his 70s, André Gide claimed: 'If I did not keep telling myself my age over and over again, I am sure I should hardly be aware of it.' This attitude suggests that chronological age has little impact on how we feel or what we do. A person may experience crises, but they are caused by events – reaching puberty, losing your job, becoming pregnant, getting divorced, reaching the menopause and so on – not by the fact that the individual happens to have reached a certain age. This theory predicts, for example, that two first-time mothers will have more in common, whatever their ages, than two 30-year-old women, one a new mother and the other still childless.

Does it really make that much difference how old you are? The media certainly seem to think so. The headline, 'Mother, 34, Runs Amok In Supermarket', carries the clear implication that the woman's age somehow explains her behaviour.

There is little doubt that age can be vitally important for people in certain walks of life. Sportsmen are an obvious example. So are actors, which may explain why Shakespeare was so bitter about the ageing process. However, research suggests that most of us are not slaves to our age.

A large study carried out in East Anglia discovered that most people reject the idea that their age has anything to do with what sort of people they are or how they behave. The 550 people interviewed simply did not accept that their essential nature was changing as they got older. As one elderly lady in Colchester put it: 'I still feel the same inside, whatever my face looks like in the mirror.'

'I still feel the same inside, whatever my face looks like in the mirror'

When we are invited to think about it, most of us make a distinction between an outside shell (what we look like), functional performance (what we are capable of doing) and our actual selves. Of course you know how old you are, but it does not obsess you – except perhaps on certain key birthdays. Most of us view age philosophically, as a process which helps us come to terms with ourselves. As we get older we tend to get better at this and increasingly confident that we will be able to deal with other people – one of the great bonuses of advancing years.

There are, however, certain points in life when we are particularly sensitive about the ageing process. Being a psy-chological concern it cannot become a major worry until we start to think psychologically, at about the same time we reach puberty. But the enormous significance of this landmark, coupled with the fact that different children reach it at such different ages, creates an enormous interest in the subject among teenagers. The age of consent and the official school leaving age may convince the developing adolescent that the adult world is age-struck.

Many teenagers have elder brothers or sisters in the Young Adult age bracket (17-25), a period in which concern about age is reinforced by two factors: an unjustified panic about options closing and the fact that this is when people spend more time exclusively with their contemporaries than at any other point in their lives (more life-long friendships are formed during the Young Adult years than at any other time).

By coincidence, teenagers also tend to have parents in their 40s, the decade when we are arguably more conscious of our age than any other. There are two reasons for this. First, whatever we may be feeling, we undeniably start to *look* different. Eyelids are beginning to look wrinkled and eyes to sink. Skin which has been exposed to the elements is becoming thinner and flatter. We also lose strength, and experience a small but perceptible decline in such things as lung capacity, grip and eyesight. Don Marquis described the 40s as 'the time when a man is always thinking that in a week or two he will feel as good as ever'.

How much do we really change as we get older? As a general observation, the old saying '*Si jeunesse savoit, si vieillesse pouvoit*' (If only the young understood, if only the old were capable) still holds good. But the balance between the two provides ground for optimism. For example, the consensus among people in their 40s is that although they regret being past their physical peak this feeling is more than compensated for by increased emotional stability, a feeling of being more at ease and greater satisfaction with life generally.

So far as personality is concerned, the period of young adulthood brings as much change as any other single period of life. At this age, people tend to become more giving and productive, less gregarious, less prone to fantasise and better able to cope with frustrations. As they move into their 30s, women describe themselves as less tolerant, more irritable and less tranquil. All these changes can be traced directly to the presence of young children. At this age, however, only one woman in three regards herself as less physically attractive than she was 10 years earlier. For men, this figure falls to 15 per cent – the same number now consider themselves to have become *more* attractive.

The 30s are also a time when people say they find it easier to accept new ideas, and easier to control their lives, than a decade earlier. What makes this period particularly interesting is that it is when most older people consider that they finally acquired their adult personalities.

Subsequent change is not all for the worse. As Ezra Pound observed: 'One of the pleasures of middle age is to find out that one *was* right and that one was much righter than one knew at say 17 or 23.'

'It is very noticeable that people in their 50s rarely hanker after being young again'

After the turbulence of the 40s, middle age (which most of us now consider begins at about 50) is a period of mixed fortunes. You certainly need to take on board Jung's warning that you cannot live in the afternoon of life according to the programme of the morning. But it is fairly clear what adjustments need to be made. You have to convince yourself that wisdom can be as desirable as strength or beauty. In other words, a change of body image is called for. In personal relationships, you should be preparing for a change of emphasis from sexuality to sociability. You need to broaden your emotional investment too, to include new people, new activities and different roles.

Men in their 50s often re-discover a gift for friendship, both with people younger than themselves (mentor relationships with younger colleagues at work who no longer represent a threat) and with older neighbours, perhaps to get a foretaste of retired life.

Many women get a new lease of life, particularly those actively involved in a career who may either have missed out or have been made to feel guilty while their children were younger. They can

now devote themselves full time to an important concern in their lives.

Perhaps as a result of this, and the looming retirement of their (generally older) husbands, there is often a shift in the balance of power between a couple. Both sexes tend to become happier in their marriages once the children leave home. During the 50s women are much less satisfied with their husbands, although the divorce rate does fall abruptly after 50. By 60, both sexes have become equally pleased with their partners (by this age, most cases of real dissatisfaction will presumably have ended in separation or divorce). It is also noticeable that people in their 50s rarely hanker after being young again.

The final psychological ingredient in the recipe for a happy middle age is mental flexibility – you must try to accept new ideas and new solutions to problems, in the home as well as at work. People in their 50s are less worried about health problems than those 10 years younger. In our research 42 per cent of men and 28 per cent of women in their 50s described their health as excellent compared with 34 per cent and 17 per cent of those in their 40s.

The difference is subjective. In his late 50s, Mr Average can do hard physical work at only 60 per cent of his performance as a 40-year-old. But he and Mrs Average are no longer carrying the awesome burden of emotional and financial responsibility for the generations above and beneath them. As a result, they now feel free to admit to physical weakness. If they become ill, there is no longer the worry that their world will fall apart around them.

The responsibilities that cause this feeling have led to the popular notion of the Mid-Life Crisis. Most researchers have found very little evidence of any such phenomenon in Britain – whatever may be going on in California. Where people do find their 40s a difficult period, it is almost always due to specific events – marriage breakdown or redundancy – rather than age.

Asked to look back on our lives, most of us find it difficult to pinpoint any age as particularly awkward. Other people's ages are a different matter. Caring professionals, for example, are very age-conscious on behalf of their clients. Teachers (like parents) tend to take a gloomy view of adolescence. Statistics, however, tell a different story. Less than a quarter of us look back on adolescence as a time of rebellion. Since only 12 per cent of teenage boys and 7 per cent of girls ever stay out of the house or refuse to do things with the rest of the family, it is simply inaccurate to describe such defiant gestures as 'typically adolescent'.

The most feared age of all comes at the other end of life. According to the popular stereotype old people are unintelligent, unemployable, crazy and asexual. Once again the reality seems to be less fearsome than its anticipation. There is no single recipe for a successful old age but the most useful characteristics seem to be flexibility – again – and acceptance. Changes have to be made and death must be faced up to. How successfully we do this can to some extent be predicted by how well we have managed earlier adjustments: for example, to develop intimate relationships in our 20s or to make the shift towards becoming more generative and giving in our 40s.

So far as present circumstances are concerned, close friendships and good health are probably the most important guarantees of a rewarding old age. Having a confidant reduces an old person's chances of suffering mental illness, while the death rate among both sexes during the year after they are widowed is 10 times higher than among people of the same age whose partners are still alive. Perfect physical health is an even better recipe but sadly one enjoyed by only a tiny fraction of the very old.

Younger people often complain that the old ramble on about the past. But

research shows that the tendency to review the events of your life can be therapeutic because it increases your chance of facing death with equanimity. Some of the strongest fears of death are actually expressed by people in their teens and 20s. Among the old, advancing age seems to produce a greater interest in death but certainly no greater fear. As one old lady put it: 'I feel that from the day you are born your life is mapped out for you. As for death, well, whatever way that comes I cannot stop it, so it does not worry me.'

Age actually has remarkably little impact at any stage in life on how we think of ourselves or on how we view the world. An 80-year-old Colchester woman put it like this: 'I don't put things into blocks. If you just think, "Well, I am only one day older than I was", you do not feel very much different.' And if you live your life on the assumption that you are as old as you feel, the proposition becomes true – for you.

Do you find it frightening to watch the physical process of ageing? It is probably the worst thing about it: the experience of ageing is far less unpleasant. The drawbacks of being less fit, having less strength, and looking less attractive are more than compensated for by psychological gains.

Most of us draw a distinction between the outer shell of our appearance, the kind of physical performance we are capable of, and an inner, essential core.

The reason we expect things to get worse as we get older is that we have been programmed to think that way. Even the most original thinker is shackled by generations of social programming.

There is some truth that we turn into our parents, not just because we share their genes, but because of all those hours when we watched them and learned. They taught us the maxim 'You are as old as you feel', and it is as true today as it ever was. With it we can accept every birthday as a happy one.

SELF-IMAGE

Who do you think you are? Few of us present a simple, consistent face to the world, or even to ourselves. You can check your self-image against other people's perceptions of you – and escape from your own self-doubts

What do you think of yourself? If you are in doubt, make a list of 10 people you know who play a significant part in your life – friends, relatives, colleagues etc. Include your own name. Write each name on a postcard, and arrange the cards in sequence – the least valuable person on the left, then the others in ascending order to the most valuable on the right. The position of your own name will give you a rough indication of how good you feel about yourself.

But what criteria do we use to judge ourselves? How do we know what kind of people we are? The notion of self divides into two parts. There is 'I', a conscious agent who does things, makes decisions and has an identifiable style or sameness. Then there is 'Me', who elicits reactions from other people. These reactions provide the basis of what sort of people we think we are (self-image) and also of how good we feel about ourselves (self-esteem).

It is impossible to overestimate this influence – it starts very early. The origins of self-esteem lie in the message that children receive from their parents. Are they valued for their own sake, or merely for their achievements? Parents who exploit their child's hunger for approval by granting it only when specified targets are met are playing with fire. It is a reliable formula for producing enterprising adults. But such people can be horribly vulnerable when circumstances frustrate their ambitions or place them in a situation where there are no longer mountains to be climbed. Retirement, for example, is particularly demoralizing for those whose sense of self-worth has always rested on *doing* rather than *being*.

Other adults – especially teachers – also have an influence on how children start to think of themselves. The first crude overtures of friendship are even more significant. They mark the beginning of a lifetime habit: using peers and partners as sounding boards to test the validity of our ideas and of our essential worth. Arguably the greatest benefit friends offer is their role in the following argument.

My friend is a fine person. He or she likes me. Therefore I must be a fine person.

It may not be great logic, but it is marvellously comforting. In fact for most of us it is one of the articles of faith on which our belief in ourselves is based.

Developing self-awareness

As children we first become self-aware by comparing ourselves with other people. We observe that we are different from them. Initial perceptions are based on body image: what we look like, how we move, and so on. Later, social and psychological attributes become more important. However, the connection between how we look and how we feel never disappears. We soon learn that other people judge us at least partly on physical appearances. We realize that it is important how tall or strong other children are. Girls look different from boys. And if someone else's skin is a different colour, or if they have a squint or a spectacularly beautiful head of hair, this has an effect on how they are treated – by teachers as well as by other children.

A few years later, adolescent *angst* stems from a desperate need to establish

a coherent picture of what sort of person you are, compounded by the physical awkwardness of puberty and the growth-spurt. It is at this age that you start to think psychologically. And it is not easy to feel good about yourself when you keep knocking things over and growing out of clothes! There is a conflict, too, between wanting to develop a unique personality and the horror of being rejected by the gang.

One way to pin down an indistinct adolescent self-image is to use props and symbols. Casual shirts and brand-names (later, it is done with credit cards and Barbours) are an effective way of saying how you see yourself – and how you would like others to see you. However, that is only part of their function. Uniforms and fashions create in-groups and out-groups, divide those-in-the-know from those who will not or cannot ride with the pack. They may be a trap for the unwary, but following fashion probably helps people with a shaky self-image.

It is actually more accurate to talk about self-images in the plural, since few of us present a simple, consistent face – even to ourselves. We change with the passage of time according to fluctuating circumstances. This is especially marked in the teenage years, but even among adults, chameleonism is commonplace – most visibly in the sitcom caricature of the ruthless businessman who undergoes a daily transformation into besotted father/henpecked husband in the time it takes him to drive between the office and home.

So it is a mistake to see self-image or self-esteem as entirely fixed. There is – or should be – a stable core, but there is also a series of more peripheral self-perceptions, usually based on relationships with other people. To confuse matters further, some of us develop an artificially exaggerated self-regard to compensate for deeper feelings of doubt, or even the suspicion that we are worthless. Others take the opposite route, cultivating a line in self-deprecation that seems to bear no resemblance to other people's assessment of their value.

Different perceptions of you

How closely do other people's views correspond to your view of yourself? To find out, sit down with a group of friends and get everyone to write (or type to disguise their handwriting) a self-descriptive paragraph. You should avoid referring to physical characteristics, or to events that would immediately identify you. Collect the descriptions and redistribute them at random. Then get each person to read out the paragraph he or she has been handed, and see if you can identify its author. The exercise is more difficult than you would imagine. It also offers two different kinds of revelation: it tells you how people you think you know well see themselves, and also how they imagine you see yourself.

The latter may come as an unpleasant surprise. If so, there are three ways of taking it. The first is simply to dismiss your friends' judgement: more fools they for not understanding you better. On the other hand, you could swallow their view hook, line and sinker and accept that you have been deluding yourself – although you have to be very unsure of yourself to find this option attractive.

Have they got you wrong?
The third strategy combines elements of the other two. You may decide that you do not agree with your friends' view of you, but nevertheless find their perception interesting – and useful. Ask yourself, why have they got you wrong? Don't they realize that your habit of dominating the conversation conceals a fear that no one would pay you any attention if you just stood there and listened? Answer, apparently not. This is a reminder that, to other people, there is no 'true' you. They will see you through the filter of their own psyche. They cannot see directly into yours, and to a large extent will regard what you do as what you are. What you say, what you wear, what use you make of any of the other props available, will all contribute to their perception. You can ring the changes from one situation to another, dressing (and acting) respectably for the bank-manager, but presenting a quite different image later in the day.

In other words, you are in a position to influence how other people regard you, which must of course determine how they treat you. Given our starting-point – that a person's self-image is based largely on the way others react to them – it becomes clear that there is no need to be the prisoner of other people's perceptions, or of your own self-doubts.

DRESSING THE TRUTH

Most people say they wear what they do for practical reasons such as comfort or warmth. But the truth is more complex. Like it or not, our clothes are personal statements — and we might not always mean what they say

Those of us who live surrounded by strangers – which in Britain in the 20th century is increasingly the norm – have to develop our skills of non-verbal communication in what the sociologist Irving Goffman has called *The Presentation of Self in Everyday Life*. Just as people have differing abilities in most things, there are obviously experts in this art – the geniuses of the street who can spot a genuine Rolex or a pair of original Levi 501s at 100 yards. But it is also true that *all of us* require basic skills to enable us to read the messages of the walking billboards around us and, just as importantly, to select appropriate items for use in our own personal image management.

These personal advertisements are not necessarily 'legal, decent, honest and truthful'. If asked to check out the claims made by our walking billboards, the Advertising Standards Authority would probably take most of us to court. We dress to impress, to

◄RESPECTABLE OR FLASH►

Respectable is neat, clean, tidy, sensible, presentable. For women it means knee-length skirts, high-necked blouses, flesh-coloured tights, low-heeled shoes, discreet make-up and jewellery. For men: dark suits, plain white shirts, sober ties and lace-up shoes. The message is 'I am a pillar of the community – moral, upright, honest, God-fearing, worthy, honourable and virtuous.'

Flash is lurex, lamé, sequins, satin, fringes, rhinestones, fun-furs, garish-colours, skin-tight trousers, ostentatious jewellery and dyed hair. For women it means micro-minis, hot-pants, cleavage, fishnets, stilettos, feather boas, disco boots, heavy make-up, false eyelashes. For men: exposed chests, medallions, padded crotches. The message is: 'I'm sexy, fun, extrovert and exciting.' Because of our jobs, and fears about what the neighbours might think, most of us have to maintain a respectable image. It is only on special occasions that we let our hair down in public. The alternative is to live out our fantasies in private. Britain leads the world in mail-order lingerie and 'glamourwear'...

The conformist wears 'normal' clothes which do not stand out and attract attention. Anything bought from a chain store will generally do the trick. The message is: 'I'm a team player, one of the boys/girls – average, conventional and middle-of-the-road.' He blends with his surroundings.

The individual wears whatever is unusual, unconventional, personal and distinctive. The message is: 'I'm special, unique, creative, one in a million.' Individuality and conformity are always relative. A punk with a vibrant Mohican hairstyle would stand out in most crowds, but at a Clash concert would blend invisibly into the background. Yet even where conformity is demanded, the urge to stand out need not be totally frustrated. Among business-suited commuters, a pair of bright tartan socks or a floral tie is bound to attract attention. In the animal world, the bird of paradise can be seen a mile off; the chameleon hides from view. But we humans have a choice. Leigh Bowery (shown left in his own clothes and above in Marks and Spencer's) is, however, one of a kind, devoted to the pursuit of individuality.

confuse and to deceive (if only ourselves). Whether we utilize the skills of an undercover cop to blend into our surroundings or those of a pop star to stand out, there is generally a considerable gap between what we project in our appearance and the reality of our situation in life. It may be only when dressing for, say, a job interview or a first date that we are aware of our capacity for visual deceit but we are, in fact, at it all the time.

Dressing for effect is a game we all play. It is also a very serious business – not just in the sense that the clothing and make-up industries are big business (clothing manufacture is Britain's fourth biggest employer) but also because our own personal, economic, social and romantic relationships so often derive from effective image management. Except for the minority of people who live out their lives in small, rural communities where everyone knows everyone else, we inevitably build our relationships upon a foundation of fleeting initial visual encounters. It is a cliché that 'Appearances Matter' but it is nonè the less true. At a party, on the street, in the office, at a disco, when visiting the bank manager, verbal communication is only one aspect of our interaction – and frequently (perhaps surprisingly) it is often the least important source of information. How many important relationships in all of our lives would have never developed to the verbal level if we had not surmounted the initial hurdle of visual compatibility?

The other side of the coin is our ability to interpret the appearances of others in order to avoid unpleasant or even dangerous encounters. On a dark, sparsely populated street the distant glimpse of a 'dodgy looking character' may make us cross to the other side or even retreat in the opposite direction – often without justification. Our prejudices about appearances frequently interfere with our logic. Muggers, pick-pockets, rapists and con-men rarely, in real life, look like the stereotypes we expect. Usually it is only very subtle inconsistencies of style and manner that are the clues we should look out for.

And if the interpretation of appearances is a complex game, the task of projecting to the world our own personal self-advertisements is no less so.

▼HARD OR SOFT▼

Hard is tailored, sharp, angular, severe, minimalist, strong solid colours, bold stripes, pointed collars, black leather, studs and metal trimming. The message is: 'I'm efficient, businesslike, sharp, strong, aggressive, decisive, urban, sophisticated and in control.'

Soft is flowing, unstructured, woolly, casual, pastel shades, muted patterns, fussy, fine fabrics, lace, floral prints, frills, bows, suede, mohair and ribbons. The message is: 'I'm caring, nice, gentle, friendly, relaxed, innocent, passive and rural.'

The choice between projecting a hard or a soft image is a question of strategy. Hard signals 'Don't mess with me', while soft invites others to lower their guard. Beware the wolf in sheep's clothing.

Buying a new wardrobe – or even a pair of socks – is no easy matter, but the choices we make (yes, even in socks) are among our most important decisions. Many people who have abundant skills at anything from computer programming to writing pop songs are held back in life because they have never taken the time to develop their skills of image management. Yet it is not difficult to do so.

The first point to grasp is that items of clothing, make-up, hairstyles, etc. are *symbols*. Just as in learning the vocabulary of a foreign language, one has to learn the meanings of these everyday style symbols. Unfortunately there are no dictionaries of these things (their meanings are too ephemeral for that) but simply by taking note of what other people are 'saying' with what garments, you can become fluent enough to begin to evaluate what you are communicating through your own appearance.

To make this process a little easier,

◄ELITIST OR EGALITARIAN▲

Elitist means expensive fabrics, bespoke tailoring, couture, hand-made shoes, the family jewels, formal dress. The message is: 'I'm a member of an exclusive coterie, not one of the hoi polloi.'

Egalitarian means work clothes, army surplus, practical fabrics, donkey jackets, Dr Martens, overalls, badges. The message is: 'I'm a proud proletarian, salt of the earth, left wing, "Up the workers".'

This is where style meets politics. Through our choice of clothes and accessories we can present ourselves as either a member of the elite or one of the common people. To the Manor Born or EastEnders. Money has nothing to do with it. A second-hand outfit from Hackett (such as the one our model is wearing) can cost a lot less than some of the designer un-chic worn by pop stars like Bob Geldof or Jimmy Somerville of the Communards. Either way, you are wearing your political affiliations on your sleeve. It was in the late 1960s that dressing down caught on in a big way. Suddenly everyone affected a look which suggested they had been born the wrong side of the tracks.

we present here in graphic form some of the things which people frequently attempt to communicate through the medium of their appearance, and invite you to consider how you and people you know fit into this scheme of things. Remember: What we illustrate here are the extremes – most of us fall somewhere in between them on a graduated scale.

The messages which we *think* we are transmitting are often not the ones which others actually read in our appearance. Get someone else to evaluate you. Then, independently evaluate yourself and compare your appearance profiles.

Do not expect the message which you are sending out to correspond too closely to your real life situation. The presentation of self is the act of creating a public fiction about a character who happens to have your name. The only thing that matters is whether the fiction which you project is the one which you want the world to read.

◄ TRADITIONAL
OR TRENDY ▲

Traditional is classic – anything which is timeless and does not date. The message is: 'I'm reliable, steadfast, not fickle.'

Trendy is anything which is in fashion. The message is: 'I'm up-to-the-minute, going places, not stuck in a rut, progressive and in with the in crowd.'

Back in the 1960s, practically everyone had to be a dedicated follower of fashion. Today, more and more of us are happy not just to ignore trends but to flaunt our anti-fashion timelessness. Even some 'fashion' designers have re-

jected flavour-of-the-month trendiness. Jean Muir has publicly stated that she aims to produce timeless garments (like the classic black dress, left) which will still be wearable in 20 or 30 years' time. Generally speaking, it is people with prospects who believe they will benefit from change, who are drawn to fashion. Those who think they have it made prefer to proclaim the desirability of keeping things just as they are.

MIND▶
▼ OR BODY

Mind-dressing means loose-fitting, carelessly assembled, slightly rumpled clothes which do not show much flesh, briefcase bulging with books, spectacles. The message is: I'm an intellectual, concerned with ideas not appearances, reasoning, rational, thoughtful, civilized and introspective.'

Body-dressing means sportswear, dance clothes, muscle T-shirts, body-hugging stretch fabrics, suntan. The message is: 'I'm fit, sensual, instinctual, natural, intuitive.'

Do you prefer to be appreciated for your mind or for your body? The choice is yours. Psychological research has shown that anyone wearing spectacles is presumed to be more intelligent, and a slightly rumpled appearance suggests that your mind is on higher things. Alternatively, if you want people to see you as the physical type but can never find time to work out, an artificial tan, designer sportswear, the right sort of windblown or still-wet-from-the-shower hairstyle and a little care with your posture can do the trick. Getting physical is a state of mind. What you have got is less important than how you package it.

HAIR STYLE

Change your hairstyle and you change the personality you project.
You can express conformity, individuality, tribal membership –
even your attitude to sex

The message of the mane is as clear and straightforward as the style itself. It reached a peak of popularity with the female (and some male) pop stars of the 1960s (Marianne Faithfull and Mary Travers of Peter, Paul and Mary) but has never really been away. Classically it always looks freshly washed and is forever on the move, being played with, tossed about, and, most importantly, hidden behind. The signals are deliberately confusing and conflicting. It is essentially a young look, with a hint of virginity about it (later in life, hair tends to lose its texture and looks good long only when worn 'up'). Yet, on the other hand, hair is also a powerful sexual symbol. The more there is of it, the louder the sexual summons. This style says: take me, I am an independent agent, free from conventional constraints – a child of nature, but with a capacity to surprise.

Its antithesis is the modern neat and casual look in the next picture – short and slick (old days) or made spiky with gel (modern). The key messages here are neatness and professionalism. On men and women alike, it works better on dark hair (Ronald Reagan's variant in its way is just as effective as Elvis Presley's), perhaps because it is important to see how each individual tuft makes its contribution to the overall effect. The look is casual rather than formal, but do not be fooled. Make no mistake: what we have here is a control freak. Nothing is left to chance, and – despite the improbability of wind damage – frequent mirror-glances will be needed to confirm that all is still in order, together with regular applications of gel, mousse or hairspray to keep it casually tousled and spiked in the right places.

The mane (left) stands for freedom, the slicked look for professionalism.

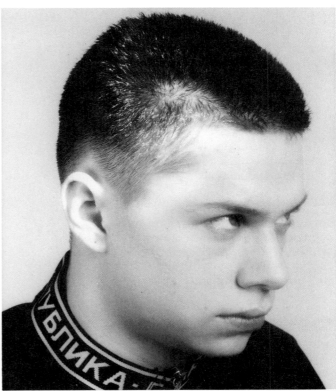

What is the first thing you say when asked to describe a friend who is bald? Yes, it is that important. Baldies try to cheer themselves up by quoting research that indicates a link between hair-loss and virility. But most of them do not really believe it. You can tell by the care with which they adjust the line of their parting to extract the maximum mileage from their diminishing assets (a tendency known as Charltonitis or Scargillism, depending on your age and/or politics). A luxuriant growth indicates youth and vigour; balding signals age and decay –

As long as there is baldness, there will be wigs.

which is why some men go to such lengths to conceal it. Hence the enduring popularity of the wig (shown here) or a subtle, well-fitted toupee.

The news for unreconstructed bald-tops is not all bad, though. There is something disarming about an exposed scalp (echoes of babyhood, perhaps?) that cunning operators learn to exploit. Paradoxically, 'artificial' baldness induced by close shaving is usually seen as sinister.

Direct opposites: the short-top-with-sides (left) and the guardsman-plus-crest.

The short-top-with-sides look dates from the early 1970s and is much favoured by rock stars and footballers. Without long hair, rock stars when viewed from the back of the hall tend to look like children, dwarfed by their instruments and equipment. Long hair is the easiest way to convey sexuality and personality at a distance. But performers do not want to spoil their act by getting hair in their eyes, so the length is all in the back and sides. For them, it is a sensible compromise. On fans it looks like muddled thinking. Copying the great has its compensations, but the price you pay here is a look of sheepish irresolution.

The reverse of this – a look pioneered in London art colleges – is the guardsman severity from the neck up, topped by a crest. It has echoes of punk and, further back, of the crewcut, with the shaven neck suggesting almost Puritan asceticism – the ideal look, perhaps, for the age of Aids. It suggests discipline, too, with its over-the-top exaggeration of an army barber's clipper-work. The look is more striking than flattering – a demand rather than a request for attention. Surprise is the key. Even wearers of the style often look as if they cannot quite believe it.

ANY BODY THERE

Some of us pamper our bodies, some of us torment them. Others simply ignore them. Here eight contrasting individuals consider their fitness

POSTURES NEW

Anthony Sher, 37, actor, says he does not enjoy exercise. But, three years ago, when he was playing the Fool in **King Lear** – and playing him as a cripple – his distorted body position caused an Achilles tendon to snap. 'It made me rethink my use of the body, as a dancer or athlete would.' Now, he goes to a gym at least three times a week for an hour's circuit training. For certain roles he will consider which part of the body will be most stressed and train accordingly. 'In **Richard III**, for example, there is going to be some form of distortion whatever way you play it. And there is always the factor of physical and emotional endurance.'

WHEELS OF POWER

Chris Hallam, 24, wheelchair athlete, like most disabled sportsmen, is intensely competitive. He was a member of the Welsh swimming squad when he suffered a motor-bike accident. He has been back on a motor-bike since then, with some assistance, and he has been skiing. '... instead of travelling at 40mph on my feet, I go at 50mph sitting on the floor.' He has even been piggy-backed up to a high-diving board and launched himself into authentic somersault dives.

Wheelchair racing is attractive. It is 'the nearest thing to running because you're moving at speed'. And the big marathons attract more public attention than the track racing at the Disabled Games. Chris Hallam won the first London Marathon wheelchair race, and has recently brought his time down to

2hr 1 min. Now his ambitions lie in the big American marathons. He regards his training as his work and, supporting himself with social security and disability benefits, he lives in his own house, rather than with his family. Says his 'wheelie' friend John Harris, with admiration: 'Chris is like a horse with blinkers on. All he can see is the winning post.'

FIT FOR THE PART

Jo Mills, 20, model, started weight training two years ago when she was skinny and wanted to gain a stone. In theory, it is a bit like the cup of tea which is warming if you are cold and cooling if you are hot. Jo went along with a friend who wanted to lose a stone. Eventually, Jo gained half a stone but was told by her Greek agent that she was getting too 'muscly' for the swimwear modelling and the 'natural' look which is her speciality. He suggested that she switch the emphasis from weight-training to aerobics.

Now she mixes sessions of weight-training and aerobics. Like many other models, she finds that going from one assignment to another tends to mean a lot of walking, and that this also helps to keep her in trim.

In her work-outs Jo concentrates on keeping buttocks and chest in good shape. Further motivation comes from having a boyfriend who keeps very fit with regular weight-training sessions. But she does not pay any special attention to the food she eats.

She says she trains 'to look good and feel good — obviously I do it mainly for the effect, but I do also enjoy it.' Her one regret is that she cannot continue with the team games like netball, tennis and hockey, which she used to play for her school. Unfortunately, they call for a commitment to evening practice which her busy schedule will not allow. She thinks it is a pity there are not any team sports that can be pursued in adult years on a more casual basis.

But she is resolved to make her exercise a permanent commitment. 'I've seen how people sag when they get to their forties and then try to get themselves back in shape. Surely it's better not to let yourself sag in the first place.'

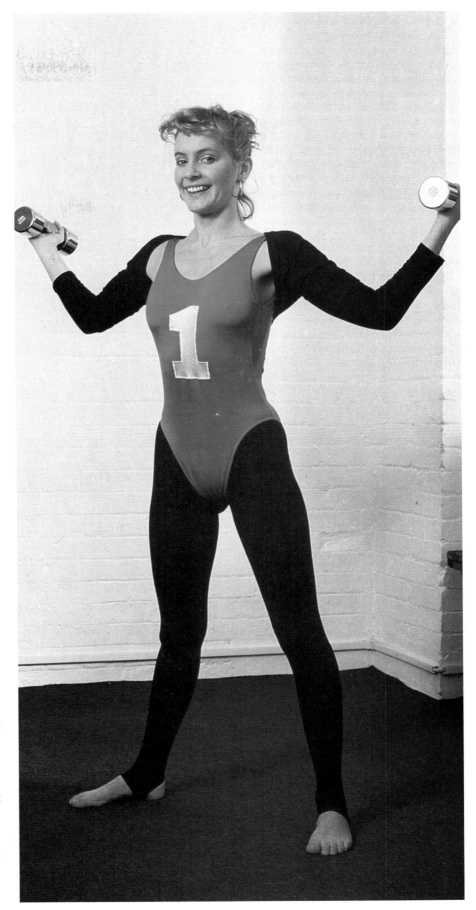

IN THE LONG RUN

Lis Forrester, 47, social worker, volunteered four years ago to join a year-long fitness project. She was an ex-smoker with bronchial problems that she wanted to cure, and she felt she needed some incentive to get fit. When she was told she would have to run, it was a most unattractive prospect. The family thought her running was a joke. She herself thought it was 'pathetic'. After four years she still regards it as hard work. But the psychological impact has compelled her to keep at it; and she has sustained her motivation by joining the London Road Runners Club and running in a Paris half-marathon last summer.

'Some people think I'm obsessive. I'm not. I just know that I need to keep running because it's a way of keeping myself feeling good, more positive, more in control. I am more prepared to do things that I dodged before, like learning to ski. I don't put off doing things so much. I say to myself, "If I can do a half-marathon I can do all these other things." '

THE VOICE OF ASCENT

Chris Gore, 28, professional climber. They do not wear breeches, boots and red socks in Chris Gore's world of climbing, but aerobic tights, and they train like gymnasts. Instead of 26,000ft mountains there are rock faces perhaps 70ft high, which a competition climber like Gore will scale in an intense surge of energy lasting around 10-15 minutes. Equally challenging is the so-called Flash ascent which is made 'on sight' – the climber never having seen it before – and the ascent that is so difficult that every move has to be pre-practised.

There is also the risk element, especially as some competition climbs are done without ropes. 'That adds to the excitement.' But, above all, Chris Gore sees himself as an athlete: 'You work on stamina and power, trying to keep your body weight down and become very powerful for your weight.' And for this type of athlete the reward is the sort of feeling that comes with the completion of a fast Flash ascent: 'Amazing body fatigue coupled with great elation.'

The contestants are judged on technique rather than on time. 'You pit yourself against the rock, against other people, against yourself. But the biggest challenge is to do it in better style than the person who established the route.' And the **ultimate** climb? 'One that's totally sustained, where you're at the limit of your ability and only get up by the skin of your teeth. But you always improve: the route that was beyond you a year ago, you now do easily. You go on looking for the perfect climb.'

THE JOKER IN THE PACK

Jimmy Savile, 60, celebrity, ran for charity in the first London marathon and has now totalled over 50 full marathons.

'I love all the pre-race activity, the sparkle. And the pinnacle of life is when I finish and can relax in the back seat of a Rolls with a big carton of orange juice.'

PINTS AHEAD

'Jocky' Wilson, 37, professional darts player, was as thin as a rake at school in Scotland, where he played football and cricket. But his weight increased and his health suffered when he took up darts. 'Darts is a tiring, professional job with long hours and travelling.' His diet used to consist of little more than vodka and coke. But then he switched to lager, consuming 10 to 12 pints an evening. At best, food was a curry late in the evening. His weight went up to 17 stone and he developed an ulcer. Now he drinks less — four or five bottles of Pils lager — and his weight has dropped to 15 1/2 stone. 'I feel a lot better,' he says. 'I might still be a bit overweight but I'm happy.'

THE OLD MAN OF THE SKY

James Decker, 84, widower, made his first parachute jump last year, in spite of his doctor's concern for his rheumatic knees. 'I've always liked a challenge, and I thought it was just my cup of tea.' He swims — over 30 lengths three times a week — with an occasional dive from the high board, and cycles, too, often 10 to 20 miles. In addition to the yoga which he does to maintain his flexibility he has taken up T'ai Chi dancing. And now he is keen to sponsor himself in some new activity. He would like it to be scuba diving.

YOUR GARDEN STYLE

Gardens can vary from a shrub-packed back yard to a wilderness of nettles or rosebushes. Whatever they look like, they make precise statements about their owners

Your garden says a great deal about your character – and what it says is not always flattering. The most damning evidence of sloth, for example, is that unmitigated and unromantic horror, the urban wilderness – all flesh-ripping bramble and spiteful nettle, as inhospitable to wildlife as it is to man. And those of timid and unsure temperament, needing reassurance through order, betray their unimaginative conventionality by marshalling their plants in strict and widely-spaced lines, producing an effect of devastating tedium.

With just a little thought, however, it is not difficult to plan the kind of garden which will help foster the self-image you would prefer to promote. All works of art to some degree are deceptions and, like any other kind of artist, the gardener will increase his chance of success if he is

quite definite about the message he wants to project, and excludes anything which might obscure it.

The number of character types is almost as broad as the number of gardeners, but it is possible to identify a range of the most common ones:

The plantsman
This is the garden elitist who turns his plot into something of a miniature botanic garden by arranging the plants in their beds according to botanical order. With members of the same family displaying widely diverse characteristics, there is plenty of opportunity for informed discussion with interested visitors.

The health fanatic
Enthusiasts for the wholefood organic creed will make their philosophy plain by filling their gardens with deep and

attractively arranged compost-fed beds of vegetables. The compost heaps and water butt to catch unpolluted rainwater from the roof will be prominent features.

The romantic
Those wishing to proclaim that their spirit is not constrained by mundanities will obscure their boundaries with mystifying screens of foliage. Cascades of leafy and flowering climbers extend the sense of mystery by making it impossible to view the whole of the garden from any single point. Enormous clumps of shrub roses fountain all over the place and perfume the air.

The family man
Here facilities are the key, with a swing and climbing frame mandatory. The barbecue is the obvious focal point, with a plank-walled jacuzzi running it a close second in the Volvo belt. Space and money dictate just how far the image can be extended. A heated swimming pool, with or without canopy, and a handball or badminton net for the lawn are the next priorities. A tennis court is still the ultimate symbol of health and status.

The formal aesthete
The giveaway is a strong architectural design, probably featuring a temple or gazebo in the classical mould set on a ballustraded terrace of symmetrically-cut stone slabs. Stone urns and vases, or the busts of emperors or poets, serve as decoration in a cool, uncluttered and well-proportioned scheme.

The executive
Anyone wanting to establish a reputation for absolute reliability will opt for the conventional villa garden with its obligatory ingredients: well-mown lawn with tightly-clipped edges, deep well-weeded herbaceous borders, sunken formal beds of hybrid tea roses, a swatch of shrubbery and a crazy-paved terrace.

The futurist
Avant garde swingers will consider the whole garden as a giant abstract and asymmetrical sculpture. Typically it will be constructed on several levels and cast in shuttered concrete. Heavy timberwork and unusual water features will provide a soothing contrast to the harsh basic material, as will the foliage and flowers in raised beds.

YOUR HOME STYLE

Houses are silent witnesses to their occupants' self-image. What are your curtains and cushion-covers saying about you? How far do you identify with the facade you live behind?

Exterior deception: the front of an apparently ordinary house does not prepare you for the Victorian parlour within.

Even in choosing a kettle you make a statement about your self-image. You may be a comfort-loving copper-kettle sort of a person; or a forward-looking type with a plastic plug-in jug; or an absolute conformist hooked on stainless steel.

There is no escape. Now that our lives are littered with brightly coloured plastics, chintzes, antiques, Italian chairs that look like exploding insects and repro everything, your choice of home and the way you dress it are unavoidably expensive. Postwar conformity – in which class had a great deal more say, as did cleanliness, tidiness, economy and respectability – has been replaced by style, or at least the search for it.

The trend towards self-expression has implications for the furnishing and building trades, just as much as for the ambitious home-maker.

The mass market in off-the-peg images (trendy young executives at Habitat; country cottage at Laura Ashley; moneyed taste at Osborne & Little) has knocked the old department store and corner curtain-maker into the shadows and forced individuals more than ever before to decide how they want to package themselves.

Buying a brand new home shows that you are a practical type who likes to know that everything will work properly, and the cleanness of the walls and carpets has obvious appeal for perfectionists. Buying an older home shows you to be more of a romantic – more interested in ideas than absolute efficiency.

Your home: a reflection of you?
An established home inevitably exposes a mass of information about its owner.

Mid-eighteenth-century smoking room in Spitalfields

The cushion covers on their own say whether you are obsessively tidy, casual, a lover of beautiful things or visually illiterate. For it is not simply a matter of money. No matter how tight your budget, you are still the architect of your own atmosphere. However, it is wise not to redecorate the moment you move house. Far better simply to live in it for a while to see how it works and which rooms are most important to you. Then the changes will spring naturally from your experience instead of being merely an adopted style that you pick up and put on like a mask.

Every home has to be a compromise between your public and private selves. You may use your dining room for entertaining, but it may also have to do duty as your study, where you need peace and quiet. Colours, too, have their own messages. Pinks, apparently, show you want to look or be looked after; primary colours indicate a bold and positive nature; and black and white shows you want to be taken seriously.

Following fashion has its perils. Some people become time-locked. For example, the craze in the late 1960s to paint the bedroom chocolate brown, or to have one maroon wall, still lingers in some houses like the aroma of old joss sticks. And there are those at the forefront of fashion who fall victim to what Peter Thornton, former Keeper of Furniture at the Victoria and Albert Museum, calls 'the false start'. These risk-takers stylistically isolate themselves because it takes the rest of us at least a decade to get used to any zany new styles.

Interior designers
People of really uncertain dispositions – at least, those with the money to afford them – turn for help to interior designers. Jeremy Eldridge, who runs an Interior Design course at Middlesex Polytechnic, finds it immensely worrying that there are now 'such vast armies of interior designers'. They may be trained in co-ordinating patterns and colours, he says, but they cannot reflect our emotional and cultural needs.

Sir Terence Conran, who has pulled Britain by the nose into the design era, also condemns the trend in which he sees us becoming 'like those awful Americans who employ a decorator, and the decorator becomes the psychiatrist and puts you on the walls'.

His particular *bêtes noires* are the couple who pass through some kind of horrible sea-change in their mid-thirties, switching from Habitat to repro Georgian, what-the-neighbours-think and colour safety. And then there are what he calls the 'sheep', who are the backbone of the swirly carpet market.

'It is so practical because it doesn't show the dirt, is what they say. But the idea of disguising dirt is quite appalling. One reason people buy these excruciating things is so that other people can be sick on them without leaving a mark.'

Another designer with considerable influence is David Davies, who projected the Next image shop interiors and catalogues, and is currently remodelling the Design Council's image in its shop in London's Haymarket.

While visual illiteracy can be forgiven, lack of comfort cannot be. And failing to find the time to make your own decisions, he says, is utterly depressing. It is likely to mean that your creative self has been hijacked by the office or some obsessive hobby. Conran agrees. 'If you cannot make up your mind, you are probably not a very interesting person,' he says.

Conran believes the home has already been neglected, and lays the blame at the door of the average British high street shop, which he says is 'extremely dull, dreary and undesirable'.

He believes, however, that the age of self-expression through the home has arrived at last. People have more leisure time and larger disposable incomes, and stay at home for long periods to watch television or entertain. As a result, they are investing more in interior decorating, and the DIY stores are going from strength to strength.

The marketing men may have us all profiled right down to our shopping habits. Ordinary folk shop at Tesco and Finefare; the aspiring Volvo owners prefer Sainsbury and Safeway; careerists buy their pre-packed *cordon bleu* at Marks and Spencer, and famous faces clash trolleys at Waitrose.

It is Davies's ambition to encourage people to break out of these moulds. 'We can be more eclectic now,' he says. 'My own house (a bleached artisan's dwelling in Battersea) is so tasteful I am sick of it. I want an eclectic bedsit with some exquisite furniture and some revolting furniture.'

At 35 he *is* exactly the right age for a sea-change.

Knowing your place

Your home indelibly carries the thumb-print of your psyche. You can disguise, but not eliminate, your personality – and you say as much about yourself when you open your door as you do when you open your mouth. Which of these styles most closely reflects your own?

1 Intelligentsia You want your home to express the eclecticism of your mind. Books must line the sitting room, preferably floor-to-ceiling and preferably visible from the road. Large shabby armchairs show that you place comfort above style, and there is evidence that you prefer reading to housework. You may be a bit time-locked (Arts and Crafts movement, for example), so the William Morris curtains will be showing their age. Such an easy-going atmosphere *could* show that you feel very comfortable with yourself; but it could equally conceal an extreme intolerance of other people's ways of living.

2 High-tech You are bursting to express yourself but are frustrated by the conservatism of most house-builders. Typically, you may buy an old house but completely smash through the walls to create the space you want. Then you fill it with *objects* rather than books. The 'false start' trap is particularly evident here. Symptoms of it are metal window blinds, ribbed aluminium flooring, lights on stalks and the kind of furniture that visitors would rather talk about and view with interest than sit upon.

3 Stockbroker Tudor You are house-proud, practical and terribly British. You demand all the conveniences of modern life – draughtproof windows, fitted carpets and electronic kitchen – but you want a touch of the vernacular, too. Hence you favour oak beams and leaded windows. Tidiness is more important than originality, however, so you are particularly fond of reproduction furniture, fake fireplaces and polish. Your need for comfort and safety is served by silver-framed family photographs, nests of coffee tables, ruffled curtains and gin and tonic.

4 Fogey You bother about things like conservation, reading the right newspaper and eating enough fresh fruit – and you may be just a little bit snobbish about how 'original' your house must be, no matter how impractical it might be. New Victorians go to extraordinary lengths to find the 'right' fireplaces, baths (with feet), fabrics and colours – even the right Christmas tree decorations. Meanwhile, the New Georgians, Thirties freaks and Country Cottagers are all at it in their own way, too.

5 Suburban Net curtains ensure you get the privacy you need. You are practical, so you like swirly-patterned carpets (they do not show the dirt) and easy-wash furniture covers. Instead of books you display ornaments and mementoes, so valued bits of your life are always within easy reach; and the television set has the prominence and significance of an altar.

6 Sloane Net curtains are clearly infra dig, but you may use some tall plants in their place. Properly-lined curtains from Peter Jones are almost more important than the curtains themselves. People are likely to think of you as snobbish but conventional – you are not fighting battles with your house like the hi-tech enthusiast. Creams and beiges and good taste are what matter to you, though you may pretend to adopt an offhand attitude, deprecatingly describing your home as 'just a tiny town house in Fulham'.

PSYCHOLOGY OF THE CAR

How well do you fit the image of your car? Do you become a different person behind its wheel? What does it say about your life style and your personality?

Some men run up against a psychological impasse when they buy a Porsche. Law-abiding to a fault, one man had been ignored by the police throughout 23 blameless years at the wheel of various saloons. Within a year of buying the Porsche, however, he had been stopped 14 times and lost count of what he could only describe as harassments. He was breathalized twice (negatively) and repeatedly flagged down – 'Just a routine check, sir. Is this your car?'

He was a victim of prejudice at its purest – a truth confirmed by a motorway police patrolman who said: 'People don't buy Porsches to do 70 on the inside lane. They are what we call nine-out-of-ten cars. Nine out of ten of them are speeding. If they're doing less than 80, it's only because they've seen you.

'There are eight-out-of-ten cars, too – Saabs, BMWs mostly. They're nearly all speeders. Old Capris are the ones that won't be taxed or insured. Stop a Mercedes and the driver will threaten to report you.'

Both these views reinforce popular perceptions. That policemen should deal heavy-handedly with drivers of fast cars is hardly surprising. A MORI poll conducted for *Road and Car* magazine (published jointly by *The Sunday Times* and the RAC) revealed that one adult in three thought Lotus drivers more aggressive than others, more likely to have a high self-opinion, and probably young, status-conscious and trendy.

Certain cars do undeniably make statements about their drivers. It is not really any use pretending that people as a rule do not buy Porsches to drive fast – or at least to *pretend* they do for they are not all driven at illegal speeds, as any motorway journey will confirm. There are harassed people who buy a Porsche in middle age to fulfil a lifelong ambition and rarely exceed 60mph.

Their cars are a means of declaring themselves socially. As much as their clothes, house and furniture, the Porsche is a personal display of taste and power. It implies conspicuous leisure. A chauffeur-driven limousine might equally imply wealth, but something else, too – a preoccupation with self that leaves no room for anything so mundane as driving a car; or a preoccupation with business that leaves no time for it.

A sports car is like casual clothing, a respectable saloon like a city suit. It says something about one's style of life and also, in the eyes of the insurance companies, about one's style of driving. Experience tells them that cars badged GT and capable of 120mph tend to have more accidents than GLs capable of 95mph, and they base their insurance groupings accordingly. They see no need to wait for a new model to establish its own track record.

A committee decides the insurance group in advance, and it rarely finds any need to change its mind. The anomaly is that this should penalize a car such as the Lotus, which probably has the best handling, braking and roadholding in the world, and encourages the view that drivers of fast cars will always run closer to the threshold of disaster. Even this is probably too simplistic, though the records suggest MORI may be right and Lotus drivers *are* more aggressive. The insurance industry has been under pressure for years to insure the driver, not the car, but no reliable system for doing this has yet been devised.

Henry Ford was one of the first to underestimate the importance of image in a car. He could never understand why customers stopped buying his Model T and went instead for Chevrolets. He kept the Model T in production years longer than commercial good sense should have dictated, in the belief that all people wanted was transport.

Ford nearly foundered as a result, the Model A being rushed out only just in time to stave off the Chevrolet challenge. Ford never forgot the lesson, but Volkswagen had to relearn it the hard way. The Beetle was kept running far too long before, in the nick of time, the company at last found a new model, the Golf, to nourish the customer's vanity. General Motors (Vauxhall/Opel) found a way of winning buyers with annual model changes – playing on the fear of seeming old-fashioned.

As the MORI poll shows, image advertising has conditioned us to 'match' cars and drivers to such an extent that the truth of the matter is obscured rather than clarified. In image terms it is no longer possible to know which came first, the driver or the car. Are Volvo drivers *really* all middle-aged respectable family people, ordinary and unglamorous? Or is that simply the image they want to project?　　　E.D.

**What do you drive?
Wheels talk.
What are yours saying
about you?**

Cars dominate our lives. It is not just that there are a lot of them about (one for every 20 yards of paved road in Britain), nor that they are the second largest purchase most of us ever make after buying a house. Of course they are useful – the only sure means of being able to go *where* you want *when* you want. However, this is not why we are obsessed with them.

To understand that, you have to swallow a simple, and to many, unpalatable truth: *wheels talk* – to us and about us. The direct message is a potent one. Driving puts real power at your fingertips, not just to get Up, Up and Away, but to maim or kill. There is danger, to yourself as well as others, plus the feeling that you are at the mercy of fate and the incompetence of other road-users.

So driving is stressful, which must explain why ordinary folk sometimes

	VW Golf GTi convertible	Citroen 2CV	Morris Minor Tvllr	Austin Metro	Rover 3500	Volvo 240 Estate	Ford Cortina	Lotus Esprit Turbo
Male	45	18	30	32	57	39	33	52
Female	17	36	18	28	6	11	20	9
With a family	7	22	51	34	20	70	42	2
High self-opinion	18	2	1	5	20	4	4	33
Aggressive	9	2	1	2	5	1	3	22
Young	45	25	8	21	15	8	21	41
Middle-aged	8	20	33	27	31	34	33	6
Old	1	8	20	7	2	3	7	2
Sporty	53	2	1	7	22	2	3	56
Status-conscious	14	3	2	11	31	11	8	32
Home-loving	3	16	30	14	4	23	20	2
Glamorous	14	1	*	3	8	1	2	25
Warm and friendly	5	16	23	11	3	11	15	2
Wealthy	17	1	2	11	34	18	5	46
Ambitious	16	2	2	13	22	9	12	27
Rather conservative	4	12	21	16	15	18	17	7
Careful with money	4	35	27	18	5	11	17	2
Successful	17	2	4	18	39	25	13	34
Ordinary	4	28	32	24	3	14	35	2
Trendy	37	9	2	8	11	2	5	38
Gimmick-loving	16	5	1	4	5	1	3	26
Not well off	4	29	22	3	2	3	10	2
Professional	10	5	6	23	40	27	19	22

Respondents in a MORI poll were asked: Which of these adjectives/phrases would you say best describe the kind of person who would own one of these cars?   *Denotes less than 1 per cent

transform into maniacs behind the wheel. Tiny discourtesies are blown up into mortal insults. Mild-mannered Maestro drivers swerve off their route to track down the Porsche that cut in on them at the lights. Why should being outpaced by a car three times more powerful and four times more expensive than yours cause loss of face? What will the loyal supporter of the domestic motor industry actually *do* if he manages to track down his Teutonic tormentor? Logical questions remain unasked when the siren voice of the motor goddess is whispering in your ear.

There is not much more logic in the message conveyed by the type of car you drive, though it still comes through loud and clear. Today's cars are significantly safer, faster and better built than they were 20 years ago. And from an objective viewpoint there is also much less to choose between the different marques. But who views cars objectively? Not the advertising industry which has responded to the challenge of vanishing brand differentiation by emphasising (and occasionally inventing) particular characteristics in their products to appeal to different people.

The admen classify us according to age, income, sex and personality. As a result of their efforts, male 'Yuppies' buy Volkswagen Golf GTI's, females Renault 5s. The BMW 3 series is acceptable to successful young executives of either sex – even though many objective observers regard the cars as overpriced and indifferently manufactured. Where income fails to match ambition, Citroens or Metros may be acceptable alternatives.

Our perceptions of different cars
Where personality is concerned, we class cars by their country of origin. While British cars are a source of pride if they are Jaguar and an embarrassment if they stir any other memories of what people still think of as BL (no amount of name-changing seems to change this), 'British' (i.e. American-owned and European-manufactured marques like Ford and Vauxhall) cars are judged more on price than image factors. Swedish cars, on the other hand, are seen as rugged, enduring and respectable; Japanese cars represent no-nonsense reliability; German origin indicates reliability plus prestige (and engineering innovation) while cars made behind the Iron Curtain are simply cheap (new cars at second-hand prices). Italian marques are still regarded as drivers' cars which fall to pieces. The French, however, are slowly losing their reputation for building bizarre cars for *Guardian* readers, thanks to the success of the Peugeot 205 and the new generation of Renaults – clever cars for clever people.

Research shows that long, square bonnets are perceived as masculine, though not young. A rounded bonnet is seen as more youthful, while the low-slung look indicates sophistication. But these are glosses. Cars are about function and style, and at the root of all our thinking about them is the association between power and sex. Again, there is not much reason to it. Most people regard Porsche as the ultimate automotive status symbol. The generally functional appearance of the marque is mitigated by some clever 'feminine' touches. The effect is of restrained menace, and the drive is hard but habit-forming. But the origins of the Porsche success story are serendipitous – and distinctly morbid. It was a silver Porsche 550 Spyder, with the legend 'Little Bastard' plastered across its back, in which Fifties screen idol James Dean met his end. The romantic circumstances of the crash made the reputation of man and car alike.

Just as illogical is our habit of giving cars human nicknames (Betsy or Bessie is Britain's favourite). Psychologists speculate that we do this to assert authority over our cars or to charm them into doing what they are told. Under hypnosis, people constantly compare driving to sexual activity. Asked about their ideal car, they describe an impossible hybrid: a fast car that can go anywhere, with all the comfort and sophisticated amenities of the perfect home – speed and power, sex and money. Fantasists to a man and woman, motorists must be the answer to an adman's dream.   J.N.

HOW DID YOU SCORE?

Check your answers from pages 12-13

1 Happiness

For questions 3, 5, 7, 9 and 10, score 2 points for each YES answer, and zero for every NO. For questions 1, 2, 4, 6 and 8, score 2 points for each NO and zero for each YES. The higher your score, the happier you are. A score of 14 or more suggests you are pretty cheerful, optimistic and at peace with the world. That's not to say that life couldn't improve, but it's obviously quite rewarding at present. A score of less than 8 indicates that you are a pessimisitic, rather depressed individual who feels at odds with the world.

2 Self-esteem

For questions 1, 4, 6, 8 and 9, score 2 points for each TRUE answer; zero for every FALSE. For questions 2, 3, 5, 7 and 10, score 2 points for each FALSE and zero for each TRUE. The higher your score, the better the opinion you have of yourself. A score of 14 or more suggests that you are quite confident; not necessarily conceited, but certainly you like yourself. A score of 8 or less suggests that you need a bit of psychological stroking, and are probably ready for some changes.

3 Aggressiveness

For questions 2, 3, 5, 7 and 10, score 2 points for each YES answer, and zero for every NO. For questions 1, 4, 6, 8 and 9, score 2 points for each NO and zero for each YES. The higher your score, the more aggressive you are. A score of 10 or more suggests you are prone to direct or indirect expressions of aggression, e.g. through temper tantrums or violent arguments. You don't take any nonsense from anyone and have a powerful urge to get revenge on anyone who annoys you. A score of 4 or less indicates you have a gentle, even-tempered disposition and are not drawn towards aggression, either physical or verbal.

4 Assertiveness

For questions 2, 4, 5, 9 and 10 score 2 points for each YES answer, and zero for every NO. For questions 1, 3, 6, 7 and 8, score 2 points for each NO and zero for each YES. The higher your score, the more assertive you are. A score of 14 or more suggests that you have what is sometimes called a strong personality. You insist on other people respecting your rights, and may even be seen as 'pushy'. A score of 8 or less indicates that you are submissive, a follower rather than a leader, and easily taken advantage of. Assertiveness can be seen as the acceptable face of aggressiveness. It involves standing up for your legitimate rights, whereas aggression involves trying to deprive other people of their legitimate rights.

5 Sensation-seeking

For questions 1, 3, 4, 6 and 9, score 2 points for each YES answer, and zero for every NO. For questions 2, 5, 7, 8 and 10, score 2 points for each NO and zero for each YES. The higher your score, the stronger your thirst for new experiences and the lower your boredom threshold. A score of 12 or more may make you rather a tiring person to live with. A score of less than 6 indicates a degree of inertia which will not make it easy for you to change yourself.

6 Anxiety

For questions 1, 4, 6, 9 and 10, score 2 points for each YES answer, and zero for every NO. For questions 2, 3, 5, 7 and 8, score 2 points for each NO and zero for each YES. The higher your score, the more anxious you are. A score of 16 or more suggests that you are very anxious, while a score or 8 or less indicates that you are quite well armoured against anxiety.

7 Adaptability

For questions 2, 3, 5, 6 and 8, score 2 points for each TRUE answer and zero for every FALSE. For questions 1, 4, 7, 9 and 10, score 2 points for each FALSE, and zero for each TRUE. The higher your score, the more flexible you are. A score of 14 or more suggests that you are quite well-equipped to handle change, while a score of 6 or less implies a degree of rigidity and a reluctance to consider alterations which may make it difficult for you to change yourself.

8 Do you care what you look like?

Score 1 point for each answer as follows: question 1, YES; 2, NO; 3, YES; 4, YES; 5, YES; 6, YES; 7, NO; 8, NO; 9, NO; 10, NO; 11, YES; 12, YES; 13, NO; 14, YES; 15, YES; 16, YES; 17, YES; 18, YES; 19, YES; 20, NO.

If your score is between 0 and 5, it suggests you really don't give a damn about your appearance. This attitude may be holding you back at work and in your relationships. 6 – 10: you have just about enough concern about your appearance to get by, but you are going through life with a handicap. 11 – 15: you have a healthy concern for your appearance. 16 – 20: some would say you are too concerned about your appearance, that you are vain – but don't worry about it unless it is dominating your life. If it is, try to get it under control.

YOUR LIFE

1 Ambition

YES NO   YES NO

1 Do you set your aspirations low in order to avoid disappointment?

2 Do you try to do things immediately rather than put them off until later?

3 Do days sometimes go by without your having achieved a thing?

4 Do you find it difficult to enjoy a holiday because you would prefer to be at work?

5 Do you find it difficult to concentrate on an important job when people around you are chatting?

6 Are you inclined to be very envious of the success of other people?

7 Do you try to enjoy work from day to day rather than struggling to improve your position?

8 Do you often compare your ability and performance on a job with that of other people?

9 Would you very much enjoy being 'in the public eye'?

10 Do you let an escalator carry you along without walking yourself?

2 Technophobia

TRUE FALSE   TRUE FALSE

1 When I find myself talking to a telephone answering machine, I usually hang up without leaving a message.

2 I can't help laughing at people who believe that microwave ovens are harmful.

3 I think it's wonderful the way tiny speakers in modern hi-fi systems sound just as good as the big old ones.

4 Whenever I read about a new electronic device for use in the home, I can't wait to try it out.

5 I'd hate to have to rely on one of those 'hole-in-the-wall' cash dispensers if I needed money urgently.

6 I can't understand why some people have problems getting the right programme taped on their video cassette recorder.

7 I like these new automatic checkout systems in supermarkets because they reduce the risk of human error.

8 I've given up trying to find out how to transfer calls on the new telephone system they've installed at work.

9 Home computers are all very well for the kids, but no one over 30 has a chance of learning how to work them.

10 Digital watches may suit some people, but I'd never feel easy if I couldn't see the whole watch-face.

3 Financial security

YES NO   YES NO

1 Do you know how much is in your current account?

2 Do you go into the red at the end of every month?

3 Do you pay bank charges?

4 Have you got three or more credit/store cards?

5 With credit cards, do you (tick one):

a Pay off the full amount each month?

b Pay the minimum?

c Pay whatever you can afford?

6 An unexpected tax bill for £2700 lands on your doormat: can you pay it?

7 If you and your partner were both out of a job tomorrow, could you carry on paying your debts indefinitely?

8 If you walked under a bus tomorrow, could your spouse/children/parents/friends cope financially without you?

9 If your spouse walked under a bus tomorrow, would you be able to carry on financially?

10 Have you any idea how you're going to manage when you retire?

11 If you walked under a bus tomorrow and ended up in hospital for the next year and a half, would this mean financial ruin?

12 If your house – and everything in it – was reduced to ashes or rubble, would your insurance policy be sufficient to replace it all?

13 Is your mortgage for more than £40,000?

14 If yes, does it represent more than twice your salary?

15 If not, does it represent more than two and a half times your salary?

16 Are you expecting some major item of expenditure in the next five years – school fees/second home?

17 If yes, are you relying on increases in income to fund it?

18 Do you know what your basic monthly outgoings – rates, heating, lighting, food, travel – add up to on average?

19 Do you have investments in shares, unit trusts, investment bonds?

20 If these investments halved in value, would you have to get a second job to make up the difference?

Lives are blighted by wrong choices, and the blight deepened by the mistaken belief that bad decisions cannot be reversed. Being in the wrong job, for example, is a dark well of misery that can spill into the lives of all who know you, and contribute to problems far beyond the workplace. Failing to make the most of your leisure time, too, is an offence against those who have to live with you: 'workaholism' is a weakness, not a strength as many people mistakenly imagine. This section of Lifeplan is essentially about control and, through control, security. Control your finances and feel safe about your future; control your fears, phobias and addictions and give yourself the space to lead a richer, fuller and more contented life.

See page 83 for interpretation of your answers

4 Household management

YES NO   YES NO

1 Do you usually clean up or tidy up before guests arrive? □□ □□

2 Can you find your dentist's address, your NHS number, a clean flower vase, a safety pin, a sticking plaster, a rubbish bag and a new light bulb in seven minutes? Ready, steady, go! □□ □□

3 Given a choice, do you do most of your household shopping at a supermarket? □□ □□

4 Do you worry about dust under the bed? □□ □□

5 Can you improvise a hot, well-balanced meal for four in less than half an hour? □□ □□

6 Do you give enough attention and affection to close friends and members of your family? □□ □□

7 Is your bathtub spotless? □□ □□

8 Are there some clothes in your wardrobe which you don't wear because they need cleaning, mending or ironing? Or because they don't fit? □□ □□

9 Do you spend enough time each day relaxing and doing your own thing? □□ □□

10 Do you argue about who should do the household chores, or about when they need doing? □□ □□

5 Job satisfaction

TRUE FALSE   TRUE FALSE

1 If I won the pools, I certainly wouldn't carry on working where I am now. □□ □□

2 The most important things that happen to me involve work. □□ □□

3 I try to think of ways of doing my job more effectively. □□ □□

4 When I get into difficulty at work, there's no one I can turn to for help. □□ □□

5 Even if another employer offered me a lot of money, I would not seriously think of changing my present job. □□ □□

6 In all honesty, I couldn't advise a friend to join my company. □□ □□

7 I often find myself looking on a day's work with a sense of a job well done. □□

8 I am too embarrassed to tell people who I work for. □□ □□

9 If I had my life over again, I wouldn't choose to do the job I'm doing. □□ □□

10 It makes me unhappy when my work is not up to its usual standard. □□ □□

6 Drinking

During the last three months:

YES NO   YES NO

1 Have you ever woken up and found yourself unable to remember some of the things you did while drinking the night before? □□ □□

2 Have you found your hands shaking in the morning after drinking the previous evening? □□ □□

3 Has your work suffered in any way because of drinking? □□ □□

4 Has there been any occasion when you felt unable to stop drinking? □□ □□

5 Have you feared that you were becoming dependent on alcohol? □□ □□

6 Have you needed a drink to face certain situations or problems? □□ □□

7 Have you concealed the amount you drink from those close to you? □□ □□

8 Have you had a drink first thing in the morning to steady your nerves or to get rid of a hangover? □□ □□

9 Have you been involved in arguments with your family or friends because of your drinking? □□ □□

10 Have you found yourself neglecting your responsibilities because of drinking? □□ □□

7 Risk-taking

YES NO   YES NO

1 Would you prefer a job involving change, travel and variety even though it was risky and insecure? □□ □□

2 Do your tend to lock up your house carefully at night? □□ □□

3 Do you think young children should have to learn to cross roads by themselves? □□ □□

4 Would you agree that an element of risk adds spice to life? □□ □□

5 Do you think people spend too little time safeguarding their future with savings and insurances? □□ □□

6 Would you always be careful to declare everything at the customs when returning from a trip abroad? □□ □□

7 When you are catching a train, do you often arrive at the last minute? □□ □□

8 Would you make quite sure you had another job to go to before giving up your old one? □□ □□

9 Do you find that you have often crossed a road leaving your more careful companions on the other side? □□ □□

10 Do you avoid 'thrill' rides such as the roller-coaster when at the fair? □□ □□

WORK: PAIN OR PLEASURE?

Does your job give you the satisfaction you need, or are you trapped in a daily routine of frustration? Here you can learn how your pleasure in work can be increased – and four Lifeplan volunteers describe how they have improved their prospects

TO MAKE your job work for you, instead of vice versa, you need to achieve two things. First, you have to manoeuvre yourself into the right job. Then you have to set about doing it in a way which suits you.

Your response to that may be a hollow laugh. You have probably noticed that while jobs these days are in rather short supply, the queue of candidates eager to fill them is as long as ever. What you may not know, however, is that there is almost as much dissatisfaction on the *other* side of the desk, among personnel officers and others who have to fill the vacancies. Their complaint is a *shortage* of good candidates.

With so much pressure to find jobs, and employers so worried about making wrong choices, we obviously should be applying much more thought to the business of matching the right people to the right jobs. Perhaps the best way to start is by asking exactly what it is that people *get* from their work, for job dissatisfaction often seems to result from unrealistic expectations.

You must accept, for example, that no job will be equally enjoyable every day. Indeed, ups and downs are probably an essential part of the pleasure which people who like their work actually derive from it. What are the other ingredients?

Money is certainly important, although it actually features much more prominently on the list of what people dislike about their jobs than it does among the things they say they like. When a job offers other rewards, the financial aspect seems to lose much of its significance.

Alternative sources of gratification include social benefits – most of us meet the majority of our friends through work – and valuable psychological assets, such as a sense of purpose, the pleasure of carrying out a worthwhile task, the feeling of being in control, and the reassurance that comes from someone we respect acknowledging that we have done well. It is the loss of these, at least as much as the financial penalty, which can make the experience of being without work not just unpleasant but a serious threat to psychological and physical health.

Different professions, and different jobs within the same profession, offer different packages of rewards, psychological as well as financial, just as they require different skills. So you have to make sure your job fits your needs as well as your qualifications. To do this you have to know what sort of person you are. For example, a recent study carried out within the civil service suggests that extroverts are happiest in jobs which have the following characteristics: variety, complexity, learning new skills, making decisions, a fast pace, efficient use of time, clear goals, immediate acknowledgement of a job well done and good pay – but also a belief that the job would be worth doing even without pay.

JO POWER, 26, network control administrator, London.
Jo's ambition is simple – or at least simply stated: 'To earn lots of money'. She readily accepted our invitation to attend a Young People at Work residential course run by the Industrial Society at Plas Menai in north Wales, where she and about 20 others were put through a rigorous programme of canoeing, orienteering and abseiling, with lectures and assessments in the evening.
The aim of the course is to demonstrate the importance of good communication and leadership.
Jo responded by returning to work and successfully seeking an interview to discuss promotion. Before the course, she says, she would not have taken such an initiative.

You and your job

WORK, according to Thomas Carlyle, is a grand cure for all the miseries and maladies that ever beset mankind. Lifeplanners, however, need to be a bit more precise than this, because work can also be a major source of unhappiness. To get an idea of your general attitude towards your job, see what you make of the following four sets of statements. Read through each set, indicating which of the three statements (a, b, or c) most closely resembles your way of thinking.

1 a) I often feel uncomfortably tense at work.

b) I see work as a way to fulfil myself.

c) By the end of a holiday, I can't wait to get back to work.

2 a) I blame myself for every small mistake I make at work.

b) You have to accept that everyone makes mistakes occasionally.

c) When there are mistakes, it's usually colleagues who make them.

3 a) I have to work longer hours than other people, just to keep up.

b) I'm always careful to take regular breaks at work.

c) Sometimes I find myself worrying about work I have to do tomorrow before finishing today's tasks.

4 a) I only work because I have to.

b) I work for mental stimulation/ because I enjoy it/because the job I do is useful.

c) The best thing about my job is the power/prestige it gives me.

How did you score?

Your job: if you have ticked mostly 'a' answers, someone is making dangerously high demands on you at work. Is it your boss, is it the organization – or is it you? Whoever it is, you're not coping well. You need to change either the job or the way you do it.

A majority of 'c' answers suggests you may be a workaholic. You're probably doing well at your job, but not so well at getting a healthy balance between your work and the rest of your life. A majority of 'b' answers indicates a healthier balance between a satisfying work-life and sufficiently rewarding interests away from work.

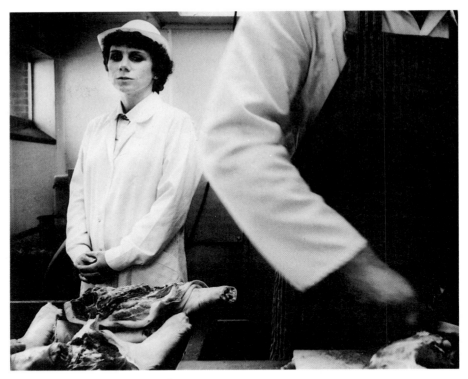

DINAH SIMMONDS, 26, sales director, Coalville, Leics.

Dinah wants to be a managing director – an ambition boosted last month even as she was completing the application form for the Runge Effective Leadership Course. The sales director of her firm, the Belvoir Bacon Company, announced his intention to leave, and she was promoted to succeed him.

The Runge course, organized by the Industrial Society, is for high-fliers – future directors and managers – with the aim of improving manager-worker relations.

One of her tasks on the course was to deliver, in exactly three minutes, a 500-word report on the subject of company communications – a stern task in which her assessor (Mike Judge, Peugeot-Talbot's director of industrial relations and personnel) said she acquitted herself well. She found the course 'tough' but stimulating, and says it gave her the confidence to tackle her new job effectively. She began by exercising her new expertise in communications with a 7am meeting between the night and day shifts, and the dispatch department.

If you want a rough idea of how much of an extrovert you are, answer yes or no to the following six questions:

● Do you prefer action to planning for action?

● Do you usually take the initiative in making new friends?

● Would you call yourself a lively individual?

● Would you be miserable if you were stopped from meeting lots of new people?

● Are you generally quick and sure in your actions?

● Are you happiest when you're involved in a project which calls for rapid action?

The more positive answers you have given, the more extroverted you are, and hence the more important it will be that you should find a job which has at least most of the characteristics listed above.

The penalties for making wrong choices can be severe. 'It was just like being a round peg in a square hole. I felt my face didn't fit.' This is the most common kind of complaint uttered by people leaving their jobs. But there are other sources of job dissatisfaction. Many of us, for example, complain of simple frustration – either with the company we work for or with those working around us. You can test your own present frustration index by using the questionnaire on this page.

Frustration of this kind stems from interference with how you carry out your work. Surprisingly, however, researchers find it to be a comparatively insignificant source of anxiety or job dissatisfaction. Nor is this the only respect in which scientific research contradicts popular wisdom. For example, we hear a lot about the dangers of executive stress. Not only are top business people believed to work too hard for the good of their health, but they are also supposed to be put at risk by having to make too many decisions.

As a matter of fact, stress-linked illnesses are more common on the shop-floor than they are in the boardroom (unfortunately, social class differences in smoking make this finding difficult to interpret). It has also become clear that people with too little to do at work, and not enough say in how they do it, suffer more stress than those with heavy responsibilities.

The most dangerous combination, according to the results of a recent survey of tranquillizer-consumption among electricity workers, is a heavy workload and minimal autonomy. A high degree of responsibility for their own work was found to increase job satisfaction among workers whose goals were money, security, interest or achievement; the only exceptions were those who gave 'the pursuit of happiness' as their main reason for working. Perhaps it was such people that Henry Ford Senior had in mind when he made his cynical assessment of the average American auto worker in the 1920s: 'Above all, he wants a job in which he does not have to think?'

Another very common complaint at work arises from simply not knowing what you are supposed to be doing. It is surprising how difficult even senior executives find it to answer the simple question: What is the main point of what you do? The reason it makes people uneasy is not just that it reminds them they have never been given a formal job description, although this frequently is so. It also forces them to impose priorities on the vast array of small tasks that most jobs consist of. When they do discover exactly what it is they are meant to be doing, they often realize how badly equipped they are to do it.

The answer ought to lie in training, but unfortunately this is an area in

which most British companies fall far short of their foreign competitors (the current expenditure on training in the average UK company is 0.15 per cent of sales turnover, compared with more than 2 per cent in the US, and 3.8 per cent in Japan).

Very often, however, the reason people do not get the training they need is that they do not *ask* for it. Which brings us to another very important aspect of planning for success at work. Success and job satisfaction tend to go to those who see it as their business to make what they want actually happen.

In fact, Getting the Most out of Your Boss ought to be an important topic on every management course. So should Getting the Most out of

WALTER GREGG, 37, sports clothing representative, Prestwick.
Walter, who is the Scottish over-35 squash champion, went on a Tack course on selling techniques. Tack teaches a 'thoughtful' approach to selling, using the image of a mirror to teach students to understand their own personal image and, where necessary, change their attitudes. A week after returning to work, Walter finds he is able to analyse his methods and achievements much more effectively than he could before. His employers, Nike, have asked him to give a report on the course to other members of staff so that they, too, can learn from his experience and improve their technique.

DAWN GIBBS, secretary, London.

Dawn works for the chairman, managing director and financial manager of a small company specializing in oil and gas exploration, so the Monadnock course on Understanding Business Finance was the perfect choice for her. The course tutor used the accounts of established companies to inject 'wit and enthusiasm' into the study of potentially dry subjects such as profit-and-loss accounts, fundamental accounting concepts and policies, and auditors' reports. At the end, she was given a huge workbook, covering all the subjects discussed during the three-day non-residential course. On her return to work, she said, she felt immediate benefit from her greater understanding of the company's financial transactions.

How frustrated are you at work?
Answer true or false:
1 Quite often other people stop me doing my job as well as I could.
2 There aren't too many petty rules at work.
3 There are times at work when things really get my back up.
4 Sometimes at work I am forced to put up with other people's incompetence.
5 I don't often run into obstacles trying to get things done at work.
6 Things hardly ever annoy me at work.
7 In my job, people who get the blame usually deserve it.
8 Often the system at work prevents me doing things the most efficient way.
9 It's not often that I feel thwarted in my efforts to do a good job.
10 There are times when I'd like to be able to tell some people at work what I really think of them.
Interpretation
Frustration: for questions 1,3,4,8 and 10, score 2 points for each True answer; zero for every False. For questions 2,5,6,7 and 9, score two points for each False answer; zero for every True. The higher your score, the more frustration you experience at work. Most people score quite highly on this test. It is only those with a score of 14 or more who need on this evidence to examine their suitability for their job.

Your Colleagues. Both would teach the same elementary lesson of life: when people do not do what you would like them to do there is a sporting chance it is because they did not know what you wanted. As often as not they are quite happy to play ball – so long as you explain what you would like to happen and why. The skills required to do so are no more than a basic ability to communicate – plus the imagination to recognize when it needs to be used.

There are two other common reasons why people fail to make the most of themselves at work. The first concerns response to problems. A major function of many jobs, particularly in the service sector, is to deal with problems as they arise. Sometimes it is the only reason the job exists. And yet, when problems occur, even professional problem-solvers sometimes throw up their hands in horror, as if the occurrence were a personal affront or the act of a malevolent deity, instead of being the entire point of their professional existence.

Clearly an important spin-off from any analysis of your job should be the development of attitudes and expectations which will improve your performance and hence your satisfaction.

Finally, many people find it difficult to get the balance right between commitment to a job and other areas in their lives. Some believe that success at work inevitably threatens family relationships and restricts involvement in all outside activities.

The relationship between professional success and private failure is observed too often to be denied. But it is by no means a necessary one. Indeed, a little intelligent Lifeplanning may be able to reverse the relationship. Why? Because many of the skills required of the top manager are the same as those needed to sustain a successful long-term relationship. Being aware of your own strengths and weaknesses; establishing other people's needs and communicating your own; sharing information; planning the use of time and accepting the need for change; all these are cases in point. And I doubt whether Lifeplanners will need a psychologist to point out that neither obsessional commitment to work nor a hopelessly tangled emotional life constitutes the ideal platform on which to build lasting professional success.

A WOMAN'S WORK IS NEVER DONE

Are you sitting comfortably? Then the chances are you are a man. In spite of the fact that 50 per cent of women have jobs outside the home, they are still responsible for most domestic chores

The stark reality of housework – or, as feminists would prefer, 'the division of labour within the home' – is that it is boring, repetitive, lonely, undervalued, unpaid, unstructured and up in the air. Nobody knows exactly how much we ought to scrub and bake, or how women and men should divide the work.

The subject is no longer considered serious. Gone are the ringing tones of Mrs Beeton, laying down the law on everything from choosing a house to polishing a teaspoon and organizing the bedtime rota. 'Children should go early and at regular times to their beds, and the servants as soon as possible after a reasonable hour.'

Advances in social equality have abolished the domestic servant and made housework classless. The kitchen has been taken over by machines and the fish finger has usurped the boiled pudding. And yet – though it remains vital to our sense of well-being – housework has lost its place in the order of things.

While many of the barriers between men and women have been eroded, one rock remains apparently inviolable against the tide. Despite the fact that nearly 50 per cent of women now *also* have jobs outside the home, the cleaning and administration of the house is still almost universally assumed to be the responsibility of the woman.

The leading academic expert on the subject, Ann Oakley, deputy director of the Thomas Coram Research Unit, believes that housework on its own is an intensely demanding and complex job. 'The housewife', as marketing managers persist in describing her, is not only the family's emotional springboard but also chief, nanny and manual labourer. As an organizer she needs the judgement and concentration of an air traffic controller; while at the ironing board she is shackled to a job as tedious – and as tiring – as anything on an industrial production line.

Oakley's research shows that ironing is the most universally loathed of regular household tasks, followed closely by washing up and cleaning. The crispness of the sheets lends a little more satisfaction to the laundry; and shopping, being spiced with social contacts, is the most popular job – or least disliked – and therefore more frequently done.

The most distressing thing about housework is the fragmented nature of the job; it is *never* finished, and schedules are constantly frustrated and interrupted by children. Pausing in mid-task to ride a bucking bronco is both exhausting and debilitating unless you are in an extremely positive frame of mind. It is no great surprise that a survey of mothers at home with under-fives in Camberwell, South London, found that 50 per cent of them were clinically depressed.

More surprising, perhaps, is that despite the technological revolution, the week has *not* been reduced. Research studies in different countries produce extraordinarily similar results. In 1929, for example, rural housewives in the United States claimed a 64-hour working week. Thirty years later in France it was 67 hours. In Britain in 1950 it was 70 hours, which by 1971 had risen to an incredible 77.

Married men tend to overstate the extent to which they share: 14 per cent claim to share equal responsibility for household chores. Only 7 per cent of married women agreed. (All figures from the Central Statistical Office)

Sexual kitchen stereotypes

Some things, however, seem never to change. When Addis asked women whether they would prefer an extra hour of help from their husbands or a new machine, 52 per cent of them thought the machine would be more use. Twenty per cent of arguments in the home revolved specifically around the subject of men not helping enough.

Renate Olins, Director of the London Marriage Guidance Council, says results like these are a perfect illustration of how women are hoist with their own petards. They are too reluctant to relinquish control of the kitchen and too unwilling to let their partners make 'mistakes' in the process of learning. It is too easy for a woman to convince herself that she is the only person she can rely on, and to slip into the role of martyr. The Perfect Mother and the Perfect Housewife are both fantastical concepts which need to be ruthlessly buried.

Men, too, contribute to the imbalance by allowing themselves to be treated as children. A wife might say, 'My husband is very good. He sometimes cooks the evening meal', in the tone she might use to tell a bedtime story. In any other context it would be sarcastic or condescending.

The treatment of children has its impact, too. While sons are praised for emptying the rubbish bin or changing the batteries in the radio, daughters are expected to help with all the household chores. It sows the seeds of inequality for the future.

Renate Olins says housework features largely in marriage guidance counselling, though wives' complaints about it are often symptomatic of discontent rather than the cause of it. Often the woman herself makes tactical errors. She may resent being left to do the evening washing-up, for instance, but not say anything until her temper snaps and she accuses the man of never helping. He is taken off balance and leaps to his own defence. The matter is unresolved; both of them are angry and they go to bed feeding on the injustice.

The wiser woman is honest from the start. She sees at once that there is a problem to be talked about, and does not shrink from doing so. She does not accuse the man, but points out that they are *both* tired after a day at work, and the washing-up is a joint responsibility they might either take in turns or share.

The Marriage Guidance Council believes most men are well-intentioned, but now that the clear guidelines of the old-fashioned marriage have been replaced by the more vaguely defined equal partnerships of today, the tension is greater simply *because* of the equality. Most women are liberated enough to feel some sense of injustice, but few are prepared to insist that the man should do an equal share. Most women still

thank the man for 'helping', as if he has done them a favour.

Projections show that by the 1990s, 60 per cent of women will be in work. If they continue at the same time to carry the overall responsibility for housework, redecoration and entertaining in the home (dinner parties in the age of Mrs Beeton were unthinkable without servants), then they will be imposing a dangerous strain on their sanity.

Reducing the workload
Why on earth is it that house-workers are not relaxing a little more? One reason is that the figures all include child-care, a never-ending task which no-one has yet found a way of mechanizing. And the labour-saving machines themselves *demand* to be used. For example, we wash our clothes much more than we used to; and recipe book sales are forever climbing as cooks struggle to keep pace with the insatiable appetite of the food processor. The problem is that housework is infinitely expandable, and a spare hour is more likely to be spent 'getting ahead' than relaxing with a book. To avoid chasing your own tail, you have to impose a proper work structure, create leisure hours and *not* feel guilty about it. Otherwise you become obsessional and deceive yourself by calling it being houseproud.

After all, the load *should* have been reduced. Even convenience foods have gone up-market – *coq au vin* for the Volvo owners. (The 'frozen recipe dish' market, as the trade calls it, grew 76 per cent in 1985 and 30 per cent in 1986

and is now a £100m-a-year business.)

A 'Kitchen Report' sponsored by Addis in 1986 made comparisons over a 30-year span and revealed what is probably the most significant trend of all. In 1956 *very* few women worked outside the home. Instead, they reckoned to do a five-day week in the home as part of the marriage contract. It was a clear brief. Monday was washday, with the whites to be boiled and bleached. There were clothes to be knitted, stitched and darned, and hardware to be scrubbed and polished. There were bake days for bread, cakes and pies, and days for bottling and preserving.

Women's magazines then were full of a new thing called the refrigerator, which cost £80 or two months' wages for a manual worker (the equivalent of two weekly pay packets now).

The kitchen revolution of the last 30 years has been both social (it has replaced the sitting-room as the place for women to entertain their friends) and material, with the development of non-iron fabrics, non-stick ovenware and plastics absolutely everywhere – on the floor, in the sink, lining the bins, wrapping the food, even around the baby's bottom. As recently as 1982, only 12 per cent of all nappy changes were made with disposables, but now it has shot up to 50 per cent (though still well behind the rest of Europe's 75 per cent). Calculations made in 1982 showed that disposables then cost £265 per baby per year, compared with £234 for washing and drying old-fashioned towelling nappies.

SPEND AND SAVE

The average British family turns over as much money as a substantial small business. To make the most of what you have, it pays to think ahead

Being financially secure is not the same as being rich. Security means living within your income, being able to cope if something unforeseen happens and, above all, being released from the need to think about money. Most people live on a wing and a prayer as well as ready cash, taking comfort from the thought that the worst does not usually happen. But it is much more reassuring if you have got a paddle or two in reserve, just in case the financial winds are not set fair for ever.

Security starts with knowledge, so if you do not know, at least roughly, how much is in your current account, you have fallen at the first fence. Unauthorized overdrafts cost around 20 per cent

a year, and you also have to pay bank charges – all quite avoidable expenses if you can only learn to get your timing right.

You may wonder what an accumulation of credit cards (question four in the Lifeplan Financial Security questionnaire) has to do with financial security. Many people find it convenient to have a couple of cards, alternating their use to maximize the interest-free credit period they offer. But who needs

more? Credit *is not* credit (a point it is easy to ignore): it is debt. Extremely expensive debt, what is more, with interest rates of around 26 per cent on Access or Visa and 30 per cent or more on store cards. If you find you are not paying off the full amount, and that the sum owed seems to grow steadily larger – and if you find yourself being tempted into yet more schemes offering instant 'credit' – beware! Some people have even lost their homes through credit card debt.

Building financial security

Most of us have to face the occasional large, unwelcome and totally unforeseen bill. And the only way to cope is by building a layer of financial fat into the system, an emergency kitty locked away, preferably in the larder of a building society with penalty-free instant access and good rates of interest. This fat is really the first major step to real financial security.

Hard on its heels comes life assurance. Why is it that the British hate to buy life assurance? The Americans do not. Perhaps an erroneous belief that 'the state will look after me' is at the root of it; or perhaps resentment at paying out money for somebody else's benefit. If

you feel that way you can always opt for an endowment or a whole-life policy with surrender facilities: so (with luck) you can enjoy the proceeds once your children are independent.

Pensions are the next major plank in the security platform. If you know perfectly well that the only way you are going to manage is badly, then there is little that can be done for you, other than to reiterate the financial health warnings. Most people think retirement is going to be cheaper than working; but most come to realize that it can easily become more expensive: more heating, more lighting, more time to spend money.

So do try to persuade yourself that it is worth foregoing some jam today for a bit more bread tomorrow. If you are in

a company pension plan, investigate the possibility of starting an Additional Voluntary Contribution scheme (especially if you are over 40); if you are self-employed, start a pension plan now, or bump up your contributions if you have remained at the same level for the last several years.

Be warned about question number 12 in the questionnaire: if your insurance policy is not for a sufficient sum assured to replace *all* the contents of your house, and to rebuild the place if it is reduced to rubble, then you have been caught out as a cheat. Remember that the insurance company can reduce the amount of any pay-out to you by the proportion by which it calculates you are under-insured.

Mortgages and investments

Legend has it that, not so long ago, the editor of a major national newspaper was horrified to learn that most of his

staff had these major long-term debts called mortgages. These days, of course, anyone without a mortgage is likely to be condemned as a financial unsophisticate. But, like any form of credit, mortgages are debts, and mortgage problems have grown apace in the last few years.

The problem of mortgage arrears has coincided with a great leap in home ownership, extending it further down the social ladder than ever before. Whether that is the reason for the increase is a moot point. It has also coincided with a massive decrease in inflation. For much of the 1970s, people could borrow right up to the hilt and rely on the succeeding wave of inflation to make mincemeat of the original figures. That is not so any more. It is easy enough these days to find a lender who will advance up to three, or even three-and-a-half, times your income, and none dare question young couples about whether or not they intend to have children before lending on the basis of two incomes. Especially now that tax relief plays a fairly minor part in allevi-

ating the burden, it is not necessarily prudent to borrow the maximum available.

Finally, what about your investments? If all your spare money is tied up in National Savings, bank deposits or building societies, you may feel you are opting for the most secure form of investment. Yes and no: the capital value of your cash may be fixed, but by the same token there is no potential for capital growth. The only sensible *long-term* investments are outside the fixed capital arena altogether: they are company shares and property.

The trouble with these, of course, is that the capital value may fluctuate, which means that you should not be relying on that capital increasing (or even remaining stable) to fund your day-to-day financial requirements.

Where the money goes

If you still doubt whether it is worth taking time to plan and protect your financial future, just consider the size of some of your investments. At current rates, extended over 20 years, a couple with two children might typically lay out:

On the home
A £40,000 mortgage, five years into its 25-year term, will cost £103,680 gross (£82,461 net) to repay over the final 20 years.

On the car
Including servicing, tax, garaging, petrol, interest on capital and depreciation, a 2-3 litre car costs £5,935 a year to run: £118,700 over 20 years.

On holidays
At today's prices, the average British family in 20 years will spend £7,600 on British holidays and weekend breaks; £27,432 on holidays abroad.

On schooling
The school careers of two children at private day school will cost their parents a total of around £46,116; at private boarding school, £109,620.

On clothes and shoes
At 1986 prices, the average family would spend £16,557 in 20 years.

HOME SECURITY

Many people are concerned about their safety at home and in the streets. Before you suffer from the hands of a criminal think carefully about the need to take some intelligent precautions

Burglary is one of the most common serious offences dealt with by the police (most people are burgled at least once in their lives), yet it is the least understood and the least often solved.

It is also the crime most likely to provoke an intense emotional response in the victim. For the psychological effects can continue to be felt long after the event.

Most of us are conditioned to believe that the world outside our front doors is inherently hostile, but we still expect our homes to remain sacred. Unlike other Europeans, who socialize publicly, allowing children and babies to perch among the restaurant wine bottles until late into the night, the English hug the privacy of their homes.

The Englishman's castle is not simply the place where he parks his marital bed. It is his major financial investment, a sanctum into which others are allowed to step by invitation only, and where the dining-room dictator of the Sunday sirloin can impose a little order on things around him. Most of us are traumatized by burglary not so much because we mind what has been taken, but because the sanctity of our most private refuge has been violated. Not knowing who has touched the door handles, rummaged through the clothes drawers and peered into the baby's cot sends our imaginations into overdrive. Images of masked men, childhood fears of darkness and helplessness, a feeling that we have been watched and exposed, dance agonizingly through our minds. It is no wonder that in the 17th and 18th centuries burglary carried the death penalty.

In spite of the unpleasantness of the crime, however, it seems we are simply not doing enough to protect ourselves. Our feelings of helplessness are largely avoidable and self-imposed. Insurance companies' figures show that burglary in England, Scotland and Wales has boomed throughout the 1970s and 1980s. In 1973, the total payout in compensation for property stolen was £7,000,000. By 1979 it was up to £49,000,000. Last year the ever-steepening line on the graph climbed all the way to £249,900,000.

Over the same period the proportion of households making a positive effort to improve home security rose from eight per cent to 35 per cent, and those with burglar alarms from five to eight per cent.

Know the burglar's mind

Researchers have found that up to 20 per cent of Londoners feel insecure inside their homes. As the Home Office points out, *feeling* unsafe is sometimes as unsettling as experiencing the crime itself – the impact on your life is exactly the same.

While locks, grilles, doorchains and alarms are worth every penny you spend on them if they buy peace of mind, it is also worth taking a more imaginative look at ways of improving home security in the future. Until 1980, for example, there was little published work on the implications of burglary in building design. However, what is the point of designing new homes in which people are afraid to live?

Now at last there is a British Standard on the security of new homes and estate layout, and the National House-building Council has produced a useful booklet for the guidance of its members. The growing market in retirement homes has been one of the most potent factors in concentrating the builders' minds.

Of course, you cannot design effective defences against burglary unless you know something of the burglar's mind. Some of the most helpful evidence in this respect was produced by Mike Maguire, of Oxford University's Centre for Criminological Research, in his book *Burglary in a Dwelling*, published in 1982. In his analysis of 6,000 cases from police records, interviews with 300 victims and 40 persistent offenders, he found, for example, that the *position* of your house is almost as important as how opulent it looks.

If you live just off a busy main road, or have a footpath running alongside, or have a corner property, then you are particularly vulnerable. Detached houses standing in their own gardens are especially burglar friendly. It is often a positive *advantage* to surrender a little privacy and be overlooked by your neighbours, since this provides a surround of what is called good 'defensible space'.

A Home Office study similarly categorizes types of houses according to risk. The small detached house comes top, with a one in 20 annual chance of being burgled, followed by the large detached at one in 42. The bungalow comes next, at one in 68; then semis and short terraces at one in 209, and long terraces at one in 504.

Who burgles whom? It has been shown that most burglars stay within a two-mile radius of their own homes, although more professional operators may travel further afield to selected high income areas. And what sort of person is the burglar likely to be? He will probably be quite young (in 1978, 49 per cent of all people convicted or cautioned for burglary offences were under 17); he is almost certain to come from a disadvantaged background and may well have drunk a couple of pints of beer to improve his courage; but he is unlikely to carry a firearm. In 1980, fewer than 70 reported cases of burglary in Britain involved firearms.

The burglar's busiest time is during the week. Two-thirds of all burglaries take place during the day, with a peak in mid-afternoon. He usually works

late on Fridays and Saturdays only, and likes to take Sundays off. He likes your house to be empty (three-quarters of burgled houses are empty at the time of entry), and he is not usually skilled at breaking in. A quarter of burglars enter through open windows or doors, and more than half force their way in at the back of the house rather than the front.

Are you properly insured?
The intruder is likely to feel a thrill but to be very frightened while he is inside your house – at least as frightened as you would be to find him there. The last thing he wants is to be interrupted – hence the initial telephone call or ring at the doorbell to make sure you are out. Almost always he will be deterred by good locks. The Home Office estimates that in 1986 alone 200,000 attempted burglaries were foiled in this way.

Door locks ideally should be morticed – set right into the woodwork of the door – and the hinges, too, should be strong enough to resist crude assault. Costs vary widely, but you should be able to get a comprehensive package of locks, bolts, chains and a door viewer, sufficient for two ground-floor doors in an ordinary family house, for a very reasonable price; and a package of window locks, sufficient for eight windows, costs only fractionally more. Steel cladding a door, however, is quite expensive.

American researchers believe you are six times less likely to be burgled if you have an alarm. Until recently in this country, burglar alarms have been regarded as expensive or even luxury items. They can be very costly, and the industry has been riddled with cowboys. Now, however, the question of choosing the right company has been made much easier: you should make sure that your installer is a member of the National Supervisory Council for Intruder Alarms (NSCIA). Prices, too, have improved: for instance, Telecom Security (now primarily owned by British Telecom) has a complete burglar, fire and personal protection system which can be installed at reasonable cost and rented thereafter on a monthly basis. The advantage with this system is that it is wired up to a 24-hour manned monitoring centre. Technological advances mean that the alarms of the future will be largely wire-free and consequently easier to instal.

Other sensible precautions are to mark all your valuables with ultra-violet or security marker pens (burglars hate marked goods); and start or join a Neighbourhood Watch Scheme.

Most important of all, make sure that you are not under-insured. As a general rule of thumb, the contents of a two-bedroom flat should usually be insured for not less than £10,000, a three-bedroom semi for £13,000 and a four-bedroom house for £15,000. Most reputable insurance companies offer reductions on their policies of up to 10 per cent if you have the right locks or belong to a Neighbourhood Watch Scheme.

Information on crime prevention in the home is available from your local police crime prevention officer, who will also advise on the establishment of Neighbourhood Watch Schemes.

Initially you will need the co-operation of your neighbours, and the agreement of one member to act as area co-ordinator.

SELF DEFENCE

It is hard to find the courage in an emergency to defend ourselves, our property – and those we love. Confidence and determination go a long way to help

At the age of 84 my grandmother – a frail yet formidable widow – woke in the night to see the silhouette of a youth slipping across the window-sill into her darkened bedroom.

Her chins trembling with rage, she reached for her walking stick, thumped the carpet and demanded an explanation: '*What* do you think you are doing, young man?' The intending burglar fled as if he feared for his life.

A naturally assertive woman, she had felt anger rather than fear and thereby won the psychological skirmish – although I should say that this happened long enough ago for her not to have seen the endless reports of abductions, muggings and sexual assaults that make us all, young and old alike, more wary, afraid and fatalistic every day.

Almost more than anything else it is our *confidence* that is under assault, particularly among the elderly and those who live and work in inner cities. Among those striving hard to give that confidence a boost is Diana Lamplugh, the diminutive but fiercely energetic mother of Suzy Lamplugh,

the London estate agent who disappeared in 1986 after a meeting with a client. In her determination to turn personal tragedy into public service, Mrs Lamplugh has launched the Suzy Lamplugh Trust, designed to encourage people to be more aware of how they can protect themselves.

'People – especially women – need to feel they can lead their lives to the full and go about their work without feeling too constrained by fear,' she says.

The Trust has commissioned the London School of Economics to undertake research into the vulnerability of women at work – nurses and social workers are known to have particular difficulties. There is also to be a book, a training pack for schools and colleges, and a Citizens Advice Bureau video sponsored by the Kelly Girls employment agency. A Suzy Lamplugh personal screech alarm (you can purchase one from Aldbridge, Manchester) is already on the market.

Another symptom of increasing private determination is the growing

self-defence industry. Judith Low, who teaches self-defence to both elderly and young people in the London area, agrees that confidence is the key to coping with awkward situations. My grandmother's story, in her view, exemplifies the principles of good self-defence.

She believes the Rambo approach, which involves learning a five-step acrobatic hip-throw followed by a bite to the jugular, is unhelpful. Firstly, you do not want to *escalate* a confrontation; secondly, your memory is the first thing to desert you in times of stress. You should choose your teacher carefully.

'Self-defence,' says Judith Low, 'is creative rather than a question of learning physical routines. You bring out a piece of self-defence to fit the moment. A confident person will deal with something much better.'

Trust to your intuition

Women, she believes, send out signals just in the way they walk. They can make themselves look like easy victims, or they can walk proudly, which is in itself a deterrent. If you feel powerful and you have the situation in perspective, then you can control a confrontation much more effectively.

'Women do not think of themselves as having skills, but their intuition is excellent and they are very dextrous. They do not think their arms are strong. But then they pick up three toddlers, two large bags of shopping and go home to make six beds.'

Some of her pensioners come to her because they have been too afraid to go out of their flats for up to four years. She tells them they have a lifetime of experience of survival to draw on, which in many ways makes them better equipped than the young. They also have authority if they can use it.

She despairs at the newspaper articles that show terrible pictures of mugged elderly people because she believes it leads to another 1,000 deciding not to venture outdoors. Television horror movies are another *bête noir* because, she says, they show women helplessly tripping over their high heels.

'People should think about how much they are influenced by this sort

Albert Parry, robbery victim

Owning and running a newsagent's shop in Bootle on Merseyside sometimes seems to call for the rugged determination of a Wild West frontiersman. 'I don't give in easy,' says Albert Parry, whose premises in the unemployment belt have been broken into eight times, and who has been physically threatened twice.

Newsagents are notoriously vulnerable: they work long hours, often alone, and the pickings for a determined thief are relatively easy. Following the example of many others, Albert Parry has repaired his confidence and improved his security by adding extra precautions. He is now protected by a panic alarm bell and, even more dauntingly, by Rex the Alsatian.

A succession of broken windows, stolen cigarettes and visitations by two armed robbers – one with a knife, one with a gun – have not been enough to make Albert Parry give up his way of life. As a 67-year-old widower, he would rather run the shop and continue to enjoy the feeling of the neighbourhood pivoting around him than admit defeat and, as he sees it, seal himself away in the isolation of retirement. His confidence is exactly what Judith Low is aiming to instil into her elderly self-defence students.

'I'm determined by nature,' says Mr Parry, with typical true grit. 'I just try to make it difficult for them.' No one should be surprised that neither of his armed visitors got away with much.

THE HEALTHY HOME

Your home may be your castle, but is it a healthy one? Coughs, colds, headaches and depression can all stem from avoidable environmental hazards within your own four walls

Temperature

Britain in winter has one of the highest seasonal increases in death rate in the entire Western world. In the Building Research Establishment's chilling phrase, there is an 'excess mortality' in the cold months of 40,000 people – most of them elderly.

Surprisingly, perhaps, only one per cent of these can be attributed to hypo-

of thing. The idea is not to become more afraid, but to find your strengths, enlarge your horizons, trust your intuition and live in a nicer world.'

The Home Office is keeping pace with these attempts to recreate confidence in the streets and has published a new pamphlet, *Violent Crime, Police Advice for Women on How To Reduce The Risks*. Its approach is

somewhat pedestrian, but the advice is sensible and useful.

To find a suitable self-defence course, ask at your local adult education centre. The Home Office pamphlet of advice to women is being distributed by crime prevention officers and will be made available through local libraries, police stations and voluntary organizations.

thermia. More common causes of death in winter are strokes and heart disease, probably resulting from the changes in blood pressure and viscosity induced by cold. Accidents are also more common because the brain slows down in the cold, impairing physical co-ordination; and the rate of cot death doubles to a seasonal total of between 300 and 400 cases.

There is no 'safe limit', but most

people feel uncomfortable at temperatures below 18°C (65°F), and below 16°C (61°F) you may reduce the body's resistance to respiratory infection – colds, bronchitis and pneumonia. Given facts like these, the high winter mortality rate cannot seem surprising. A survey of elderly people at home revealed that 75 per cent of them kept their living rooms uncomfortably cold in winter, and more than half were below the crucial 16°C. About 10 per cent were living at only 12°C (54°F), and some even as low as at 6°C (43°F).

Humidity
Damp air is good for you, so long as it is controlled. You should keep the relative humidity of your home between 40 per cent and 70 per cent – a process aided by washing, cooking and simply breathing, all of which discharge pints of water into the atmosphere every day.

If the air becomes too dry, you increase the risk of respiratory illness. Not only do the airborne germs survive better, but your nasal passage dries out and lowers its defences against infection. That is why patients on artificial ventilators, and those with breathing difficulties, are encouraged to breathe damp air, and why mothers of babies with croup are advised to take them into steamy bathrooms.

However, it is not simply a case of the wetter the better. If the atmosphere is *too* souplike, the result is condensation on windows and other cold surfaces, and the growth of moulds and mites. Both are eliminated if the humidity is kept below 70 per cent.

An estimated three million households in Britain suffer from condensation problems, which can be put right only by adjusting the balance of heating, ventilation, thermal insulation and humidity. Heaters burning paraffin or bottled gas release particularly large volumes of moisture into the air, and are common causes of condensation problems.

One answer to a chronic dampness problem, is to instal a de-humidifier. It works on the same principle as a refrigerator. Air from the room is drawn over a cold coil, causing the water to condense and drip into a collection vessel. The dry air is then heated and released. Its performance is critically dependent on the room being suitably warm and humid in the first place. It is

of little use in cold rooms, or if its extraction capacity is less than two to four litres a day. The other drawbacks are that it is likely to be noisy, and need frequent emptying.

A typical priced example, at over £300, is the Rentokil Homedryer, which is disguised as a teak hi-fi loudspeaker and extracts 15 litres a day. Most de-humidifiers are very reasonable to run (less than £2 per week).

Signs of a dampness problem are dripping windows and clogged salt. If you want to be more precise you can take a reading with a hygrometer, available from central heating suppliers and specialist hardware shops.

Ventilation
It would be hard to over-state the importance of clean air and effective ven-

tilation. Many people virtually seal themselves into their houses, especially in the cold winter months, but your good health depends on the house getting a complete air change at least once every two hours.

At best, a stuffy house is the happiest kind of hunting ground for colds and flu. At worst, it can be fatal. Un-flued or open-flued gas or oil-fired stoves and room heaters can produce lethal build-ups of carbon monoxide in unventilated rooms. Tobacco is another particular hazard in stagnant air. The Department of Health and Social Security reports evidence to suggest that non-smokers sharing a home with a smoker have between 10 and 30 per cent greater risk of developing lung cancer than people who live in smoke-free homes. Children are said to be especially vulnerable if

one or both of their parents smoke.

There *may* also be an increased risk of lung cancer to those who live in areas (particularly granitic parts of the West Country) where radon, a radioactive gas released from uranium in the earth's crust, is present in higher than average concentrations.

Concern about radon arose because uranium miners in other parts of the world have a measurably higher risk of cancer. As yet there is *no* hard evidence to show an increased risk from build-ups of radon in the house, although research is continuing in Devon and Cornwall. Obviously, however, it is best to err on the side of safety; and good ventilation is the easiest way to guard against contamination.

Dose-meters are available free of charge to anyone living within the Devon and Cornwall survey areas, and to others to purchase from the Radon Survey Office, National Radiological Protection Board, Chilton, Didcot, Oxfordshire.

Space
It is one of the puzzles of the age that the formula defining acceptable levels of overcrowding in local authority housing (laid down in the 1957 Housing Act) makes no allowance of space for infants, and only a half an allowance for each child. How many children do you know who take up less space than their parents?

The Registrar General's definition of overcrowding is more than two people (or, presumably, four children and an infinite number of infants) per habitable room, which might equally mean a bedroom or a living room (no size limits are stipulated). The ill consequences of overcrowding are many and various. People who live on top of each other for instance are more likely to exchange colds regularly: the average cough or sneeze has an infective range of about 1m/3ft.

Not all the problems are physical – lack of privacy is one of the commonest causes of depression. The World Health Organization reports that 'lack of privacy and of freedom of movement in the house...is considered a cause of mental unrest. Shared and interconnected bedrooms, bathrooms without direct access, a family room where it is impossible to find a quiet place if so desired, windows and doors that do not permit visual privacy are typical of the deficiency that may generate feelings of irritation, resentment and frustration as a result of intrusions, interruptions and general interference.' It is important to the family's wellbeing that each member can find at least a small haven of privacy whenever he needs it.

Swedish housing experts believe that lack of play space for children actually inhibits their development.

Noise

The World Health Organization identifies noise as an important health hazard, contributing to many minor psychiatric illnesses. A huge number of complaints are made every year about noise from bad neighbours – more than are made about traffic noise – although some people do allow themselves to become more annoyed by it than others.

The current building regulations for sound insulation are modest by international standards, and, even where they have been observed strictly, studies by the Building Research Establishment show that 14 per cent of people are still disturbed by noise from next door.

Loud music, parties, barking dogs, doors banging and noise from nearby commercial or industrial buildings are all mind-benders if you are in the wrong mood, or if you need to sleep. Most such noises are more irritating than passing traffic.

There is a way of stopping it. The shock absorbers here are the local authority's environmental health officers. Ring them with your complaint and they will come to gather 'evidence'. It is an awkward thing to judge, but the noise must be bad enough, or repetitive enough, to constitute a 'nuisance'.

Noise is classified as pollution. Even if the environmental health officer has not heard it and followed it up with a notice ordering the perpetrator to cease, there is another way to seek redress. The Control of Pollution Act 1974, Section 59, allows you to take the case to the magistrates' court yourself. Offenders may be fined up to £2,000.

Thinking safe

You are more likely to have an accident at home than anywhere else, and more likely to die from an accident at home than on the roads. Three million non-fatal accidents requiring medical treatment happen at home every year, and nearly 6,000 people die.

More than half the accidents involve a fall. Young children, careless teenagers, over-reaching do-it-yourselfers and old people are all liable to misjudge their capabilities. Kitchen cupboards are often hung much too high; houses are badly lit; and people not only leave clutter lying about on the stairs but exacerbate the consequences of a fall with glass tables or glass-panelled doors at the bottom.

Think about what could happen if fire broke out. How would you escape? It is the contents of the home, not the structure itself, that catch alight and give off dangerous toxic fumes. Think very carefully before buying foam-filled furniture (now made safer by British Standard 5852): it is still likely to release harmful gas more quickly than traditional furniture.

Another essential precaution is to keep aerosol cans away from heat and fires. The butane they contain is explosive.

Lighting

Subdued or 'romantic' lighting is the enemy of good health. The Building Research Establishment estimates that 60 per cent of British homes are inadequately lit, leading in many cases to eye-strain and eventually to serious optical disorders.

In basic safety terms, poor lighting can be a killer. At the very least you should make sure you have a powerful bulb over the stairwell (and, incidentally, that the stair carpet is kept in good order to avoid the danger of tripping).

Natural light, too, is important. It influences our body rhythms including sleep pattern, ovulation and hormone secretion; and the skin needs it to produce Vitamin D, which gives us healthy bones. Sitting in a darkened room all day makes no possible sense. Throw back the curtains and let the sun shine in – far better to risk a faded carpet than damage your health.

Food storage

A refrigerator is much safer and more efficient than a larder. To retard the growth of bacteria, you should keep your food at below 10°C. Then when heated it must reach at least 60°C to kill off the bacteria.

More than two-thirds of the 150,000 cases of food poisoning reported each year are sporadic (i.e. they have nothing to do with mass catering) and most of them are caused by the same species of micro-organism – salmonella. Fresh and frozen poultry and processed meat (including sausages) are often heavily contaminated when you buy them in shops, so you must be careful to cook them properly.

Wiring

Electrical wiring should be checked by an expert at least once every five years. You can, however, make some initial judgements about it yourself. If you have modern grey or white pvc sheathed cables and modern switches and power points, it is likely to be safe. If you have round-holed sockets and round switches, then there is the likelihood that you need to rewire. If your cables are rubber or lead-sheathed you could be running a serious risk of fire.

The lavatory

As long as you wash your hands, use clean towels, keep the lavatory well aired, regularly wash the wall and floors and make sure that pipes never get blocked, there should be no serious hygiene problem. You cannot get AIDS or venereal disease from a lavatory seat.

When infections do occur (for instance, 5,000 cases of Sonne dysentery are reported every year), they are usually spread by hand from urine splashed on to the lavatory seat. (Splashing on to the buttocks is unimportant – normal skin flora deal with it.) Cistern handles and door handles may also become contaminated.

TECHNOPHOBIA

An irrational fear of modern technology is no joke. It can damage commercial efficiency and diminish the pleasure of private life. How can the fear be mastered?

The symptoms are clear. You telephone someone – even quite urgently – and hang up when an answering machine replies. You have a video recorder that can be programmed for a fortnight, but you use it only day by day. You have a hi-fi with sophisticated tone-adjustment: you leave it at a constant setting. And you are panicked by the thought of having to use a computer at work. From all this, only one diagnosis is possible. You suffer from technophobia.

It is a widespread condition which in private life is only moderately constricting. You do not *have* to use a telephone answering machine: you can always ring back later, or write a letter. And your records mostly do not sound too bad if you do not know how the graphic equalizer works (or even its function). However, for job-hunters technophobia is a severe handicap.

Typewriters are gradually going the way of the quill pen; and cash registers are computer terminals programmed for stock control and sales analysis.

Nationally, the disease is a tragedy. There are acute shortages of people with hi-tech skills – shortages quite severe enough to demand the country's commercial interests. Significantly and, to most people, surprisingly, technophobia

strikes early in life. At the University of Surrey Dr Glynis Breakwell has been looking at 13 to 18-year-olds' attitudes to hi-tech in general, and computers in particular, and has found a rich mixture. Intriguingly, her research shows that the attitudes derive from the children's background – they do not reflect innate ability. Any of us, at any time of life, can change if we want to.

Check your diagnosis

Can you...
- **Drive a car of a different make from your own?**
- **Cook from a recipe?**
- **Connect the wires correctly to an electric plug?**
- **Knit from a pattern?**
- **Set and change spark-plugs?**
Most of these things are more difficult than operating hi-tech. If you can do any of them, you can learn to use any piece of electronic equipment.

Glynis Breakwell used a questionnaire among a research sample of 4000 young people to look for 'a positive attitude to new technology'. The crucial figure in the family, she discovered, is the father. 'If his job involves high technology,' she says, 'it is a powerful positive influence. It is very likely that he will have a home computer and that the children will use it.'

Mothers' attitudes seem irrelevant and, says Dr Breakwell, 'compared with young men, young women are very unenthusiastic about hi-tech'. They are also lower in self-esteem – a quality which her research has shown generally correlates with a positive attitude to hi-tech. The 'feminine' attitude to

technology is something of a stereotype, but the truth is that in the world of work, it is mainly women who actually *use* the hi-tech equipment.

'The differences are not really sex-based at all,' says Glynis Breakwell. 'Prevailingly negative attitudes are found only in girls from co-educational schools. Girls from single-sex schools are as positive about technology as boys.' Several explanations are possible. Mixed schools do seem to encourage a very 'traditional' relationship between the sexes.

'On the other hand,' says Dr Breakwell, 'it may be simply that, in mixed schools, the boys are more aggressive in competing for the available computers.' Interestingly, there is no correlation between young women's ambitions to make careers in technology and their enthusiasm for the subject – which seems likely to produce some dull, frustrating working lives.

The Breakwell survey tends to suggest there is not too much you can do about technophobia. For most of us, it is a bit late to change either our parents or our school. To a certain extent, other psychologists agree with her conclusions. The British Psychological Society, for example, recently held a conference on information technology and people.

Dr Mike Burton, of Nottingham University, argued that it was poor systems design that caused many of the problems. 'If they were designed around the humans who were to use them,' he said, 'working in information technology would not be such a black art. The designers should take a lesson from aircraft instrument panels. So much information is contained on these that they *have* to be designed in human terms, so that the pilot can absorb it at speed. It is worth remembering that the disaster at the Three Mile Island nuclear power station in America was caused by operators who made bad decisions because they were confused by the sheer volume of information from the dials and indicators they had to watch.'From aircraft practice,' he said, 'we have learnt the value of using icons (symbols representing the information as signals).'

It would be hard to overstate the importance of this. A graphic display of the wingtip angle is much easier and quicker for the pilot to absorb than raw technical data; and the same is potentially true of many of the on-screen functions in computers. In stock control, for example, a simple 'thermometer' chart would be much more visually direct than a column of figures. It would take a fraction of the time to read and significantly reduce the risk of error.

Instruction manuals are major contributors to the problem of technophobia. Even with something as simple as hi-fi, manual and machine combine to produce obfuscation rather than enlightenment. Not every control has a self-evident function, and the more recondite ones cannot always be identified from the manual. As a result, people find a 'working setting' and stick to it, without ever using most of the flexibility for which they have paid. (It is this same problem which has led to the popularity of the automatic camera.)

Computer manuals, of course, are notorious. Even a modest machine can come with a ring-bound volume several inches thick, and a popular programme will come with the same. The suppliers recognize that there is something faulty in this approach and supply a slim brochure with some such title as *To Get You Started*. Here many people begin, and here they end. Computer manuals, incidentally, are seldom error-free: a baffled learner, of course, never expects this and presumes his own incompetence is responsible for any failure.

The Apple Macintosh computer is one of the simplest to learn to use because many of the operators are represented by icons. A set of notes or a text you are working on, for example, is shown visually as a folder lying on a desk. To call the text to the screen, you simply move an arrow to the picture and press a button. The Macintosh also successfully attacks another problem for hi-tech users by doing its best to be

charming. When you switch on, it greets you with a smiling face. If you have to wait for some process to be completed, it shows you the image of a wristwatch. And it avoids the rudeness of other computers which react angrily to mistakes with uncompromising messages like 'Error no. 217' or 'No such command'.

But operational difficulties still remain. Many people – particularly senior managers – dislike using a Querty keyboard, and even feel it is demeaning to do so. They look forward to the frequently-promised 'secretary machine', a voice-controlled word processor that will accept dictation.

But that is in the future, as computers still do not find it easy to follow complicated speech. As hi-tech devices continue to confront us with comprehension problems, the prospects for technophobes do not look good. Yet no one *need* stay phobic. Remember that be-

hind the thickets of verbiage in the manuals and on the information-laden screen there lies a simple logic. The real complexity is absorbed in the circuits, making your own task more direct and straightforward. Remember, too, that plenty of people slower than yourself, and no more highly motivated, have learnt to get along with hi-tech. It is important to realize that hi-tech equipment in general is very robust: it is difficult to damage a computer by trying to use it.

The best thing for a technophobe to have is a computer-literate friend. Get him/her to show you the elementary operational stages, and make notes. Then, once you have learnt the minimum, find out more. Learn to use the machine in ways you may never need. By doing this you will achieve a comforting feeling of mastery – and a reputation as a citizen of the age.

PHOBIAS

Are you terrified of spiders, snakes or bees? How do you react to rats, mice and aeroplanes? Irrational terrors like these are too often trivialized. They can be analysed – and cured

Patricia Hughes has been phobic about mice and rats all her life. A few years ago she was going through a bad patch and the phobia seemed to intensify: she found herself thinking about mice and rats more and more. Then at a dinner party someone told a story about a mouse and she had to leave the table. Deciding, then, to take treatment, she consulted Professor Marks at the Maudsley Hospital and, with the help of behaviour therapy, is now 95 per cent cured. 'I don't think I'll ever love them, but I can at least hold them.'

Kelly Flynn, who works with a publishing firm, has such a severe phobia of snakes that she recoiled with horror when asked even to hold a photograph of one. 'It affects where I go on holiday,' she says. 'I went to India once and was scared the whole time.' She also approaches newspapers, television programmes and books with great wariness, in case a snake is shown. She does not know how it started, but is hoping the hypnotherapy she is now undergoing will cure her sufficiently to go on a longed-for – but previously feared – holiday in Australia.

Can you understand someone who goes into hysterics at the sight of a kitten? Or someone who will not go out of the house for years because he or she is terrified at being in the street? Or would rather walk up 15 flights of stairs than take a lift? A phobia – which is what all such people suffer from – is an irrational fear. What, after all, is there to be frightened of in a kitten? Or a walk outside?

The worst problem all phobics face is that their family and friends do not understand the panic they feel when confronted with the object of their fears. When they most need support, they face only laughter.

Although some phobics know the origins of their fears – they can recall the experiences that produced them – this is not much help. Logically, they *know* their phobias are irrational but this does nothing to stop the panic when confronting the phobia.

Phobics cannot explain their reactions even to themselves. One building worker, for instance, with a phobia about spiders (arachnophobia) was so over-

come when a workmate waved one in front of him that he picked up a piece of masonry and smashed it down on the man's head. His own action so frightened him that he went to consult a psychologist. Another woman with a phobia about balloons (more common than you might think) became totally hysterical when someone deliberately brought one near her.

A phobic's life can be spoilt in other ways. One woman who was terrified of moths refused to go to the local pub on summer evenings when its outside lights were on. The subsequent rows with her pub-loving husband all but destroyed their marriage. Another arachnophobic woman spent some 20 minutes each night stripping the bed and minutely checking it for spiders. She said she could sense if a spider was nearby – even if it was 'looking at her'.

Although you can have a phobia about almost anything – from gamophobia (a fear of marriage) to pogonophobia (a fear of beards) – they fall roughly into

three broad categories. First, there is the fear of a specific object or animal, like a dog or spider. Secondly, a fear of a specific situation, like being outside the house, or in a lift, supermarket, plane, school, restaurant and so on. Thirdly, a fear of specific illness or death.

Fear of an object
This first category is frequently linked to a childhood experience, even if a forgotten one. Children can be immensely cruel to each other, stuffing a spider or fish down someone's back; or shutting a schoolmate in a cupboard. Most children forget it; but some, the more nervous ones, find the fear developing, not diminishing, in adulthood. Any stress – if a boy who is nervous of dogs, for instance, is bitten by one – can turn the fear into a phobia.

Fear of a situation
Phobias in the second category have a strong link with stress. The most common, and most debilitating, phobia is

Janet Watkins became phobic about bees and wasps after being stung at the age of four. 'Now when I see one, I just run.' Her phobia stops her from sitting in the garden in the summer and eating outdoors. She thought it might be the pain of the stings that was the cause of the fear but, after being stung again a few years ago, she found the pain bearable yet the phobia worsened. She hopes the hypno-therapist she is seeing will allow her to enjoy summer once more.

agoraphobia, fear of being out in the street. This is known as 'the calamity syndrome' as it is often a reaction – sometimes delayed – to a severe shock, like a parent's death or an operation.

Fear of illness or death

The third category can begin after a relative or friend dies of an illness like cancer. Sometimes the phobic has nursed the dying person, then gets a morbid conviction that he or she will contract the same disease.

Treatments for phobias

There are various treatments for phobias. Some sufferers may choose psychotherapy, others hypnotherapy. But it is generally acknowledged that the most successful treatment is 'behaviour therapy' – based on the idea that if you have 'learned' to fear something then you can 'unlearn' it too. Phobics are helped to relax; then over a series of sessions they are introduced by degrees to the feared situation until they can overcome it. A cat phobic, for instance, may be shown a cat at the end of the room, half hidden in a cardboard box and gradually, over further sessions, learn to accept it being brought nearer until he or she can actually touch it or tolerate it being loose in the room.

The same treatment works with agoraphobics. Classically, they withdraw into the home after suffering panic attacks in the street – staying there in some extreme cases for 20 or 30 years. Many are unaware that the attacks are caused by stress, which may have been accumulating for years. In the end the nervous system can stand no more and the result is a panic attack – pounding heart, dizziness or fainting, sweating, breathlessness. The sensations are so strong that many people mistake it for a heart attack.

In behaviour therapy, the standard practice is for a group of agoraphobics to be taken slowly, over a number of sessions, step by step along the street. Each time anyone thinks he or she is going to faint, the whole group stops until the individual has been reassured by the therapist. (One mother, tired of her daughter's slow progress said, 'Well, faint, then,' and the girl found she couldn't.) Ultimately, agoraphobics learn to get on buses, enter shops and so on.

Britain's leading phobia guru is Isaac Marks, Professor of Experimental

Alan Cooper, a sports marketing consultant, was phobic about flying before he ever flew. He managed his first flight – on honeymoon – but, after two more short trips, stopped. He is also claustrophobic – he walks upstairs rather than taking the lift and avoids the Underground. Like similar sufferers, his fear is mainly that of not being in control. Being unable to fly affects his work and, in particular, where the family can go on holiday. He is going to a behaviour therapist for help – but the complication now is that his wife says that she has 'caught' his phobia. Once able to fly herself, she, too, now panics at the thought.

Psychopathology at the Maudsley Hospital, who is currently conducting an extensive study on agoraphobia, testing the value of various treatments – drugs, or behaviour therapy, for example, both singly and in combination. As a result, treatment can now be offered more quickly and referrals to the Maudsley are welcomed. 'We have done other work showing that self-treatment has more possibilities than we thought,' he says.

'Self-treatment' involves patients in practising the exercises Professor Marks gives in his highly practical book, *Living with Fear*. He suggests, for instance, that hyper-ventilation (or 'over-breathing') caused by panic can be overcome by breathing into a paper bag. This creates carbon dioxide, which stops the dizzy feeling caused by over-inhaling oxygen.

Agoraphobia is regarded as being almost entirely a 'female' phobia, but this may be because men are socially conditioned not to admit fear, and so use strategies to get round it. One countryman, for instance, who could manage to walk only a few yards from his house, bought a 50ft leash so that his dog at least could get some proper exercise.

The problem in curing agoraphobia is, first, to deal with the stress that originally caused it; and, second, to adjust the relationship between the cured phobic and his partner. The phobic relies totally on her husband to shop, collect the children from school and so on; and the male partner in turn may need this dependence to sustain his own self-esteem. The psychological department at an Essex hospital managed to cure a group of women agoraphobics – only to find that three of their husbands, faced unexpectedly with independent, coping wives, became impotent.

Despite this particular unhappy ending, phobics need to know that they can be cured – though hoping the phobia will go away, or just avoiding the feared situation or object, will not work. More often, it spreads: one woman's phobia about flying, for instance, worsened to the stage that if she heard a plane flying over while she was in her bath, she would leap out and dress so that she would not be found naked in the wreckage.

It is a cautionary tale, well worth remembering.

ADDICTIONS

The hardest part of coming to grips with an addiction is admitting that you have one. Many people who consider themselves to be 'only social drinkers' may consume enough alcohol to bring them up to danger level and beyond. Think before you drink – and smoke, and swallow that pill

Alcohol

The stereotyped picture of an alcoholic is of someone staggering around the street singing Nellie Dean. It is never ourselves. Yet the amount we can drink safely is always revised downwards as yet more is learned about the harm alcohol can cause.

According to the Office of Health Economics, the latest danger level for men is five bottles of wine a week (or 17 pints of beer). Anyone drinking that amount should at once cut down to a maximum of three bottles of wine. For women, the danger level is three bottles of wine (or 10 pints of beer) a week. They should aim to cut back to no more than two bottles of wine.

Those who cannot cut down should recognize that, whether or not their repertoire includes Nellie Dean, they are alcoholics. As such they are twice as likely to die from alcohol-related illness – cirrhosis of the liver, for example – as moderate drinkers.

The two rising groups of drinkers are women and teenagers. 'The full extent of the problems is hard to judge,' says Betsy Thom, a sociologist working in the Addiction Research Unit at the Maudsley Hospital. 'So many people either don't recognize it, or are not prepared to admit it.'

Drinking too much is usually explained by social and psychological problems, though individual tolerances do vary. Job stress (or, these days, lack of a job) is clearly identified as one of the main causes for male drinking.

● Between 1950 and 1984, per capita beer-drinking in England and Wales rose 40 per cent, spirit-drinking 135 per cent and wine drinking 250 per cent.

● Heavy drinkers carry twice the average death risk. Pub landlords are 15 times more likely to die from cirrhosis of the liver than the average person; fishermen are six times, and doctors three times more likely.

● At 16–17 litres of pure alcohol per person per year, France easily tops the European drinking league. It is followed by Spain (14 litres), West Germany (13), England and Wales (7½–8), Sweden (5) and Norway (3).

Women are more likely to drink because of relationship difficulties.

Organizations which help alcoholics – usually by giving advice and holding meetings – tend to be in the larger towns and cities. 'Obviously the first thing we have to do is try to get them to stop drinking,' says Betsy Thom. 'Here they tend to do it by counselling, by providing support and by liaising with their GP. If it is thought the person is going to suffer withdrawal, a drug may be used to help them, though drug treatment is not used here.'

Because so many who drink over the safety limit indignantly refuse to go to anywhere labelled 'for alcoholics', an organization with the deliberately innocuous name of Drinkwatchers was set up in London, aimed at helping drinkers to cut down before it becomes impossible. It has proved a successful gamble, and should be extended. Sadly, few people manage to cut down without help.

Tranquillizers

When tranquillizers first came on to the market in the 1960s, they were given chirpy and confident epithets like 'The happiness pill' or 'Mother's Little Helper'. It was not until the 1980s that the public became aware that tranquillizers were not happy-ever-after pills.

By then they had become a way of life – a crutch without which many people could not face the day. Tranquillizers deadened all life's crises, from bereavement to unemployment, from pressure at work to pressure at home. Doctors, faced with more and more patients complaining of stress, and themselves untrained for the role of counsellor, were only too delighted to have something at last to prescribe.

There seemed no harm in tranquillizers: doctors accepted that patients suffering from anxiety might have to be on them for life. Repeat prescriptions multiplied. Today in Britain more than 21 million tranquillizers are still being prescribed every year. In 1980 the Committee on the Review of Medicines published a report warning doctors that there was no proof that tranquillizers remained effective after four months of continuous use. By then, some patients had been on tranquillizers for up to 20 years, cocooning themselves from life. And what many then found was that they were addicted, and that when they tried to give them up they suffered withdrawal symptoms.

The words 'addiction' and 'withdrawal' in relation to tranquillizers at first sounded ludicrous, and users were shocked to see references in the press to 'middle-class junkies'. Most of the continuous users were quite unaware that they were dependent on them. (Warning signs for those who are still unsure are: being unable to cope without them; needing to take more to get the same effect; and getting strong reactions when you try to stop taking them, like shakiness or nausea, which disappear when you go back on them.)

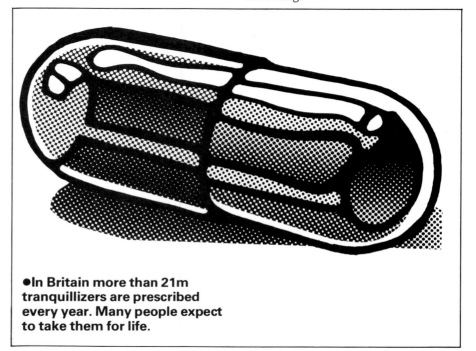

●In Britain more than 21m tranquillizers are prescribed every year. Many people expect to take them for life.

If you have been continuously taking tranquillizers for over six months, and now intend to give them up, do not stop them abruptly, or you may get unpleasant withdrawal symptoms and snatch up the bottle again. Instead, work out a programme of gradual reduction with your doctor.

You must be prepared for some withdrawal symptoms and you will need plenty of moral support.

Do not add to your anxieties by worrying over whether you should take the occasional tranquillizer. It is only long-term use that causes the problems. There is nothing wrong with the occasional use of tranquillizers, to tide you over a crisis, but do *not* let them become a permanent crutch.

If you think that any of these categories applies to you and you want to come off tranquillizers, then you should consult your doctor and talk to an organization like TRANX which has a network of support groups and special telephone help lines. Your family and friends can be supportive too if they understand why you want to stop and the problems you may face. Slow withdrawal is usually recommended and is the most successful route for most people. The advantages are that you do not need constant medical supervision and you can deal with it one day at a time at home with your family and your friends. You will be advised to do the following:

1 Stay busy – do not allow yourself any spare time to sit around and do nothing. Try to take up some form of exercise or sport.

2 Do not expect it to be easy. It will take time but you will get and feel better eventually. Meanwhile, just accept the withdrawal symptoms for what they are and cope as they arise.

3 Try not to develop an alternative addiction by drinking or smoking instead.

4 Join a group of other people who are experiencing or have known what you are going through. They will provide support and encouragement when you feel at your lowest ebb.

5 There is no need to feel ashamed, guilty or frightened. You *will* come through and *will* be rewarded by a greater awareness of life.

Smoking

One executive in London who entertains frequently has a 'No Smoking' sign on the pathway to his house, and several more inside. Although this is rather extreme, it does show how growing awareness of the health dangers has started to make smoking socially unacceptable.

The Royal College of Physicians estimates that 100,000 people in the UK are killed by smoking each year. Despite this, 13 million adults in the UK still smoke. Martin Jarvis, of the Addiction Research Unit at the Institute of Psychiatry, says, 'If you have to give one single reason for people continuing to smoke, it is dependence on nicotine. Nicotine is addictive, and many who want to give it up find they are beaten by their craving to smoke, and the edginess and bad temper they face without their drug.'

Dr Alan Norris, a psychologist who set up a clinic in 1979 to help patients give up smoking in Walsall, says that in his experience health is the most common reason why people want to stop smoking, followed by cost, then dislike of dependence on a drug and being made to feel anti-social. Before deciding on what type of treatment to use, Dr Norris examined the reasons why smokers who wanted to break the habit had failed to do so. 'The most common single factor was stress,' he said. 'The ex-smoker may have a row, or a nasty shock, or someone upsets them – and they turn to cigarettes. Nicotine acts fast: seven seconds between inhaling and the drug reaching the brain.

'The next reason was simple craving for cigarettes – particularly in the early stages. And then there are social occasions, parties and so on. There is a difference between the sexes over smoking. While men smoke to enhance their enjoyment of the situation, women are more likely to smoke to relieve feelings of boredom and depression.'

Dr Norris developed a six-week practical learning course on how to give up, designed to prepare people for obstacles. His strategies for dealing with difficult situations are:

Stress

Relax by using breathing techniques, thinking positively.

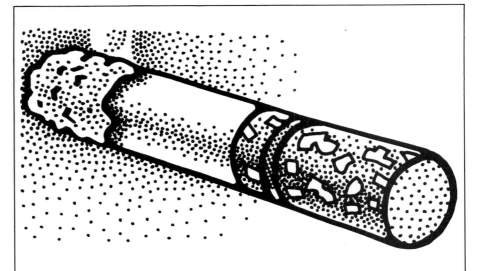

- **Thirteen million adults in the United Kingdom smoke.**

- **On average, someone who smokes 20 cigarettes a day shortens his or her life by five years. Forty per cent of heavy smokers – those smoking over 20 cigarettes a day – die before retirement age. For non-smokers, the pre-retirement death rate is only 15 per cent.**

- **Between 1960 and 1984, male smokers dropped from 61 to 36 per cent of the adult population, and female smokers from 42 to 20 per cent.**

- **About one in five children at secondary school now smokes.**

Craving

Tell yourself you will have a cigarette in exactly five minutes. Cravings will pass and at the end of the time you may well feel differently. If not, give yourself another five minutes. Or try Nicorette chewing gum, available on prescription from your GP.

Social pressures

Learn to assert yourself and say no politely, firmly and in a friendly way when you are offered cigarettes by fellow smokers, especially in social situations such as parties. Rehearse in advance.

Boredom/depression

This is often because of inactivity. Give yourself a small task to do, like washing the car or cleaning your shoes to stop yourself reaching automatically for a cigarette.

Such clinics around the country are comparatively few in number. Some smokers try hypnotherapy; some go to homeopathic doctors, who look at their entire physical and emotional state of health. Others have found that making a bet with a friend, or being sponsored to give it up (through, for instance, the National Heart Hospital) helps, as a financial penalty is involved. But in the end, it all comes down to willpower. It *is* hard to break the habit of a lifetime, but it is well worth it in terms of your health. And it is marvellous when you finally succeed.

Giving-up bonuses

The benefits of stopping smoking start the very day you throw away your cigarettes. You will save money – a powerful incentive! Add up your weekly cigarette bill, save the money and treat yourself to something which really lasts.

You will be much more attractive: your breath, hair, skin and clothes will smell fresher, and there will be no more nicotine stains to disfigure your hands and teeth. You will feel fitter and healthier: you will suffer fewer colds and chest infections, and you will have more breath when running to catch a bus or when climbing stairs.

Your family will be healthier too: your children will be less likely to get colds and even pneumonia if they live in a smokeless home.

LEISURE: HOLIDAYS

Holidays should be a pleasure. But all too often delayed journeys, shoddy hotels, crowded beaches, turn the ideal break into a total nightmare. How can we prevent the packaged ordeal?

Most people manage to return from their holidays with a wallet full of happy-snaps and a couple of believably jolly anecdotes. Not many care to admit they have had a bad time.

But very few holidaymakers survive without at least a private grievance or two – a fact acknowledged by, among others, BUPA, whose standard stress test awards extra stress-points to any patient who has recently endured a holiday.

Leaving aside genuine matters of complaint – overbooked airlines, shoddy hotels, shabby resorts – most people who suffer bad holidays have only themselves to blame. Almost always, they have failed to match their choice of destination, or type of holiday, closely enough to their family's needs.

Holiday planning
Of course, it is part of the joy of planning a holiday that it promises a complete break from everyday routine. But you should not fall into the trap of seeing this as some kind of annual metamorphosis, obliging you to pursue all sorts of activities you would avoid like the plague at home. Why, for instance, does the philistine who never sets a weekend foot inside a British museum or stately home inexplicably feel compelled to troop around a succession of Romanesque churches, or embark on a tour pickled in antiquities instead of more honestly enjoying a good lounge on a beach? How come the 40-fags-a-day, sedentary life style suddenly feels physiologically equipped to handle a hiking, cross-country skiing or scuba diving holiday?

An early American travel brochure once advertised a Caribbean holiday by telling prospective punters that they would visit eight islands in 10 days and 'fly real low over four others'. Over-ambitious schedules are another common cause of disappointment. Although time is invariably scarce, no itinerary should be built around the 'if this is Tuesday it must be Belgium' kind of timetable. This way, ulcers lie. Drivers should consider not only their own fatigue, but the misery that mammoth mileages inflict on the rest of the family

Holidays

	YES	NO
1 Do you often end up working instead of going away?	☐	☐
2 Do you forget to take all your days off?	☐	☐
3 Do you leave it too late to shop around for the most suitable holiday?	☐	☐
4 Do you usually return from a holiday feeling exhausted by your family?	☐	☐
5 Do you always go on holiday to the same place out of habit?	☐	☐
6 Do you feel that you just cannot be bothered with 'active' holidays?	☐	☐
7 Do you usually spend your holiday decorating the house?	☐	☐
8 Do you tend to find yourself on the sort of holiday which suits your partner much better than you?	☐	☐
9 Would you really prefer to take your holidays with someone different?	☐	☐
10 Looking back on your holidays, do you often catch yourself thinking you would rather have done something else?	☐	☐

A positive answer to **any** of these questions suggests that you need to rethink your holiday philosophy.

How well do you travel?

1 There is no sign of your luggage when you arrive at your destination in the middle of the night. Do you:
a) think what a terrible start to the holiday and decide to stay at the airport until it turns up?
b) take a telephone number and ring back in the morning?
c) do nothing and wait for the courier to sort things out?
d) grab a taxi and tell the driver to take you to the nearest bar?

2 At the hotel you are shown a room that has neither the balcony nor the sea-view for which you have asked and paid. Do you:
a) take what you are offered for the moment, but determine to get what you want in the morning?
b) refuse to accept the room and camp in the lounge?
c) smile knowingly and turn up the volume on your Walkman (you knew things would go wrong)?
d) take the room, certain you will be able to swap?

3 The bar at your hotel turns out to be ridiculously expensive. Do you:
a) drink without flinching, because there must be some way to get it off tax?
b) pay up, but moan non-stop?
c) decide to give up drinking for the duration?
d) find a cheaper bar a couple of streets away?

4 The weather is lousy. Do you:
a) see if there is any chance of an earlier flight home?
b) stay in your room and listen to the Walkman?
c) organize trips to museums and galleries until it gets better?
d) make for the beach anyway? (You once read an article that said the sun can tan you even through thick clouds.)

5 When you arrive at the beach, you find it is tar-ridden and there is a plague of jellyfish. Do you:
a) spend the fortnight lying on your balcony?
b) ask about transport to another beach?
c) complain bitterly to the courier and ask why nothing was said about this in the brochure?
d) use the beach regardless – a jellyfish sting cannot be all that bad.

who are condemned to an endless scenario of juggernauts and an occasional leg-stretch in the autobahn *Restplatz*. Never lose sight of the geographical realities. When poring over the atlas, for instance, the whole of Australia may look manageable in a two-week whip-round. The lunacy of the enterprise becomes apparent only when distances are more tangibly translated – when you realize, for instance, that Perth is nearer to Singapore than it is to Sydney.

Such holidays are every bit as daft as they sound, but not as uncommon as you might think. In recent years, travel companies have succeeded in selling us the idea that the further we go, the better our holiday will be. Do not be seduced. Why travel halfway round the globe when all you really want from your summer holiday can be had close by? Nowhere in the world has a better summer climate than the Mediterranean, so why pay more if all you want to do is soak up the sun and swim?

Snobbery and one-upmanship can play a distorting role in travel plans. Do not sniffily dismiss the obvious destinations. Behind even the brassiest of chart-busters you will discover worlds where those hard-flogged brochure superlatives really do apply.

The cost of your holiday

Sky-high resort prices and other unforeseen expenses are a perennial cause of complaint. But too many people fail to read the brochure's small print, lazily assuming that the quoted price is really 'all-in', including all meals, airport taxes, fuel surcharges, the use of the hotel sports facilities – even the sunbeds around the pool. It often is not, so always check.

The purchasing power of the pound, taking into account shifts in exchange rates and relative levels of inflation within the holiday country, will also make a staggering difference to on-the-spot expenses.

When and where?

It always makes sense to spread your holidays throughout the year. Wise travellers, for example, will always take their main, most expensive holiday in the winter. If all you need is a change of scenery, the Mediterranean out of the season will not let you down. Nor will the prices, with half-board packages at around £150 a week. But the weather is a gamble. In January, for example, there is a 50:50 chance of rain on any day in Corfu, Istanbul is no hotter than Torquay and it is as dry in Dublin as it is in Dubrovnik. For guaranteed heat you have to travel at least as far as the Canaries, southern Israel, Egypt or the Gambia.

There are other reasons, too, why the calendar deserves careful scrutiny. Most importantly, if you neither have children of your own nor teach them

6 Doing your accounts at the end of the first day, you realise you handed over a 2,000 instead of a 200 denomination note for lunch.
Do you:
a) go back to the restaurant, certain they will give you a refund once you explain what has happened?
b) curse all foreigners and never leave another tip all holiday?
c) shrug your shoulders and write it off to experience?
d) have an enormous blow-out at an expensive restaurant to show that you will not let your holiday be spoilt by a little thing like money?

7 Having tried all the restaurants, you are forced to acknowledge that the local cuisine is appalling.
Do you:
a) thank your lucky stars that at least the fruit and salads are delicious, and resolve to stick to them?
b) complain bitterly, and eat lots of ice-cream and sweets between meals – even though neither is particularly appetizing?
c) wash your hands of the local cuisine and go on a crash diet?
d) reckon you have just been unlucky so far, and give the restaurants another try?

8 You go on a whole-day coach-trip with regular stops for drinks, meals and sightseeing. The rest of the party do not look like the sort of people you would mix with at home. Do you:
a) talk only to your holiday companion and thank God you both brought books?
b) bitterly regret your mistake and spend the whole day in a huff?
c) identify anyone who looks remotely congenial and see if you can engage them in conversation?
d) make yourself the life and soul of the party?

continued over...

for a living, try to avoid the school summer holidays. These are the busiest, most expensive and generally hottest times to travel, and need the most advanced booking. Try to incorporate the year's quota of bank holidays into your plans, carefully judging the dates in order to effectively make your holidays grow without eating into your official allowance – freeloading in the nicest sense of the word.

Think, too, about taking one of the increasing number of 10-day trips, which involve taking only a week off work, or a Friday-to-Monday mini-break, which is much more of a tonic than the short time-span might suggest. The more holidays you can manage, the more compromises you can make with the needs of your partner or children, indulging each other's interests or even taking the occasional separate break without it seeming like the prelude to divorce.

'People go barmy on holiday,' one insurance claims assessor reported. 'If they don't get coronaries they do daft things like fall off balconies or dive into empty swimming pools.' Last year insurance claims included the replacement of dentures broken by a nail in a doughnut, and a pair of spectacles stolen by an ape in Gibraltar, as well as thousands of other less derisory accidents and injustices. Always buy adequate holiday insurance, but never forget that the most fundamental insurance against disaster is to be sure of where you are going.

9 Too late, you discover that the tourist police are having a blitz on illegally-parked hire-cars. Their English is not good, but eventually you realise you are being asked to accompany them to the police station. Do you:
a) suggest they ring your hotel so that the receptionist can vouch for you and help overcome the language problem?
b) rely on your own charm to deal with the situation?
c) fold your arms, smile, turn up the volume on your Walkman, and wait for them to get bored?
d) insist that they send for the British consul, refuse to answer any questions until he arrives, and resolve to go to jail before you will pay even the smallest fine?

10 When you go away on holiday, do you:
a) hardly think about what is going on at home from the moment you leave until the moment you return?
b) know there is absolutely no point in worrying about not having finished the project you were working on before you came away because someone else is bound to have coped with it?
c) wake up most mornings worrying about how on earth they are coping without you?
d) send postcards to a few close friends, but not until the second week of the holiday?

Interpretation
In the questionnaire each answer is awarded a key letter. For question **1**, note down the letter **Z** if you chose answer (a), **W** if you chose (b), **X** if you chose (c), **Y** if you chose (d). Then treat the other questions in the same way: **2** (a) **W**, (b) **Z**, (c) **Y**, (d) **X**. **3** (a) **X**, (b) **Z**, (c) **Y**, (d) **W**. **4** (a) **Z**, (b) **Y**, (c) **W**, (d) **X**. **5** (a) **Y**, (b) **W**, (c) **Z**, (d) **X**. **6** (a) **X**, (b) **Z**, (c) **W**, (d) **Y**. **7** (a) **W**, (b) **Z**, (c) **Y**, (d) **X**. **8** (a) **Y**, (b) **Z**, (c) **W**, (d) **X**. **9** (a) **W**, (b) **X**, (c) **Y**, (d) **Z**. **10** (a) **Y**, (b) **X**, (c) **Z**, (d) **W**.
There are at least four different ways of behaving on holiday and most people display elements of more than one. Each of us, however, has a particular tendency. If your answers have a predominance of **W** options, it shows you are a Good Holiday Person – flexible, adaptable and capable of improvization in awkward situations, everyone's ideal companion. A predominance of **X** answers reveals a Blind Optimist – given the right breaks, your blindness to reality may see you through, though you tend to be a very wearying holiday companion. A majority of **Y**s indicates a Selfish Hedonist – determined to carry on with what you want to do irrespective of what is happening around you. While you are capable of having a good time on even the most calamitous of holidays, you do not contribute to anyone else's enjoyment. If **Z** answers predominate, you are an Autodestructive Grumbler – seeing trouble where none exists, and biting off your nose to spite your face.

LEISURE:BOOKS

The pleasures of the page can outshine many others. Here the distinguished writer Frederic Raphael tells us why he believes 'it is far from closing time in the libraries and bookshops of the West'

'They say that life's the thing,' Logan Pearsall Smith once wrote, 'but I prefer books.' It is hardly a universal preference. How many contemporary homes contain more than half a dozen volumes? Even authors sometimes feel guilty about their dedication to letters. Why put your whole mind and body at the disposal of mere words? The number of works devoted, down the centuries, to the glorification of warriors and sportsmen emphasizes this unease. Rudyard Kipling had a far from secret respect for Gunga Din; Ernest Hemingway preferred a Purdy to a pen; even Aeschylus wanted to be remembered not as a great tragedian, but as one of the Athenian infantrymen who defeated the Persians at Marathon. Who would choose to read, or compose, a love poem, if he could be making love instead?

The book, in truth, has not been an unmitigated blessing to man. The Bible itself – the Book of Books – has been too demanding a text to excite thoroughgoing gratitude. It conveys a message whose promises can be as intimidating as its threats. Randolph Churchill, reading it for the first time, on Evelyn Waugh's suggestion, while marooned in wartime Yugoslavia, was heard to exclaim, 'What a shit God is!' The Gospel is not all good news. We need scarcely be surprised that mankind has tried, again and again, to free itself from the trammels of The Word. Books, it can be argued, put us in the power of those who translate, interpret and pervert their meanings. Literacy can be another name for the dominion of shysters and mountebanks. Marshall McLuhan claimed, not so long ago, that the Age of Print was coming to an end (he used a book to make the claim, of course). Electronic media, he thought,

would prove less socially divisive than the one-at-a-time linearity of the printing press.

In his cool-gospelling zeal, McLuhan did not care to observe that communal thinking is nearly always crass. Homogeneity of culture – everyone watching the same programme and singing the same chorus – is another name for mass stupidity. Individualism is not the enemy of progress, but its necessary means. Luckily, the pundit's predictions have proved vacuous. It is far from closing time in the libraries and bookshops of the West. (Literature alone, and its furtive reproduction, has continued to remind the East of what it is missing in the way of liberty and conscience.) Despite the ingenious marketing of huge quantities of trash by our publishers, there are more than enough good new books. (Samuel Rogers, Byron's sour friend, used to say that whenever he heard of a good new book, he rushed out and bought an old one, but a literature without innovation loses its savour.) No one, however diligent, will ever read all the available masterpieces. Those who feel guilty about not having got round to *Lost Souls* or even *David Copperfield* are bound to be in good company: we all have shameful gaps in our reading. The last man to know everything died at the end of the eighteenth century. He will never be replaced: we are doomed, by the fertility of human invention, to incurable partiality. The growth of knowledge entails the growth of ignorance: there will, inevitably, be more and more of both.

My father was always telling me how essential it was to be well-read, though that cannot have been the only reason why I was reluctant, during my childhood, to open a book. Part of the problem was laziness, part an aversion to Dickens, whom he venerated. (I still prefer Trollope, and his inspiration, *The Memoirs of Charles Greville*.) The only reason I used to go to the library at Charterhouse School was that it was reasonably warm in the winter of 1946-47. By chance I started to look at *The Spectator* and so became addicted to Harold Nicolson's weekly column, 'Marginal Comment'. Nicolson was a snob, but he was not condescending. He wrote with perspicuous clarity and he had the gift of transmitting enthusiasm. He loved books and he recommended them with generous eagerness in his journalism. He and other literary journalists, like Cyril Connolly and Peter Quennell (foolishly underemployed), gave my generation steadily good advice, for which they were reviled by academic puritans.

If I am asked to recommend a way of turning the proverbial Young Person to the pleasures of literature, I flinch from offering lists of Good Books. Kenneth McLeish and I once tried, for not wholly venal motives, to compile a sort of Michelin Guide to the Library. We were as abused as if we had sought to hawk courses on egg-sucking. I mention this not in order to promote our list of books (now safely out of print), but to apologize for a failure to reproduce it here. If you cannot stand Stendhal or Proust, are disgusted by Nabokov or O'Hara, think Italo Svevo and Thomas Mann sadly dated, and if you have not got time for Gibbon, or Runciman on the Crusades, or Edel on Henry James, if Cavafy's poems seem parochial or Homer dusty, what can I do about it, or for you? If you are waiting for arguments to turn you from the cant of leading articles to the study of Schopenhauer or Nietzsche, or trouble-making moderns like Russell or A. J. P. Taylor, or even Karl Popper

or René Girard, what can I say to convince you? Those who see merit in the detective stories of that brilliant ex-jockey, or really want to know who Smiley's People are, will doubtless think me an envious prig for suggesting there may be better trails to follow.

Let me make an uncharacteristic suggestion: to find a thread to take you through the librarian's maze, first latch on to a congenial critic. Harold Nicolson's articles may not have been collected in a single volume, but if I must offer a one-volume incentive to reading, it would be Edmund Wilson's *Classics and Commercials* (with the hope that his other works, like *Axel's Castle* and *To The Finland Station*, would soon prove equally attractive). If anyone fails to be attracted by Wilson's curmudgeonly enthusiasm for literature, there is no conceivable reason to despair. (Connolly's *The Evening Colonnade*, for delectable instance, offers the kind of sumptuous menu to give an anchorite an appetite, though dryer souls may prefer the anathemas of Leavis or the *parti pris* of a Terry Eagleton.) The important thing, whatever guide you use, is to go on to read the texts themselves. Of contemporary *hajis*, none is more encouraging than Anthony Burgess. I sometimes think that his ephemeral articles will last longer than his masterpieces. Certainly he has been, over the years, our most generous and perceptive Sunday reviewer (not that he fails to appear on most other days of the week). His responses to other people's books are a model of attentive courtesy and contributive intelligence. The worst kind of critic is like the Ravidus whom Catullus despised, one who hopes to make his name by abusing his betters. Critics should be used like Wittgenstein's ladder: as soon as they have helped you to a higher level, pitch them away. Arthur Koestler once advised people to read nothing they found boring or tiresome: there was too great a choice available to persist in tedium. On the other hand, man cannot live by placebos alone. The long-windedness of Proust or the rant of Dostoevsky can suddenly be transformed into uplifting genius beyond the scope of the season's latest sensation. It is rather ignoble to pose, with alpenstock and flag, on the summit of a transitory molehill, when there are real mountains to climb.

MUSIC

Norman Lebrecht offers a beginner's guide to recorded music of the modern age and the classical past

Music is a sea of sound without beginning or end. Where you dip in will depend on which coast is closest. The traditional method is to splash novices with the sprightly tunes of Mozart and Haydn, take them forward a little to the depths of Beethoven, back a bit to clear-blue Bach, far ahead to big-band Brahms. Then let go and watch them sink or swim.

That kind of baptism may still be valid if you are middle-aged and raised in a world of comfortable sonorities. But if you are 21 going on Level 42, and believe sound starts at 90 decibels, then you may find Bartok and Birtwistle more palatable than the Viennese pastries Richard Baker rolls out on the wireless.

So where to begin? Stravinsky's *Rite of Spring*. A fiercely feral piece of paganry that in 1913 transformed the sound of the century, provoking riots on the Champs-Elysées and dread in the Tsar's palace. With Firebird for good measure, Claudio Abbado and the LSO (DG 415 854-2) offer top value.

Let us take it for granted that you are buying compact discs. The LP is dead, DAT supertapes will take at least five years to build a backlist of recordings, and cassettes cannot match the precise digitation of hi-tech rainbow discs. (They are, however, portable and half the price; almost all these selections are available on tape too.) Many of the CDs in the new crop of discount releases are from Pickwick and the PolyGram labels.

'Is Mr Beethoven still composing?' Beecham was once asked by a schoolboy. 'I should think by now he is decomposing,' rasped Sir Thomas. Well, composers do not have to be dead to be good. Steve Reich and John Adams, flourishing on opposite coasts of America, have captivated popular musicians like Brian Eno and Glenn Branca with their repetitively minimalist sounds. Provocative, attractive, amusing, infuriating, there is an hour's worth on EMI (CDC 7 47331-2).

Shostakovich has been dead for a decade but his caustic commentaries apply to prevailing political evils. Try the coruscating quintet and trio (Chandos CHAN 8342) or, for more luscious listening, Yo-Yo Ma in the cello concerto (CBS MK 37840).

The idea that music can analyse and criticize contemporary society stems from Gustav Mahler, whose symphonies are currently the biggest pull in British concert halls. Newcomers to Mahler start with the snappy fourth – Bernard Haitink comes inexpensively on Philips (420 350-2) – or with Eliahu Inbal's dare-devil Fifth (Denon 33CO-1088), with its *Death in Venice adagietto*.

Mahler's protégé, Arnold Schoenberg, tore up the tonal rule book and created a new order, known as 12-tone music serialism. Taken neat, serialism can be tough on the ear and the brain. But Schoenberg's disciple, Alban Berg, blended Bach and recent bereavement into a compelling violin concerto, passionately performed by Kyung Wha Chung, and coupled on Decca with Bartok's tender-loving First Concerto (411 804-2).

The fiddle plucks direct on the heartstrings, as Tchaikovsky and Mendelssohn knew only too well. Their concertos are meltingly played by Nathan Milstein (DG 419 067-2). This should be your first Tchaikovsky disc, perhaps your only one. In the Brahms and Beethoven concertos you will never hear the like of Jascha Heifetz (RCA RD 85402); accept no cheap substitutes.

What Beethoven to buy? His 135 opus numbers have been recorded innumerable times, often wretchedly. Do not start with Karajan's powerful, inexpensive Ninth on DG (415 832-2): wait until you can read the supreme composer's mind before approaching his summits. Enter instead by way of the piano sonatas (Wilhelm Kempff on DG 415 834-2), then progress to Klaus Tennstedt's scintillating performance of the Pastoral and Eighth Symphonies (EMI CDC 747459-2).

Mozart loved the piano above all instruments: Alfred Brendel's account of his 27th and last Concerto is unsurpassed (Philips 420 487-2). Eine Kleine Nachtmusik, the piece everyone knows, is sold with delicious divertimenti on Marks and Spencer's first release (2584/5730).

Handel offers astonishing variety. Most would start with the Water Music (Pickwick PCD 826), but a little extra money also buys you the celestial vocal delights of the Ode for St Cecilia's Day (DG Archiv 419 220-2).

For Bach, the late Brandenburg concertos are a good entry point. The English Chamber Orchestra gives fine middle-of-the-road performances with Raymond Leppard on Philips (420 346-2) and, sounding brighter, with Philip Ledger on Pickwick (PCD 845).

If you cannot live without Vivaldi's Four Seasons, I Musici play them (Philips 420 356-2) as proficiently as anyone else and throw in two extra concertos for free. Further back into the 17th century, you enter the specialist realm of Early Music, a subject separate unto itself. To sample it, try Italian madrigals by Monteverdi, Gesualdo, Gabrieli and others on Pickwick (PCD 822).

So this is Italian singing? you protest. All right, get the full-bodied real thing with a large white handkerchief on Primo Tenore (417 713 2), a Decca cheapie from Luciano Pavarotti. Do not seek your introduction to opera on record; see it live.

You have now acquired more than 20 hours of basic listening. Now treat yourself to the very best of British – 20th century orchestra pieces by Britten, Bridge and Bax inspired by the sea and its sounds (Chandos CHAN 8473).

The London Symphony Orchestra, conductor John Georgiadis, playing in Muscat by the invitation of the Sultan of Oman.

LEISURE:TV

Is your life ruled by television? Is it here to stay or on its way out? Does it enrich your life or paralyse you into inactivity? Have you become its slave?

Television as we know it today is on its way out. In the 40 or so years since it found its way into our living rooms, it has taken an increasingly prominent place in our recreation patterns, offering more channels and more, and still more, viewing hours. All of which we have squeezed readily into our lifestyles – usually by switching on earlier and staying up later. It is indisputably the primary leisure activity of the 20th century.

Why, then, is it on its way out? The answer, according to Robin McCron, Head of Special Projects at the BBC, is that it is being superseded by the 'multi-media video display screen'.

You may already have an early model of one of these in your home. It still performs the traditional function of receiving the main TV channels, but nowadays with a VCR you can record and replay whatever you select, whenever you wish. Perhaps you are linked into a cable system, at least doubling the number of channels available, and with more to follow.

Before long a satellite dish will enable you to tune into the mass media of just about anywhere from the USSR to Kuwait. You will be able to filter the messages you pick up through your hi-fi, taking advantage of increasingly common stereo broadcasts. You could check the news, weather or other information on teletex. With the latest screen projection facilities you could enlarge all this to fill the living-room wall, creating the effect of a cinema at home.

When you are bored with the broadcast options, you could watch edited highlights of last summer's holiday or your sister's wedding, recorded on your pocket-sized camera. Or you might prefer to connect your micro to the screen. Home-made computer graphics or DIY cartoons set to your own sound-track might already seem a faintly unambitious use of the monitor when compared with the interactive games on sale in the US, allowing the operator to battle with aliens from outer Hollywood. And how long before the telephone link will multiply the directions in which the images and messages flow? Facilities which 10 years ago were the stuff of futuristic fantasies are now commonplace in domestic media.

How much do you watch?

Television of course is not so much dying as multiplying, giving birth to something with even greater implications for our leisure time. The impact of the current revolution in mass communications threatens to be as significant as television's own impact on previous generations. If you are thinking of making a life-change, it is worth considering what place you will afford the box in the corner. There is every prospect that it will attract yet more of your time and attention.

As a simple check on your current use of the set, you might care to make a viewing log. Take a typical week and write down each day how many hours you spend viewing. In a second column write down what you think you *should* have been doing with the time; then in a third column what you *could* have been doing. This, in effect, is your profit-and-loss account. Only you can know whether or not it is a satisfactory one, although it is always interesting to contrast your performance with others'.

Add up your week's total and see how it compares with the latest figures produced by the British Audience Research Bureau (BARB). These show that the average person in the UK spends about 30 hours every week in front of the television. Multiply your own weekly total by 52 to find a rough annual total; then multiply that by the number of years you have been watching. Now you know how much television consumes of your life.

The history of TV viewing predicts that the more there is, the more we will watch. And on the basis of past evidence, the consequences will be mixed. The bad news is that everything you dislike in television will be available soon in more generous supply. The reason is that somebody else likes it, and there are people who find it profitable to pander to their tastes. There will be more violence, more propaganda, more miscellaneous trash floating through our air space than ever before – and some people will be revelling in it. A few of them will then go out and emulate what they have seen, and occasionally the results will be horrendous.

Is TV beneficial?

Fortunately not many TV viewers are, or are likely to become, psychotics. For most of us, TV has become integrated into our daily lives in more subtle ways. Its contributions, like the set itself, are best not viewed in black and white: there are benefits, and there are liabilities.

We tend to think of television-watching as a passive use of spare time, and one that displaces other recreational and household pursuits. But Audience Research suggests that it is an over-simplification to imagine that turning on the set invariably stops us from doing anything else. If people want to do something else instead of watching television, then they tend to do it. BARB figures, for example, demonstrate seasonal variations in viewing hours in Britain with an average reduction during the summer months of some five hours per week.

TV and other activities

An imaginative study by Oxford University psychologists Peter Collett and Roger Lamb revealed that people continue to conduct many other aspects of their leisure lives *alongside* television. The researchers installed video cameras in volunteers' living-rooms, and programmed them to activate automatically whenever the television sets were switched on. By this means they obtained visible proof that just about anything that *can* be done within four walls *is* done when the television is on.

Despite the popular conception of inert masses slumped in front of the box, television has never been the direct enemy of active physical leisure. On the contrary, erstwhile minority sports such as squash, bowls and snooker have been boosted to unprecedented levels by television exposure. The huge growth

of entrants for the London marathon similarly attests to the impact of television coverage. The proliferation of cable channels is likely to increase coverage of minority and local leisure interests and stimulate involvement in a wider range of them. The multi-media screen could be keying people into the real world, rather than insulating them from it.

For some people, television provides unqualified enrichment of their daily lives. One of the most poignant pieces of psychological research ever undertaken was a study of audience reactions to a religious broadcast called House Communion. The programme took place in the homes of worshippers, showing families and friends taking part in a service, with the minister directly addressing the viewer as if he or she were present. This was very much a minority appeal programme, but for a significant minority – the housebound elderly – it was an event which they said gave meaning to their existence

and helped sustain the feeling of contact with their faiths and fellow communicants which otherwise would have been impossible. The multi-media set (for those who can afford it) can only add to the quality of life for such viewers.

Television offers a range of services which different people exploit in different ways. These include keeping the kids quiet on a Saturday morning, escaping to Southfork instead of facing the latest demand for your overdue rates bill, avoiding (or fuelling) marital dispute, and many more. But its essential benefits are entertainment, information and, for many people, wider social contact. All the developments in the technology of the multi-media age promise to add to the uses and abuses to which human beings put their technologies. Most of us have the choice of deciding how to extract the benefits of the media – though experience suggests that we might just wait for a good programme to tell us how to do it.

Attitudes to television

We rarely question our attitude towards things we take for granted. Take TV – we all watch it for a mixture of positive and negative reasons. How satisfied are you with the role it plays in your life? To find out, say which of the following statements you agree with.

TRUE FALSE

1 I often find myself regretting having watched a programme when it is over. ☐ ☐

2 Watching TV is much less involving than my other pastimes. ☐ ☐

3 If I had to live without my TV, I just do not know how I would get through the week. ☐ ☐

4 When I think about it, it is surprising how many of my conversations revolve around TV programmes and personalities. ☐ ☐

5 I watch TV because it shows how other people deal with the same problems I have. ☐ ☐

6 There is so much on TV these days, the family very rarely sits down at a table together to eat the evening meal. ☐ ☐

7 TV is good because it takes you out of yourself. ☐ ☐

8 Watching TV gives you something to do. ☐ ☐

9 Once the TV is on, it usually stays on for the rest of the evening. ☐ ☐

10 We quite often switch on the TV to see a programme that tells us what is going on in the world. ☐ ☐

Interpretation

Score two points for each of the following answers you ticked: Question 1 False; 2 True; 3 False; 4 False; 5 True; 6 False; 7 True; 8 True; 9 False; 10 True. Add up your score, then subtract from it the total obtained by giving yourself two points for each of the following answers you ticked: Question 1, True; 2, False; 3, True; 4, True; 5, False; 6, True; 7, False; 8, False; 9, True; 10, False. If your final score is positive, your attitude towards TV is fairly healthy; if negative, there is a tendency for it to control you rather than vice versa!

HOW DID YOU SCORE?

Check your answers from pages 52-3

1 Ambition

For questions 2, 4, 6, 8 and 9, score 2 points for each YES answer, and zero for every NO. For questions 1, 3, 5, 7, and 10, score 2 points for each NO and zero for each YES. The higher your score, the more ambitious you are. A score of 12 or more suggests you are hard-working, competitive and keen to improve your social standing. A score of 6 or less indicates that you place little value on competitive performance and may tend towards apathy.

2 Technophobia

For questions 1, 5, 8, 9 and 10, score 2 points for each TRUE answer and zero for every FALSE. For questions 2, 3, 4, 6 and 7, score 2 points for every FALSE, and zero for each TRUE. The higher your score, the more affected you are by technophobia. A score of 14 or more suggests that you are conducting a Canute-like struggle aginst the tide of technological development. A score of 4 or less implies that you are enviably well-adapted to today's (and probably tomorrow's) world. Most people float in the area between, at ease with those aspects of the new technology that they have made an effort to come to terms with, but still suspicious of those outside their experience.

3 Financial security

For question:

1 YES, 1 NO, −1	9 YES, 1 NO, −1
2 YES, −2 NO, 0	10 YES, 1 NO, −1
3 YES, −1 NO, 1	11 YES, −4 NO, 3
4 YES, 0 NO, 1 (−1 for each care in excess of three)	12 YES, 2 NO, −1
	13 YES, 0 NO, 1
5 (a) 6	14 YES, −1 NO, 1
(b) −6	15 YES, −1 NO, 1
(c) 3	16 YES, −1 NO, 0
	17 YES, −2 NO, 2
6 YES, 3 NO, 0	18 YES, 2 NO, −2
7 YES, 10 NO, 0	19 YES, 1 NO, 0
8 YES, 2 NO, −2	20 YES, −2 NO, 1

If you score 30 or more, you can count yourself financially secure. 18-29: you're on the road to financial security, though there remains room for improvement. 13-17: while all goes well your financial situation may seem fine. If things start going wrong, however, you could find yourself in deep trouble. Start planning now. Minus 12 to plus 12: danger signals are looming. It looks as if you don't really care what happens to you. Fair enough, but what about your family? Less than minus 12: get help fast.

4 Household management

For question:

1 YES, 10 NO, 0	6 YES, 10 NO, 0
2 YES, 10 NO, 0	7 YES, 10 NO, 0
3 YES, 10 NO, 0	8 YES, 0 NO, 10
4 YES, 10 NO, 0	9 YES, 10 NO, 0
5 YES, 10 NO, 0	10 YES, 0 NO, 10

Award yourself a glass of champagne if you've scored 100 and haven't cheated, but consider whether your fastidiousness is at the expense of spending time with those close to you. Above 80 means you're pretty fastidious and well-organised; 50-80 is a happy medium, but you should analyse your weaknesses and take action; less than 50 suggests that you are either cheerfully disorganised or miserably disintegrating into squalor. Decide which, and act accordingly.

5 Job satisfaction

For questions 2, 3, 5, 7 and 10, score 2 points for each TRUE answer, and zero for each FALSE. For questions 1, 4, 6, 8 and 9, score 2 points for each FALSE and zero for each TRUE. The higher your score, the more satisfied you are. A score of 12 or more suggests that you find your job rewarding in a psychological as well as a financial sense; a score of 6 or less indicates that you are getting less pleasure from it than most people – and less than is healthy for you.

6 Drinking

A positive answer to *any* of these questions implies that drink is causing a problem in your life.

7 Risk-taking

For questions 1, 3, 4, 7 and 9, score 2 points for each YES answer, and zero for every NO. For questions 2, 5, 6, 8 and 10, score 2 points for each NO and zero for each YES. The higher your score, the more of a risk-taker you are. A score of 10 or more suggests you enjoy living dangerously. A score of 6 or less suggests that your attachment to the safe and the familiar is so powerful that you may find change quite threatening.

OTHER PEOPLE

1 Manipulativeness

1 The best way to handle people is to tell them what they want to hear.
2 Anyone who completely trusts anyone else is asking for trouble.
3 It's hard to get ahead without cutting corners here and there.
4 Never tell anyone the real reason you did something unless it's useful to do so.
5 It's wise to flatter important people.
6 There's a sucker born every minute.
7 When you ask someone to do something for you, it's best not to give your real reasons for wanting it, but the reasons likely to carry the most weight.
8 The biggest difference between most criminals and other people is that criminals are stupid enough to get caught.
9 Fools deserve to be parted from their money.
10 Unfortunately, you sometimes have to hurt other people in order to get what you want.

2 Shyness

1 I rarely worry about making a good impression.
2 Generally, I am very aware of myself.
3 I am concerned about my style of doing things.
4 I am not often the subject of my fantasies.
5 One of the last things I do before I leave the house is look in the mirror.
6 I don't often stop to examine my motives.
7 I don't much care what other people think of me.
8 I sometimes feel that I'm off somewhere watching myself.

9 The good thing about being shy is that it gives you a chance to stand back, observe others and then act more intelligently.
10 When I start talking to someone, I always seem to find something to say.

3 Running your own life

1 Is there some habit, such as smoking, that you would like to break but cannot?
2 Do you take steps to control your figure by exercise and diet?
3 Do you believe your own personality was laid down firmly by childhood experiences, so that there isn't anything you can do to change this?
4 Do you make your own decisions regardless of what other people say?
5 Do you find it a waste of time planning ahead, because in the end something always turns up causing you to change plans?
6 If something goes wrong, do you usually reckon it's your own fault rather than just bad luck?
7 Are most of the things you do designed to please other people?
8 Do you often feel you are the victim of outside forces you cannot control?
9 Do you usually manage to resist being persuaded by other people's arguments?
10 Do you laugh at people who read horoscopes to find out what they ought to do?

4 Relationships

1 These days women don't always have to wait for a man to make the first move.

2 Basically what females want out of males is a meal-ticket.
3 No one's perfect, so you have to make allowances with new people.
4 I generally wait for other people to initiate relationships with me.
5 I'm careful not to judge people too quickly when I first meet them.
6 When I try to start a relationship, I am very afraid of being rejected.
7 I usually find it quite easy to show people that I like them.
8 I don't know what to say to new people.
9 I find it a challenge to meet someone new.
10 I am very fixed in my ways and unwilling to take risks.

5 Getting on with your partner

1 Coming back from work, or while waiting for my partner, I become irritable and negative about the evening ahead.
2 When my partner addresses a 'ridiculous' remark to me, I become upset that he/she needs to talk to me like that.
3 When I have a row with my partner, I become depressed and concerned about the relationship breaking up.
4 In a group with my partner on social occasions, I tend to mock what he/she has to say.
5 When discussing problems with my partner, I soon drop the subject because it's clear there's no interest on his/her side.

Improving your knowledge of yourself has an important by-product – an improved understanding of other people. Armed with this new awareness you can, with increased confidence, set about both establishing new relationships and renewing old ones. Many shy and lonely people – in some cases with expert help – can learn to overcome their disability and then break free of self-imposed constraints. In all long-term relationships, sexual and otherwise, the vital thing is not to overburden yourself with unrealistic expectations.

See page 107 for interpretation of your answers

6 When I sense that my partner wants a row, I make an excuse to leave because rows make me uncomfortable.

7 If I thought my partner was starting a relationship with someone else, I would look for an opportunity to start one first.

8 I would like to find some outside interest which would take me away from the home once or twice a week, but know my partner would not only not support me but would also make fun of me.

9 When discussing financial matters with my partner, I am ill at ease and worried that he/she will criticise me.

10 When my partner gives me a present, my first suspicion is that something is being covered up or that I am being bought off.

6 Sexual maturity

1 A man needs to be a sexual athlete to satisfy his partner.

2 Generally speaking, foreplay is more important for women than for men.

3 If your partner has had an affair with someone else, the best thing to do is pay them back as soon as possible.

4 Many women achieve orgasm more easily by masturbation than by sex with a man.

5 If your partner truly loves you, he/she should do whatever you want sexually, regardless of his/her own likes or dislikes.

6 It is good manners for both partners to wash thoroughly before sex.

7 Most men feel threatened and get turned off if a woman starts to take an active role in sex.

8 Homosexuality is natural for some people (albeit a minority).

9 'Trial marriage' increases the likelihood that an eventual proper marriage will end in divorce.

10 It is unreasonable to expect one's partner to be in the mood for sex every time one feels aroused.

11 People who go in for mate-swapping and group sex are usually deeply unhappy and mentally unstable.

12 Contraception is the equal responsibility of the male and female partners.

13 Most women have a secret desire to be raped even though this may be unconscious.

14 Little games of spanking, bondage and restraint are harmless and widely used enhancements to love-making.

15 The Grafenberg spot is a recently discovered erogenous zone located just at the base of a woman's neck.

16 It is not necessary to flatter a partner but sincere, heartfelt compliments will maintain warmth in a relationship.

17 Sex saps energy to the extent that sportspeople should abstain for at least three days before an important event.

18 Men are more often able to separate sex from love than are women.

19 Most women today resent chivalry and regard it as outmoded, chauvinistic behaviour.

20 It is normal for both men and women to be particulary excited when a sexual activity is novel or in some way forbidden.

7 Emotional versatility

1 No one would call me a gentle person.

2 It's a good thing to be ambitious.

3 When there's an argument, I sometimes find myself giving in, even though I'm sure I'm right.

4 I'm more of an intuitive than an analytical kind of person.

5 I tend to feel self-conscious about being affectionate with other people.

6 I'm much happier not having to rely on other people.

7 People don't often come to me with their personal problems.

8 People say I have a strong personality.

9 I'm not often taken in.

10 I don't really enjoy competitive games.

11 I frequently find myself soothing other people's feelings, even though it was someone else who hurt them.

12 I'm the sort of person who'd be elected foreman of a jury.

13 I have no inhibitions about shouting to make myself heard at a party.

14 I'd hate to be thought aggressive.

15 I'm told I'm very sensitive to other people's needs.

16 I suppose I am what you would call an individualist.

17 I rarely use harsh language.

18 I don't like taking risks.

19 Other people tend to think of me as a warm, tender kind of person.

20 I hate having to make decisions.

THE FAMILY ON A TIGHTROPE

The Victorian ideal of family life was fine if you were a Victorian: when men were men, women knew their place and children were seen and not heard. But if you want to survive a modern marriage and cope with a modern family, you will need to find a modern solution. How do you match your expectations to reality?

Here is the great emotional paradox of our time: that we crave togetherness and family fulfilment as never before, yet seem increasingly to fail. Despite the myth that co-habitation has become the preferred alternative to marriage, 93 per cent of us still marry in the end, on the assumption that being 'in love' is the natural prescription for lasting happiness.

But what George Eliot called a couple's 'glorious equipment of hope and enthusiasm' now has a regrettably short shelf-life. The average first marriage lasts 10 years. One in three British marriages ends in divorce, and one in five children has experienced a parental break-up by the age of 16. Last year 54,000 couples made first-time applications for marriage guidance counselling.

The problem is that expectations of domestic life have never been so high, or so nebulous. In part, the trouble is due to better health and longer life-expectance. Before the National Health Service, relationships contracted 'until death' could seldom be expected to last 40 years; nor did families have to withstand such unrelieved intimacy. Far from abandoning Victorian values, as Mrs Thatcher laments, it is likely that we are only now reaping the full emotional harvest sown by our nineteenth century forebears.

Before the Industrial Revolution, families had a primarily social purpose. They lived and worked, ate and (unless they were very rich) slept in a common unit with relatives, lodgers, apprentices and servants. As work and home became increasingly separate domains, however, the Home Sweet Home mentality took hold. For men, the family came to be seen as a refuge and compensation for the trials and rigours of work outside the home, while for women it became increasingly the focus for emotional energy as well as practical skills.

Many researchers now believe that the emotional temperature has climbed too high to be healthy – that couples are asking too much of their private relationships and too little of the outside world. Some of the most successful marriages happen where both partners have independent outside interests and do not see too much of each other.

Do you start anew?

Early nineteenth century children were easier to raise, too. They quickly grew from being just another mouth to feed into useful co-workers. Adolescent *angst* was never a problem: young teenagers were simply sent away as servants or apprentices elsewhere. Great-grandmother never suffered the rude awakening of Erica Tate, in Alison Lurie's novel *The War Between the Tates*, when she discovered that her small, rewarding offspring had been usurped by monstrous acned changelings – 'rude, coarse, selfish, insolent, nasty, brutish and tall'. It is significant that Erica's initial reaction is not to steel herself for the transformation, but rather to have another baby while there is still time, to buy another charmed 12 years before the pubertal rot sets in.

It is easy to sympathize with the popular trend for starting anew, through another baby or another partner, rather than ploughing on with existing relationships. New relationships are in themselves little births, with the allure of heightened excitement, forgotten *frissons*.

In some circles, says Penny Mansfield, senior research officer at the UK Marriage Research Centre, 'you may have the feeling that it is almost a stigma *not* to change partners. The suggestion is that nobody else would find you attractive, or that you are simply too boring or unadventurous to try. Relationships are certainly The Great Adventure. Those few who have dared to try on moral grounds to resurrect bygone values like commitment and security have so far met with embarrassing failure. It remains to be seen whether the AIDS scare will restore them on the more acceptable grounds of health.'

Hope versus expectation

Whether or not people who soldier on with imperfect relationships are right to do so, at least it could be said that they have understood the nature of life's bargain: they never *expected* to enjoy a permanent state of happiness. And neither should any of us.

'What is this much-trumpeted happiness, anyway?' asks Renate Olins, director of the London Marriage Guidance Council. 'Is it affection, loyalty, warmth, sexual attraction? Whatever we mean by it, it is one thing to *hope*, which can be quite modest and engaging; but quite another to *expect*, which is harsh, not very lovable and takes a lot of satisfying. "I *hope* one day to cruise down the Nile; I *expect* a fridge and fitted carpets".'

Expectation does not sit comfortably with the realistic certainty that sooner or later in any relationship one or more stresses such as illness, redundancy, poverty, adultery or just a 'bad patch' will strike, and will not necessarily have the rosy Hollywood effect of bringing those affected closer together.

It is the Dream Topping of popular entertainment and fiction that encourages us to believe that 'happiness' is attainable if only we can find the right partner. So greedy are we to hear this that more Mills & Boon romances, peddling the 'And Then He Kissed Her' happy ending, are sold each year than there are adult women in the UK.

'Any night at the Opera House,' says Olins wryly, 'you can feel a highly sophisticated audience being absolutely captivated, caught up in the heightened levels of passionate romance in *Otello* or *Lucia di Lammermoor*. It is larger than life, but it is what people dream of – the love that stays true to the end. Real life is not like that.'

Not everyone agrees. Joan Collins was simply speaking for the extreme wing of the 'Some Day My Prince Will Come' lobby when she blithely announced, after a fourth divorce, that she still believed in marriage as an institution.

This is exactly the kind of thing that prompted Dr Johnson to his cynical adage that remarriage was a 'triumph of hope over experience'. Since the risk of divorce for a second-time husband is one-and-a-half times that of a bachelor bridegroom, and for a divorcee the risk is double that of a spinster bride, then the clear inference is that the same mistakes are being repeated, over and over again, by the same people. Second marriages – average term, seven years – have an even shorter life-expectancy than first, and more than half of those who divorce and remarry in their early 20s will divorce again, with men more at risk than women.

For a while in the Seventies divorce was thought to be beneficial to children, who would go on to enjoy harmony in a single-parent family rather than suffer the unpleasantness of continued conflict. Later research, however, suggests that, unless the quarrelling is pathological, children fare better with two embattled parents than they do in a broken family.

Another myth is the *Kramer versus Kramer* cameo of the toast and two-wheeler lessons. Most divorced fathers do not have custody, and most, to their emotional cost, cease regular contact with their children within a year.

Family in decline?
Despite all this, however, it would be wrong to suppose that family relationships are in the parlous decline that sensationalist headlines would suggest. After all, two-thirds of marriages do still survive, and four out of five children are raised by their own natural parents. The conventional family is alive and well – but it is having to work out its own salvation without the aid of a modern blueprint.

Obstetricians say there is no such thing as a safe delivery until after the event; the same could be said of raising a modern family. Everyone has a kind of folk memory of the 'traditional'

English Happy Family – like the one in the *Janet and John* books where Father works in the garden with John, while Janet gives Mother a hand with the rice pudding and Rover looks on with wagging tail. This is the kind of family that makes do and mends, whose shared leisure consists of fresh-air walks or board games played before a hot milky drink and bed. Theirs are children of prolonged childhood, white socks and flannel shorts worn well into their teens. Today's shared family leisure is more likely to consist of a Saturday-night takeaway and a hired video.

Good parenting today certainly means *more* parenting than it did in our parents' day, when a little healthy neglect, while we played Pooh-sticks or made mud pies, was normal. Now, in order to help our children fulfil their potential and grow up prepared (though no one can say what kind of society we are preparing them *for*), we are committed to socializing them with a continuous round of tea-parties, sleep-overs and burger suppers, and offering them endless opportunities for after-school classes in dance, drama, mini-rugby, Suzuki violin and computers. But how is time going to expand so that parents can be fulfilled as well as their children? That remains the unanswered 64,000-dollar question. Is the dual-career family that works all week and shops on Friday night so it can be at *Kinder* gym with Oliver and Charlotte (four and two) at 9am on Saturday simply doing its job?

Or is it committing a colossal crime against itself?

The healthy family
Experts, who for years have been preoccupied with families and couples who *fail*, are only now beginning to recognize the importance of looking at how *healthy* families work. Robin Skynner, co-founder of the Institute of Family Therapy, has studied some pioneer research from, of all places, Dallas. The Timberlawns Research Centre there has been examining a group of successful families and trying to identify common attributes. The key factor, it has found, is an ability to accept the world as it really is and not to chase a dream.

These parents, reports Skynner, were people whose social attitudes were positive, who made many friends and were therefore well-supported. They also shared a tremendous respect for individuality within the family, recognizing that their children could be very different people and allowing them to be so. Such parents would not feel impelled, like Ronald Reagan, to justify a son's ballet-dancing by insisting, 'We've made sure he's a man.'

The Dallas families also communicated effectively and had a very clear sense of hierarchy. There was much consultation and negotiation with the children, but neither mother nor father would shrink from making important decisions. The parents had equal, though not necessarily identical, authority, comfortably interchanging responsibilities if not roles. Together such families shared a common system of values – humanitarian if not religious – that extended well beyond their own domestic unit, and they shared, too, a great deal of fun, spontaneous laughter and *life*.

The healthy family, though, does not do *everything* together and call that closeness. It is a little like a three-ring circus, with a great deal of activity going on at once. It looks as if it might fall apart in chaos at any moment – the trick is that it never does.

Making marriage work
The urge to know more about how relationships work has brought about a sales boom in the how-to-survive-in-marriage guide-book business. Such manuals may be pretty illuminating about the mine-fields that lie ahead –

the dip in relationship satisfaction that often immediately follows marriage; the all-time low following the birth of the first child; the increase in happiness as the children become more independent and the wife may return to work; the trough when adolescence sets in, and renewed satisfaction when the children fly the nest. But this generalizing 'W' satisfaction curve cited by most of the writers conceals some critical factors.

'For example,' says Renate Olins, 'a couple *may* re-experience delight in each other once the children have gone. But equally they may have shared a common purpose in pouring money and energy into raising their family and, once they have lost that impetus, find themselves faced only with each other – and with nothing much to say.'

Whatever the books say, they cannot convey a true sense of how any individual will feel or respond in a crisis. No psychological Richter scale exists to measure the degree and the duration of pain, and it is astonishing that human beings, adept at surviving physical privations, should be so poor at handling the emotional kind. What, then, are the variable factors of chance, skill and learned experience that determine the course of a relationship?

The most important trick is to distinguish between irreconcilable deadlock and the temporary loss of balance that inevitably affects every couple from time to time.

Bob Geldof and Paula Yates in their early days together were a perfect example of this. He would come home from tours still 'plugged into' nocturnal hours, and be 'poisonous and unbearable' at home.

'At night,' says Geldof, 'I would want to go out; she would be drowsy and want to stay at home in front of the telly. She would go to bed at nine and I would be up till two, waiting to get tired. It took us a long time to readjust after these absences. We felt not exactly like strangers, but uncomfortable with one another. Still, that always passed … and we were able to build a home we both felt we had never had before.'

Sometimes, too, a couple's private life style can be ruined by their relationship with the world beyond. Thus a young father, who would like nothing better than to come home early and spend time with his small children before bed, may find himself at exactly the stage in his career at which his future prospects depend upon being seen to work late. Left at home with a screaming baby and a fretful toddler, his partner may feel frustrated and hard done by.

Perhaps it is not too surprising that an opinion poll in the late 1970s revealed that 52 per cent of wives found their husbands irritating, while only 31 per cent of men returned the charge. It is to be expected perhaps that women, who generally demand more emotional content in a marriage – more open affection, more discussion of feelings – should express disappointment more often than men. But the corollary to this, of course, is that although women may suffer more, they can also gain more from family life. A young father's responsibility when his wife is feeling frustrated by the restrictions of the nursery is at the very least to offer comfort and understanding – to acknowledge that her job is far from easy. Saying, 'Yes, it *is* a ghastly time but I do care and it *will* pass,' may not cure the affliction, but might help her endure it.

Is divorce a disaster?

For many couples there is always the passing possibility of lasting separation – often only a hair's breadth between the marriage that ends, yet was perfectly happy until it became unhappy, and the partnership that continues to put up with considerable malcontent. Couples who come within spitting distance of parting often celebrate their survival with some kind of pseudo life-change like going on safari or moving house. Yet you cannot deduce private happiness from outward appearance. Couples who come through bad patches together, and who find the rough and tumble of family life actually quite creative, may survive precisely because they have a better-than-average ability to integrate and learn from experience. The best relationships are those between people who easily accept change, are more tolerant of faults and are able to withstand a little emotional discomfort.

'If only you can accept life as a learning experience in itself,' says Robin Skynner, 'then it won't much matter what happens. It is all part of the learning.'

Robin Skynner contends, however, that divorce need not be seen as a disaster. The widening of kinship through step-parents *can* give the children more emotional variations and a wider bank of affection. Re-married parents can also benefit from having time alone while their children are away on access visits. A group of girls discussing divorce at a very exclusive American school reached the conclusion that the children of divorced parents felt more mature, self-reliant and self-sufficient than their friends. Some of the girls from more conventionally secure backgrounds even felt quite envious, believing themselves by contrast to be soft and over-protected.

Robin Skynner's most famous client is John Cleese, with whom he wrote the best-selling book, *Families and How to Survive Them* (published by Methuen). Cleese himself observes that the benefits of divorce are underrated: 'It gives you insight into the trickier aspects of marriage, the more delicate nuances, as it were, that a couple who've been together for 30 years wouldn't begin to grasp.' He has realized that he and his first wife were brought together – unhealthily – by a shared lack of self-confidence. His therapy with Skynner taught him that he had brought forward, from childhood into marriage, emotional neuroses which had been hidden even from himself.

Cleese had grown up in a family where anger, and indeed every other strong emotion, was taboo. As the beloved only son he received no clear parental authority and was not even allowed a bicycle for fear that he might hurt himself. Small wonder that he grew up to present himself as an old-fashioned, prickly, macho Englishman who thought 'scenes' destructive, who was unable to express his needs and felt little pleasure in his resounding professional success. It was being made to confront all that he had previously hidden that transformed Cleese's life. It turned him into a hugger, able freely to admit that he needed to be loved, without fearing the risk of a put-down.

In proposing to his second wife, Babs, Cleese did not wrap up his question with promises of rose gardens and eternal love. There were no pedestals set up, or impossible ideals uttered. His view of this new relationship was simple, practical and eminently reliable. 'I think you should marry me,' he said. 'Then I can sit upstairs reading and you can sit downstairs painting.' Which, as proposals go, carries the mark of genuine experience over vain hope.

SURVIVING THE FAMILY

Misunderstanding and suspicion are the two most corrosive ingredients in any troubled relationship. Too many husbands and wives, parents and children, separate because they do not understand the real cause of their problems. The answer is to seek professional advice – and to do so early. Proper help could prevent disaster

The essential step in repairing a troubled family relationship is to accept the idea of seeking help. The notion that an outside agent, like some kind of emotional loss adjuster, may be able to feed them with new insights into what is really muddying their lives remains for many people rather hard to take. They suspect they will be sent away with nothing more than the worthy but unexciting advice to 'work at it'.

Of course most people believe they do already work at it – and so they may. The problem is that without good counselling expertise they simply do not have the tools to succeed. All too often, 'working at it' is triggered by a row – usually about something which has nothing to do with the root cause of the tension but is merely symptomatic of it – and comes down to nothing more than HIS short-lived gestures towards the nappy changing and washing up, and HER (still unwilling) outing to an office social function when she would rather be at home with the children. Nothing as superficial as this is likely to plaster over the cracks for more than a week or two.

Another common reason for resisting help is the fear of exposing yourself to self-scrutiny, or opening old sores. Taking steps to change the way you act or express yourself – with the risk that this could not just stir but possibly break the family pot – requires considerable courage. As Val Smith, organizer of the London Relationships workshops observes: 'Many people are secretly attached to their problems. They feel safe with the limitations their difficulties impose.'

Three Lifeplan volunteers expressing dissatisfaction with their family relationships summarized their problems like this:
• After 20 years my wife still expects me to behave as if we had been married for three.
• I am stabbed by guilt at the unhappiness I have inflicted on my first wife and three children.

• I would like to become less snappy with my family instead of experiencing extremes of happiness and gloom.

All have one significant point in common: they all dropped out before acting on plans they had made for seeking professional help. Of course there will always be excuses – lack of time, lack of money, or the revised opinion that 'things aren't quite as bad as I thought'.

There can also be a (justifiable) feeling that family life is being spoilt by social forces beyond individual control: unemployment, lack of nursery facilities, the need for two incomes that puts impossible pressure on time and parental energies. Rather like Christopher, whose case history is told here, many parents feel that the inexorable treadmill of keeping the household functioning, children cared for, clothes clean, cars on the road and jobs under control denies them the natural joys of having a young family.

Time may restore some of that relish once the exhausted haze of the early family years have passed. But it

child's defence.

Because so many marriages reach their lowest points when there are adolescent children in the home, many local NMGC offices have set up Parents and Teenagers groups so that couples will feel less alone with their difficulties. One of the most important things is to persuade them that uncomfortable stirrings of adolescent independence do not mean that all the love and attention lavished in the past has been wasted.

'Parents should not be afraid,' says West-Meads, 'to remind their children that they, too, have needs. You understand that the children had a hard day at school, but they in turn must understand that you have had a hard day at the office and that your privacy is just as important as theirs. The continuing intimate relationship between mother and father is a key factor in giving the children the freedom they need to grow up and away. If there's a very intense three-way relationship, then a child can feel very stuck and find moving on into adulthood very problematic.'

Another scheme that can help is Exploring Parenthood (EP), a nation-wide organization which runs discussion groups of parents and counsellors. Some of its benefits were described to me by Melanie, a former

will not erase the reality (or the possible effects) of your having rammed a toddler too violently into his pram because the supermarket bill was £20 more than you expected. Nor will it necessarily unravel the habit-forming conflict between parents who insist on their 16-year-old daughter telephoning if she is going to be home late, and the rebellious teenager herself, to whom it has never been made clear that this is not just an authoritarian rule-for-the-sake-of-it, but a means of reducing tension.

The tough truth facing anyone seriously wanting to break a pattern of unsatisfactory family relationships is that there is no point blaming your childhood (though understanding its legacy may help) nor in seeking to change your partner or offspring through constant carping. Successful reconciliations – between husbands and wives, and parents and children – do occur, but seldom without pain, care and great commitment. It is this care and commitment that marriage guidance is designed to encourage. Clients are helped towards a three-way process of exploration, understanding and action.

'It's common,' says Zelda West-Meads, of the National Marriage Guidance Council, 'for people to describe a specific problem, such as having difficulties with the children.

But after exploring it for a session or two you begin to see that it is more of a marriage problem. The second stage is to help them understand exactly what is going on. It may be that a husband is not letting his wife talk enough about her view of a teenage disciplinary problem, and that she finds his handling so Victorian and bombastic that she feels impelled to come to the

Auntie Agony the Agony Auntie

Auntie Agony the Agony Auntie

Mr Writ the Divorce Lawyer

Mr Writ the Divorce Lawyer

Rev. Steeple the Vicar

Rev. Steeple the Vicar

social worker who said she had found it an absolute boon when her two daughters were tiny. One had been sleeping very little for months (a dietary problem that later proved to be an allergy to cow's milk). She and her husband reeled into an EP workshop simply, they admit, as 'a day away from the children, who we understood, rightly, would have a wonderful time in the EP creche'.

In the event, their gains were much greater. 'It was wonderful,' said Melanie, 'to talk to other parents in an intelligent and professional atmosphere. I had my doubts about a session in which, without the children, we were invited to explore play, but it was illuminating to find that I, who had never enjoyed playing about with art, could actually find pleasure from paint and paper. It was surprising how many of us found we could hardly remember being played with at all ourselves when small.'

For Melanie, the great value of the day was the promotion of the idea that here was a group of parents all doing a worthwhile job to the best of their considerable skills and experience.

Redressing the sense of being undervalued is one of EP's prime objectives. It is particularly easy for mothers with young children to lose their self-esteem and for fathers unwittingly to connive at this.

Carolyn Douglas, co-founder of Exploring Parenthood, remembers one woman who came to a workshop convinced that her whole family, and indeed those beyond it, seemed against her.

'She had a hard personality that sorted oddly with her pretty pink dress. It emerged that she had been trying to prepare her nine-year-old son for walking to school on his own. She described beautifully how she had followed him in the morning, hiding behind trees until she was sure he had arrived safely. Obviously doubts had been raised about whether he was old enough to be out alone. That afternoon, elderly neighbours saw the boy walking home, picked him up in their car and delivered him to the door. The mother was simply furious. She took it as interference, and presumed that harsh judgement was being passed on her parenting.'

By the end of the workshop day, however, the woman's whole attitude had softened. She had been led to see that her neighbours were not necessarily being critical and were only trying to help.

It is very easy to blame 'relationships' in abstract for what are in fact very personal and private dissatisfactions. Snap outbursts of anger, brooding silences and accusative disclosures of 'I've always wanted to, but

Mr Middleclass

Mr Middleclass

Mrs Oilbaron
the Soap Opera Star

Mrs Oilbaron
the Soap Opera Star

Miss Independent
the Working Mum

Miss Independent
the Working Mum

you never ...' or 'I can't because of the children ...' may blight everyone's home life, yet actually reflect one person's restlessness within his or her own skin. It follows that if you don't like yourself very much – and at some stage we all doubt our own appeal – then you may well be hard to live with. Relationships are not a cure for inner malaise, though the preoccupation of playing lover, spouse and parent may for a time divert you from it.

Expressing emotion

Perhaps you could improve your family life by tackling your own problems of personality and circumstance. It is the conviction of therapists at the Centre for Personal Construct Psychology in London's Victoria that personalities are not fixed but fluid; that individuality rather than conformity of thought should be encouraged, and that we should cease to think in moralizing terms of what is right or wrong, but consider only what works best for each individual.

For example: a working mother who feels guilty because she thinks she is neglecting her children may be asked why she thinks it is a problem. How did it happen? How would you like things to have been? A woman who has difficulty finding meaning in her life as the children leave home (her gloom may well have a knock-on effect, making her husband, too, feel dispirited and inadequate) is invited to see herself in a different way – as someone who may eventually enjoy being a grandmother, or who may now find the time she has never had before

to take up a hobby or course of study.

Gillian Edwards, of the Actors Institute in London, observes from her experience of running the institute's Mastery weekend workshops (not only for the theatrical profession, but for a wide band of managing directors, mothers, secretaries, teachers, housewives and others) how very difficult it is for many people to put a true value on themselves.

'They find it really hard when we ask them to stand up and list even one or two small contributions they have made in their lives.'

Many people, she says, are not just unwilling but actually unable to express emotions. 'Anger and passion are very closely linked, so if you can't express anger, then your passion level may be low and you may not have much enthusiasm for what you are doing or for life in general. We are fairly used to the idea that women are not very good at expressing anger, but it can be hard for men too.'

We are also, it seems, not very good at expressing emotions clearly: 'When you see people expressing love, it often looks like need, and need expressed often looks like anger. What the Mastery workshop brings out is that with a little practice (through theatrical exercises) it is possible to state these emotions without confusing the issue by too much drama.'

Val Smith, who organizes the Relationships workshops in London, feels so sure of their potency in helping people feel more fully themselves that she offers money back to anyone who finds no value. By exploring questions

like 'How did you feel when you did something for someone who did not acknowledge it?' or 'Can you remember a time when you made certain decisions that still count in your life?' you are made to realize that you have a history, but that you need not be tied to it. You have a choice.

One man recalled being turned down by six successive women and deciding therefore that he was someone who could have no success with the opposite sex. Relationships helped him see that perhaps a different complexion could be put on what happened. Perhaps he had not asked in the right way. Perhaps they were the wrong women.

In an exercise where a group was asked whom they would approach if they needed help, one woman nominated by six others was forced to reassess her own low estimation of her supportive worth.

Inevitably some people drawn to the workshop have particularly tragic backgrounds involving incest, rape, divorce. At a Relationships workshop in Switzerland, for example, a man stood up to say that here, for the first time, he could begin to throw off the bitterness he had always felt towards his father, jailed for life for having killed his mother. Deeply shocked and moved by this disclosure, some members of the group found a weight dropping from their own shoulders.

'If he can forgive something so terrible,' they thought, 'then perhaps our children/ lovers/ spouses/ parents can forgive us, who have surely done nothing quite so awful.'

LONELINESS

Are you afraid of being alone? Do you avoid spending an evening on your own? From childhood we are encouraged to spend our time together with others. So it is hardly surprising if the luxury of solitude becomes the dread of isolation

Loneliness is not just being alone, it is *minding* being alone. This means there are two ways of treating the problem. The conventional approach is to supply the tools needed to fill the emotional vacuum the sufferer is worried about. The lonely person is shown how to improve their interpersonal skills in the hope that they will find it easier to form satisfying relationships.

Social skills training courses are designed specifically for people whose lack of close friends or partners is caused by obvious social awkwardness. By simply watching themselves in conversation on film, and discussing their difficulties with other sufferers as well as therapists, many very shy adults have been able to acquire the basic linguistic and non-verbal rules of social intercourse which most of us pick up as children. The resulting self-confidence is often all it takes.

There is also a more radical approach. The *cognitive* approach encourages victims of loneliness to rethink their attitude towards the state of being alone, and the particular feelings which make up their experience of loneliness. It is a programme of self-help which starts from the clinical observation that much of the distress caused by any psychological problem stems from worrying about having the problem rather than from the problem itself.

If you regard spending time alone as (a) a sign of personal failure, (b) entirely your own fault, and (c) something only you experience, it is hardly surprising that you find it depressing.

Doug Stewart

Complications of circumstance rather than personality have eroded the social life of builder Doug Stewart and his partner Maggie: 'We are just too busy with our own three children, and with four more from previous marriages whom we encourage to visit us freely. We have two businesses between us, not to mention Maggie's amateur dramatics, my editorship of the Village Quarterly, a house in the process of ongoing extension in the middle of a field near Milton Keynes, a huge neglected garden and a swimming pool going green from lack of interest.'

When they started out together 10 years ago, their intentions were carefree: 'Whatever happened,' asks Doug, 'to our plans for going round the world in the bus that was then our home? It is all very well having a lot going on, but we wonder what the point is if you cannot stop to see friends and enjoy it.'

Lifeplan sent Doug Stewart to a two-day Time Manager course designed to 'allow people to get more out of their lives by establishing goals and planned objectives'. Although his particular course was dominated by executives sponsored by large companies, Time Manager say that the 40,000 people they train each year are drawn from a much wider profile — including secretaries, bishops, housewives and doctors.

Doug Stewart pronounced himself 'very impressed', particularly by certain key messages put across by the course instructor. He was struck by the advice to be a 'pearl fisher' — one who notices and nurtures the special things in life — rather than a 'pearl crusher', who kills off even good ideas before they have had a hearing. He had not thought before about the first four minutes of any encounter setting the tone for what followed, but recognized it would maximize what little spare time he and Maggie shared if he did not storm into the house after a bad day, thus triggering a wasted evening of argument and non-communication. He came away determined to conquer 'flapsihapsi', the Time Manager catchword for a state of muddle and disorganization when the brain is so overloaded with options and half-done tasks that it seems impossible to set priorities for anything to be completed.

Doug went home inspired. It was very unfortunate that his determination to turn theory into immediate practice was overturned: an hour before his homecoming his seven-year-old daughter, Ella, had been rushed into hospital with acute appendicitis. After surgery she developed mumps which spread to the other children. Five days later Doug reached his 40th birthday, having 'blown it' — no time to organize the hoped-for party, not even an evening out for the two of them. Nor had he come to grips with the Time Manager planning system. But a glimmering of new order could be detected: he had managed to say no to an architect who wanted a last-minute Sunday meeting, and he had earmarked a future free-ish date to sort out the swimming pool.

Once you realize that none of these three assumptions is justified, the situation becomes very different.

Since lonely people need other people to help them help themselves, their first task is to discover why they find it so difficult to make social contact. Very often a large part of the answer lies in the face they present to the world. Research shows that, compared with others, lonely people are judged to be negative, rejecting, self-absorbed, self-deprecating and unresponsive. Fortunately, none of these characteristics is irreversible, and lonely people who have difficulty in recognizing them in themselves will find social skills training an effective means of identifying and rectifying them.

The cognitive approach can be applied to any type of loneliness. But there is another option lonely people might like to consider. They can examine the significance they attach to the state which gives rise to their feelings. There is nothing inherently shameful or unnatural about being alone. In some languages (Tahitian for example), there is no word for loneliness which has negative connotations.

The social pressures in our own culture which have made a 20th-century totem out of 'togetherness' are well documented. Being alone is the price we pay for the luxury of privacy, and loneliness is first cousin to solitude – a state no sane person would want to banish from his life.

So why are we afraid of being alone? The answer lies in the way we are brought up. Of course parents are right to give their children every opportunity to develop interpersonal skills (it is actually much less harmful for them to have unsuitable friends than no friends at all). But this is not the only need children have. They require time by themselves, and the one lesson they must not be taught is to equate being alone with being a social failure. Of course adult loneliness often follows real loss, as in divorce or bereavement. However, while some people sink into helpless despair after losing a close companion, others manage to keep afloat on their own emotional resources. What distinguishes one reaction from the other is not the fact of being alone. It is the *fear* of loneliness.

Sharon Faith

Baby Joseph arrived last August to the usual small hero's welcome. But the shock of finding herself alone at home all week after years of stimulating company as a solicitor prompted his mother's approach to Lifeplan. 'One day I was able to go out and see people whenever I wanted,' said Sharon Faith. 'The next, quite suddenly, I couldn't. Having waited until I was 31 to have a child made the loss of long-accustomed freedom worse.'

The first three or four months, 'when Joseph wouldn't even give me a smile', Sharon found 'quite awful'. Her sense of isolation, of being diminished from being a busy intelligent professional with a challenging place in the scheme of things, with clients to see and colleagues to lunch with, was heightened by the suspicion that motherhood had sent her 'slightly doolally. I felt my intellectual ability impaired. I found I was fumbling for words that normally slipped off the tongue. It became a full morning's effort to read The Times.'

One obvious solution would have been to hire a nanny and rush back to her waiting case-load of matrimonial and general litigation, with the ultimate aim of becoming a partner in the firm. But there was conflict. 'Before my pregnancy I'd been 100 per cent committed to the career structure. I'd arrive at the office at 7.30am and often stay until 6.30pm. If I went back to the same job I knew I wouldn't feel able to give any less than I had before – and then I'd have no chance of being a good mother to my child in the way I hoped.'

The other natural option was for Sharon to throw herself full-time into home-based motherhood. But she could not take kindly to unstructured days and coffee mornings with other women similarly placed. 'I could not think of anything worse. I am very interested in everything my child does.' I find him delightful and fascinating. But I do not see myself as the motherly type; I am just a woman who happens to have a baby. That may give me something in common with other new mothers, but it is not the same as sharing any real empathy. I know mine cannot be an uncommon problem, because whenever I go to Brent Cross shopping centre it is crammed with mothers pushing their buggies about, filling their days with shopping because there is nothing else to do, and because they need the human contact.

Sharon has now found a contented compromise in a three-day-a-week job with a local solicitor. 'It is much less demanding but the balance is right for the moment. I like being able to think on Tuesday and Thursday evenings, "Good, I've got real work to do tomorrow", and on other evenings, "Great, tomorrow I can spend all day with my child".'

SHYNESS

Most of us find it difficult to walk into a room full of strangers or to be the sudden focus of attention. But real shyness can be a painful social problem which prevents the joys of friendship

Four out of five people are seriously affected by shyness at some time in their lives. At any given moment, however, only half that number will be currently suffering. So if you are a shy person, there is a 50 per cent chance that you will not always be – provided you *want* to change. Of course, you may not. There are advantages to being a shrinking violet. 'Unassuming' and 'retiring' are not pejorative words, whereas 'pushy' is. If no-one expects you to talk, you can sit back and observe, which may improve your judgement of what other people are saying. And when you do open your mouth, you can guarantee they will hang on your every word.

Despite this, researchers find that only one shy person in five actually enjoys being the way he or she is. These may be the ones responsible for the idea that shyness is a kind of arrogance. However, the great majority of shy people can see only the drawbacks. They find it difficult to make friends or to get on with new people. They are frustrated by not being able to communicate their ideas effectively; and they know only too well how difficult it is to avoid being underrated, at work and at home, if their tongue seizes up at the vital moment.

There are degrees of shyness. At one extreme are the lone lighthouse-keepers and arctic explorers who tend to be highly introverted characters. For them solitude seems to be a luxury rather than a deprivation. Then there is a middle range – those who feel shy in specific situations or only with certain people. Strangers, members of the opposite sex and people in author-

ity are the three groups most likely to induce shyness. The most threatening situations for a medium shy person are: being the focus of attention (especially public speaking), finding yourself in an unfamiliar situation, and having to assert yourself – for example, by arguing with a shopkeeper about defective goods. Only one person in 50 is totally shy – with *all* other people, and in *every* situation – although the figure rises to one in 10 in Japan, where shame, and hence shyness, are deliberately encouraged, and being socially forward is regarded as a sign of immaturity.

Confronted by so many potential sources of embarrassment, shy people tend to maintain a pretty low profile. Much of their time is spent in a private world. Indeed, extreme self-consciousness is the major distinguishing characteristic of the shy person. But it comes in two different forms: public and private. If you reckon you are shy, you can judge in which category you fall by seeing how many of the following statements you agree with. They come in two groups of four:

- I usually worry about making a good impression.
- I am concerned about the way I present myself.
- One of the last things I do before leaving the house is look in the mirror.
- I am concerned about what other people think of me.

Those are all manifestations of public shyness. The more statements you agree with, the more you suffer from it.

Here are some statements which

indicate private shyness:

- Generally, I am very aware of myself.
- Sometimes I get the feeling that I am off somewhere, watching myself.
- I think about myself a lot.
- I am very alert to changes in my own mood.

The more of these you agree with, the more privately shy you are.

Public shyness means you worry about *behaving* badly, while private shyness is about *feeling* bad. Most shy people suffer from both to some extent. But it is public shyness that causes more damage, since it affects how you behave and perform in front of other people, and stops you doing yourself justice. Publicly shy people rarely become leaders, because no-one notices them. Privately shy people know how to 'turn it on' in front of an audience, but they pay a price. They learn either to hide their anxiety behind a smokescreen of carefully-cultivated social skills, or else they drown it in alcohol. It may sound a contradiction to call someone a shy extrovert, but many entertainers and politicians are generating dangerously high levels of adrenalin behind an apparently self-confident exterior.

What makes people shy, and what can they do about it? Some psychologists believe that shyness is inherited. This is difficult to prove, and even if they are right, it can be only the tendency to *become* shy rather than shyness itself that is passed on through the genes. Shyness has to be a learned reaction to social events, and it can be based on three things. The first is having unfortunate experiences with other people, or watching others suffer in this way. Alternatively, it can be the result of a learning failure – not acquiring the right skills to endear yourself to other people, either through lack of practice (as happens often with children brought up in lonely country areas) or through having over-protective parents who do all the work. One of the arguments against the genetic explanation of shyness is that many shy people have parents who are too socially accomplished.

The third cause of shyness is a kind of self-fulfilling prophecy. By trying unsuccessfully to contribute to adult

Mrs Vera Veness

Although she is warm, energetic and obviously outgoing, 50-year-old Vera Veness tends to blame herself for lack of friends. 'I want desperately to be liked, but fear of being snubbed stops me making the first move. I suppose it is a form of shyness.'

During seven years in Africa with her architect husband, Vera had no problems. 'Social life was too good to be true. I was a big fish in a small pond. I ran my own typing agency. You did not have to **work** at making friends, the expatriate community came ready-made, full of professional people like us, and strong amusing characters. You could rely on weekends of wonderful weather, with people dropping in for lunch. We played bowls a lot and, as soon as we arrived in Africa, it was "Do you act? Do you sing? Join the theatrical club".'

Since returning to her childhood town of Gravesend and a job as a typist with the Inland Revenue, Vera has been depressed by the gloomy, unclubbable contrast. 'It seems to us that the English can be most unwelcoming. We have been back here ten years and made no lasting contacts.'

Since her sons, 26 and 22, have now left home, Vera feels the lack of company all the more. 'There are no more evenings of backgammon, no sport-mad audience sitting comfortably round the TV.' Vera admits to a sense of guilt that she should often feel close to tears, overcome by the feeling that the best years are behind her, when in truth she has a very happy marriage to a 'husband good enough to patent', with loving, if healthily independent sons – and no real worries whatever.

But Vera also recognizes that it is more difficult to make friends as you grow older. 'We are more choosy, my husband and I. We know very well

the sort of people we get on with – quite broad-minded, travelled, and reasonably cultured people with a sense of humour, a sense of the **ludicrous** really. But they seem to be few and far between.'

Keen to spend their spare time together, the Venesses then chose ballroom dancing as a shared group activity to enhance their Lifeplan. 'We have started going to the local dance studio one evening a week. It is great fun as we have danced before but never had instruction. We realize that we have been doing it all wrong – even the waltz! But though it is a start and there is a lovely mix of people, dancing has not proved ideal as a friendship base because you spend all your time concentrating exclusively on one another.'

What next then? 'We are thinking of a move to a smaller village where I might have more sense of belonging,' says Vera. 'Though I realize things will not change overnight.'

---

conversations, some children lose confidence and become unreasonably anxious about their social performance. The labels we pin on people are very important here. What happens, for example, when a teacher calls a child shy? The real reason why that child is not being forthcoming may simply be that they are in a situation which *any* child would find threatening – a new class, perhaps. But tell the child he is

shy often enough, and you will indeed have a shy child on your hands.

This brings us to the main difference between people who are shy and those who are not. Certain situations, like a job interview or speaking in front of a large audience, are intrinsically frightening – for everybody. But whereas non-shy people realize this and blame the situation for making them anxious, shy people blame

themselves. The first lesson taught at any shyness clinic or self-help group is that it is often perfectly rational to feel inhibited or self-conscious. Once this burden is lifted, shy people feel much better about themselves and usually find it possible to develop new social skills. They are also relieved to discover that you do not have to change your inner self to conquer shyness, only the way you behave.

COMMUNICATION

Are you angry when someone does not understand what you mean? Communication-failure is a major source of tension in both business and private life. Overcoming it requires an understanding of the pitfalls and a talent for listening

Communication is the exchange of ideas. It does not matter whether you are a politician trying to sway the floating voter, a wife reminding her husband it is his turn to walk the dog, or a teacher trying to inject some last-minute cramming.

Every act of communication contains a message aimed at an audience. The only worthwhile measure of its success is the extent to which the former influences the latter. To be an effective communicator you need to make the message interesting, appealing and comprehensible to your selected target. This calls for careful thought, not just about style and content but also about choice of medium. It also involves knowing where your audience currently stands on the subject you want to communicate. Effective communication is almost always based on research – though this often means no more than listening carefully to what is being said.

Listening, however, is a far more sophisticated skill than many people realize. And while a failure to communicate can sometimes be put down to deficiencies in the content of the message, or in the way it is put across, listening errors are at least as common a cause of communication breakdown. It is important to understand this. To communicate effectively, you have to know why communication is sometimes unsuccessful and to be aware of the rules which govern every attempt at it – particularly those concerning *responsibility*.

The problem is that we are used to the conventions of private life, where speaker and listener usually share responsibility for seeing that the lines

of communication run smoothly. Professional obligations change all that. One party often has to bear the entire responsibility for seeing that the information is transmitted, and it is not always the speaker. If a salesman rings your bell and tries to sell you double glazing, you do not have to listen. The onus is entirely on him. But if a market researcher stops you in the street it is up to him or her – i.e. the *listener* – to coax a coherent response out of you. In both cases professional status makes one party totally responsible for the way the transaction is conducted.

To make matters more complicated, in business the responsibility often varies according to the situation, even though the same two people are involved. If you sell me a car, for example, it is up to *you* to see that I fully understand the limitations of the manufacturer's warranty. If I get hold of the wrong end of the stick and later receive a bill I am not prepared for, I have every right to be furious. But if you come to me for advice about how to reorganize your company, then it is *my* job to check that you have understood exactly what I am recommending.

The fact that you may have left a manual in the boot of my car, or that I sent you an elegantly written report, is irrelevant. Neither of us absorbed the information, so both attempts at communication failed. In neither case was the style or content of the communication at fault. Failure was due to communicator error. More specifically, it was an attitude fault caused by neither of us understanding what it means to be responsible for communication.

What happens at home or in

everyday social encounters? The responsibility for making communications work is usually more evenly distributed between speaker and listener. This creates scope for even more crossed wires and broken connections at home than at work. In a family, all tends to go well at first. Newly-weds hang on to each other's words, and most parents of young children accept that it is up to them to avoid misunderstandings – *whoever* is saying what to whom. As children get older, however, their parents may come to resent this responsibility. As a result, negotiations and recriminations about things that have been done or left undone – 'even though I told you to/not to' – become a regular feature of family life.

So far as partners are concerned, familiarity may not always breed contempt. But it does usually lead to a situation where both are confident they know what the other is about to say long before he or she has finished – or sometimes started – saying it. Of course, one of the pleasures of an intimate relationship is that things can often be left unsaid. You may

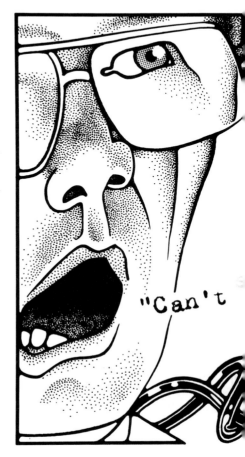

"Can't

know exactly what the other person is thinking, though it is unadvisable to rely on unspoken communication when anything really important is involved.

Then there are those little life-games which seem always to develop in long-standing relationships. Two of the most popular are pretending not to hear, and wilful misunderstanding of what has been said. The ritualized bickering which seems to hold many marriages together relies on deliberately crossing the wires. In the same way, some couples select their phrases and use conversational tricks designed to wind each other up rather than facilitate the exchange of information (see Ten Things People May Not Want to Hear). It is of course a moot point whether or not this sort of deliberate sabotage should count as a communication failure. Perhaps the real message – why are you so predictable/why do I always have to tell you that? – gets across quite effectively.

As for the various media, the important thing is to understand the different problems attached to all the most commonly used methods of communication. A letter, for example, fails most often to achieve its purpose because the writer is under the mistaken impression that letters call for a special language (usually old-fashioned business-speak). They do not. A good letter can be *spoken* to the person to whom it is addressed. So, if you are uncertain about your letter-writing ability, try reading the words aloud to someone else. If it sounds odd or unnatural, you have not got it right.

On the phone, you must make allowances for the fact that other people are not always as comfortable with the medium as you are. As a result, they can sound more anxious or aggressive than they really are. They may not be listening properly and their feelings can distort any message they are trying to convey. There are also a number of useful points of technique. For example, if you are concentrating on something when the telephone rings, take a deep breath before picking up the receiver to give your brain a chance to change gear. If you are doing written work, turn the page over while you are on

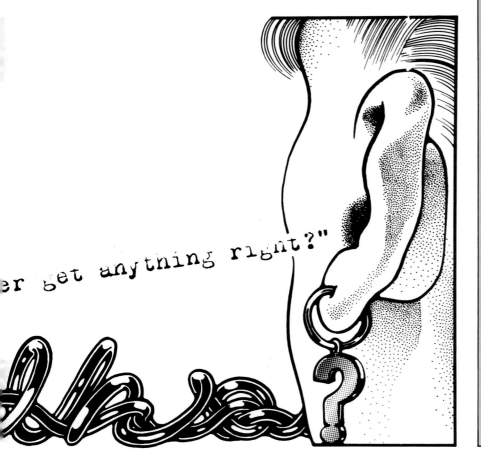

"er get anything right?"

Six golden rules for good listening

1 Stop talking – especially that internal, mental chatter – and answering back. Let the speaker finish. Hear him/her out. This is particularly important when you are in a thoroughly familiar situation. We tend to finish other people's sentences for them silently, working out our reply, on the assumption that we know exactly what they are going to say.

2 Relax. Research shows that tension and anxiety reduce the effectiveness of the auditory reception system.

3 Put the speaker at ease by showing that you are listening. The good listener does not look over someone's shoulder, or write while he is talking. If you need to take notes on what is being said, explain what you are doing. Blame your poor memory and make it clear that you are taking notes because you really want to understand what they are saying. This needs to be spelled out, because we usually rely on the expression on the other person's face to tell us how the conversation is going.

4 Remember that your aim in listening is to understand what the speaker is saying, not to win an argument.

5 Be aware of your personal prejudices and make a conscious effort to prevent them influencing your judgement of what is being said.

6 Listen with feeling as well as reason. Your main objective should be to get inside the other person's head. What would you mean if you were saying what he had just said? Similarly, be alert to what the speaker is *not* saying. Very often what is missing is more important than what is there. Again, ask yourself: what would it mean if I had left out what he has just failed to say? Remember that listening is an *active* process, never more important than when you are meeting someone for the first time. On these occasions, your objective should be to say as little as possible and learn as much as possible as quickly as you can.

the phone. It is easy to tell when the person on the other end of the line is not giving you his full attention. When you make a call, check that the person answering is not already tied up with something important. If you tell him who you are, why you are calling and how long you think the call is going to take, he can without embarrassment suggest that you call back later. He cannot expect you to know what he is doing, but he will be grateful for the consideration you have shown. Similarly, at the end of a call to somebody you do not know well, thanking them for their time creates an excellent final impression and makes it more likely that your message will be remembered.

Face to face, remember that you have two ears and one mouth. Try to use them in roughly that proportion. End your contributions to a conversation decisively, so that the other person avoids the embarrassment of replying prematurely. Some two-thirds of what we communicate to each other is conveyed non-verbally, by appearance, expression and gesture. Generally speaking, we use language to communicate facts and hard information, and non-verbal signals to show whether or not we actually *like* the person we are talking or listening to.

For example, if I am talking to you and notice that you are sitting with your chin down, arms folded in front of your chest and legs tightly crossed, then I do not need a PhD in psychology to realize that you are not enjoying what you are hearing. Other useful body language tips are: always shake hands with someone sideways on; and avoid the gesture known as a raised steeple (two sets of fingers raised and touching each other in the shape of a steeple or wigwam). Coupled with head tilted back, this gives the impression of arrogance and smugness. And remember that although there is no infallible way to tell whether another person is telling the truth, most people who are lying are in a state of tension which has to leak out somewhere. Try looking down at their feet.

Ten things people do not want to hear

Here are 10 statements that can kill a conversation. All of them can be acceptable in the right context. But more often than not they are things that people do not enjoy hearing.

'I'm interested in what is going well for you, not in what is going wrong.' This is an attempt to control what the other person is saying to you. The chances are he would prefer to control his own statements.

'I don't think you should be seeing him.' This sort of value judgement makes people clam up if you come out with it too early in the conversation.

'You started it.' Blame statements are a turn-off. If the person already knows it is his fault, he does not need you to remind him. If he does not know, then your opinion will be even less welcome.

'Can't you ever get anything right?' Statements designed to cause pain or to put people down rarely make for effective communication.

'Sex is not everything in life.' Whatever they may say, other people do not usually like to be told how to lead their lives.

'No wonder you're lonely, you need to go out and meet people.' People need to find their own solutions. By all means present them with the evidence, but let them draw the conclusions themselves.

'Don't feel so sorry for yourself.' People do not want to be told what they should be feeling.

'You can get by ... I know you can.' This sort of reassurance is usually spurious. You want them to cheer up for your sake, not theirs.

'Well I never. I wouldn't have believed it!' Such overstated displays of interest have all the conviction of a TV game show host.

'Sure, but try and tell me as quickly as you can.' If you have no time for a proper conversation, it is better not to start one. Other people want to be made to feel important, not to be told how busy you are.

Questions of tactics

Used correctly, questions are a powerful weapon in the communicator's armoury. Here are three good examples:

When dealing with a touchy subject (i.e. when you suspect there is something the other person does not want to tell you), it may be useful to put your question in the past tense. For example, don't ask: 'Do you sometimes forget to?…' Ask instead: 'Have you ever forgotten to?…' or begin 'Did you once forget to?…'

An Alternative Question can be very useful when you are dealing with somebody you would like to force into making a decision. For example, if you wanted to persuade him to spend money, you might ask him not *whether* he wanted to do so but *when*. For example: 'Would you like to take it now or would you rather make an appointment for one day next week?' 'By diverting his attention from the major decision towards an easier one about timing you will have earned gratitude – and may even have made the big decision for him.

The most effective way to end a conversation with someone too fond of the sound of his own voice without seeming rude is to use a Closed Question. This is the sort which demands a yes or no answer. Hearing himself give a one-word reply interrupts the flow and usually persuades him that it is time he shut up – especially if you reinforce the message with a decisive bit of body language, such as getting up from your chair or rubbing your hands together. Beware of using too many closed questions, however, otherwise you run the risk of sounding like the Gestapo!

YOUR FRIENDS

'The wall of friendship has to be kept in constant repair.' But building it in the first place takes perseverance, honesty and time. Have you learned the art of real friendship – and can you provide it?

Making friends does not come naturally to everyone. Nor do we all have the same need for friends. It is one of the things which distinguish the fun-loving extrovert from the more self-sufficient introvert. The more extrovert you are, the more people-hungry you are likely to be. Introverts are happier with their own company, but even they need some close friends. The average adult has about 15 people he or she thinks of as friends, and perhaps five *close* friends. But it varies according to personality, and women tend to have more close friends than men.

Where do they come from, these marvellously obliging creatures who play a vital role in holding the fabric of our lives together? Is there some magic formula for making and keeping friends? Even when you are lucky enough to meet potential friends in circumstances ideal for establishing a friendship, it will be months before you know the relationship is not going to fizzle out when you know each other better. The crucial testing period for most friendships actually comes four to six months in, when friends begin to try each other by becoming more assertive and less accommodating, and may even express outrageous opinions to see how the other person reacts.

Not that short, tempestuous friendships are necessarily a bad thing. Some people, especially extroverts, enjoy short-term relationships with people who are totally different from themselves. They like to be stimulated and provoked for a while, and then drop the friend when incompatibility becomes irritating. No

harm is done, nor is there any threat to the small body of 'real' friends, who tend to be pretty similar people to ourselves.

This brings us to the first rule of friendship. Be realistic about whom you try to become close friends with. In marriage, it is often good for partners to complement each other's strengths. But between friends the old adage about birds of a feather is usually more true than the attraction of opposites. So do not invest too much in a budding friendship until you are confident that the other person shares your view of the world and your interests. In friendship, what you do together is more important than what you look like or how you think.

Intimate disclosures

Do not make the mistake of revealing too much about yourself too soon either. Research shows that nothing is more damaging to a developing friendship than one partner pouring out his or her heart before the other is ready for intimate disclosures. Friendship thrives on honesty, plain speaking and the exchange of confidences. But premature revelations give the impression that you are gushing or indiscreet, so bide your time until the other person makes it clear that they are ready to hear what you want to tell.

Psychologists have not yet come up with an infallible recipe for making friends. But we do know that certain situations make for improbable friendships. For example, never expect too much of friendships which start on holiday: people you are attracted to when the sun is shining

and the wine flowing often lose their appeal when you are back in real life.

Some of our most intense friendships are made while we are still at school, both on a one-to-one basis and in groups and gangs. Here we learn how to keep a secret and how to gossip, how to maintain loyalties and how to betray them: lessons absorbed outside the classroom but very often more about real life and relevant to it than text book or Bunsen burner.

How do we choose our childhood friends? Proximity is obviously important, as are mutual interests and hobbies. Family networks often provide more than blood ties: a cousin may be that and best friend too, with all the similarities of background, temperament, religion and upbringing families entail.

Conversely, the increase in the divorce rate may divide siblings, throwing close family friendships open to half-brothers and half-sisters – or to ones completely outside the family where confidences and problems can be aired and discussed with greater freedom.

A surprisingly large proportion of really important friendships date from the late teens and early 20s. That is not to say that friendships formed before then are bound to fade, nor that we lose the knack of making friends after the age of 25. But it does mean that young adults should think carefully about whom they spend time with, because friends from these days are not easy to shake off and have a nasty habit of turning up ever afterwards.

The friendship drive seems to decline from about the age of 30, and does not really pick up again until just before retirement. One reason for this is that opportunities for making new friends are greatly reduced by work and family commitments. But if you want to make new friends you may be surprised by how much less difficult it seems than when you were adolescent.

As we get older, most of us gain in self-confidence and social skills, the lack of which are two of the greatest stumbling blocks for teenagers. We have learnt that friendship has to involve give and take. We also know that, as Dr Johnson said, 'the wall of friendship has to be kept in constant repair'.

BEDROOM POLITICS

The Victorians considered it acceptable for a man to marry a pre-pubescent girl, but they were shocked at the sight of a woman's ankles. Attitudes change; today the pendulum is swinging again

Attitudes to sex are constantly changing. What is normal in one century may be guaranteed to inflame the moral purifiers in another. What is fine in Tunbridge Wells might yet put you behind bars in some states in America.

In many parts of the modern world a display of breast cleavage can still cause shock. Among the supposedly prudish Victorians, however, this would not have raised an eyebrow. Their great problem was with ankles — so erotically inflammatory in their minds that the legs of grand pianos had to be covered to keep the music-room safe for the children. There have been other turnarounds too. Marriage with a pre-pubescent girl, for example, was thought perfectly acceptable (even for the Archbishop of Canterbury), but extra-marital sex with an adult woman was taboo.

The outstanding case is masturbation. In the last century it was regarded as evil, repulsive and the cause of all manner of mental and physical ills, ranging from warts to blindness and insanity. Countless treatises were written on the 'Sin of Onan,' with prescribed remedies including clitoral cauterisation and vaginal infibulation. Between 1856 and 1932, no fewer than 33 restraint devices were registered with the US Patent Office, including braces, chains, handcuffs, armoured chastity belts and inwardly spiked penis rings guaranteed to arrest incipient erections. Dr Kellogg introduced his first breakfast cereal as an antidote to masturbation, presumably in the belief that healthy regularity purifies the mind as well as the body.

Compare all this with the situation today. Masturbation is now taught in children's sex education films and recommended by therapists as treatment for sexual difficulties. Patents are issued for masturbatory aids such as vibrators and artificial vaginas.

Such radical swings show that sexual attitudes are value judgements, not moral absolutes, and that 'sophistication' must be judged against prevailing current opinion. Nevertheless, some changes in attitudes are based on improved knowledge and therefore are likely to stick. Alfred Kinsey's revelation that masturbation was practised by 92 per cent of American men and 62 per cent of women led inevitably to increased tolerance and 'normalisation'. Oral sex was regarded as a perversion until researchers demonstrated its ubiquity.

The least sophisticated stratum of society continues to be the law, with legislators failing dramatically to keep pace with prevailing views and knowledge. Oral sex, for example, is still illegal and subject to heavy penalties in many parts of the world (including some of the United States). In Canada, before Pierre Trudeau became Minister of Justice in the late 1960s, men were serving *life sentences* for such 'unnatural' acts with their wives.

In Britain, a man who buggers another man without his consent (i.e. rapes him anally) risks 10 years in jail. If he has anal sex with his wife or an animal, he is liable to *life* imprisonment.

Anomalies abound. Girls can have sex at 16 but are not permitted to marry without their parents' consent until they are 18. It is legal to ask a 16-year-old girl to have sex with you, but you may not ask a 20-year-old woman to have sex with your brother. This is 'procuring a minor'. A boy of 13 can be charged with the rape of an adult woman, although the law presumes him to be incapable of it. If the woman *consents* to intercourse, she herself commits no offence, but she must remain the passive partner and not 'touch him indecently'. A 14-year-old boy, on the other hand, can be convicted of 'passive homosexuality'.

Lesbianism has never been illegal in Britain. Initially this was because of the Church's teaching that women were naturally corrupt and inferior beings, and therefore beyond redemption. When this doctrine was replaced in the 19th century by the myth of female 'purity,', attempts to make lesbianism illegal were, ironically, dismissed by Queen Victoria on the ground that 'women could never contemplate such a thing'.

It is wrong to imagine that permissiveness inevitably continues to increase. The permissive sociey reached its acme in the 1970s — a combined result of effective contraception (producing freedom from the fear of unwanted pregnancy), antibiotics (cure of VD), and technological developments such as the motor car (mobility and privacy) and television (pictorial titillation). Recognition of the population explosion may also have assisted the recreational (as opposed to reproductive) sex lobby.

But in the 1980s there are distinct signs that the pendulum is swinging back the other way. After a brief burst of 'women's liberation' (women should emulate men, burn their bras and pursue sexual gratification without commitment), 'feminism' took over with a return to traditional female morality (men should behave like women, burn their porn and castrate the lechers). The 'new chastity' derived impetus from boredom with promiscuity ('there has to be more to life'), the herpes scare (antibiotics do not help) and especially the AIDS epidemic (not just incurable, but fatal).

What history shows us is that, however emotional it may appear, sexual morality is influenced as well as justified by pragmatic considerations. What is 'right' and 'wrong' depends upon where we are, when we are, and who we are, and this should be remembered before we become too self-righteous. What we owe to our partners, as well as to ourselves, is to be knowledgeable in the matter of sex and appreciative of the ways in which individuals differ from one another. The Lifeplan Scorechart tests sexual maturity through attitudes which are frequently distorted by prejudice and misinformation.

WHEN JOY TURNS TO AGONY

During the course of many long-term relationships, couples encounter periods of difficulty with their sexual lives. The problems are often exacerbated by misunderstanding, feelings of shame and guilt and an inability to speak frankly to each other. Here are some ways to overcome the most common kinds of problems

According to Woody Allen, 'there are only two things in life that are important. One is sex, and other is not all that important'.

Certainly no other sphere of life has the capacity to produce such joy on the one hand and such misery and distress on the other. In any discussion of sexual problems it is necessary to be frank, and useful to group them under four general headings – orientation, appetite, arousal and orgasm. Disorders of arousal are most obvious (and feared) in men, where they are manifested as impotence, or inability to obtain a satisfactory erection. (This is not the same thing as infertility, which means difficulty in reproduction, often due to sperm deficiency.)

Erection problems may be caused by a wide variety of psychological factors – stress or the fear of failure, disease or punishment – but physical factors are also important. Alcohol is so widely recognized as a cause of impotence that the condition is commonly known as 'brewer's droop'. Age and fatigue may be implicated, and so may certain diseases such as multiple sclerosis, diabetes, tumours and hormonal disturbances. Increasingly it is being recognized that some medications, especially drugs used to reduce blood pressure, may cause potency problems as a side-effect.

Sex therapists check functioning of the equipment by asking the patient if he ever wakes up with an erection in the mornings. (Erection normally occurs during dream sleep, regardless of whether the dreams are sexual in content. If it does not, something physiological has probably gone wrong.)

If a man's impotence is situation-specific, then psychological factors are clearly important. A businessman, referred by his wife to a sex therapy clinic as impotent, privately admitted stud-like prowess with his secretary. In such cases it is the relationship that is at fault, not the plumbing.

Arousal disorder in women is less public. Sometimes the problem is a straightforward lack of lubrication, easily offset by the use of oils, creams or K-Y Jelly. Thus intercourse can still occur even if (initially at least) it is less exciting. But the main problem, afflicting women much more than men, is that of orgasm failure. While a few lucky women seem capable of orgasm by fantasy alone, most require manual or oral stimulation in addition to intercourse, and some never achieve orgasm at all.

Although religious guilt, social inhibition and anxiety are frequently cited as causes of orgasm difficulty, scientific evidence for this is almost entirely lacking. For example, religious devoutness does not correlate

with orgasm failure, and anti-anxiety drugs are ineffective as treatment. The limiting factor seems to be constitution (after all, in evolutionary terms, women's orgasm is unnecessary), although all women probably have the potential for orgasm and various training exercises are helpful.

The flip-side of female orgasm difficulty is premature ejaculation, though it is not always clear whose problem this is. If a man ejaculates before getting his trousers off it is fair to say he has the problem. However, by some extreme definitions, a man is a premature ejaculator if he reaches orgasm before his partner on more than half of all occasions of intercourse, regardless of how many hours he may perform. From this viewpoint premature ejaculation is just female orgasm difficulty with the blame transferred. Most therapists operate some reasonable, intermediate definition, but where an established couple are concerned it matters little anyway. The treatment is much the same.

Disorders of appetite are increasingly recognized as important, particularly in women. A high proportion of women complain that they are just not sufficiently interested in sex to keep their partners happy; many prefer knitting, gardening and watching TV.

In Victorian days this would have been recognized as normal, and any woman with a libido approaching that of the average man would have been called a 'nymphomaniac'. Today, with a powerful myth of male/female identity, women who have little interest in sex are made to wonder what is wrong with them.

In a sense, it is unjust that lack of desire should be a problem attributed

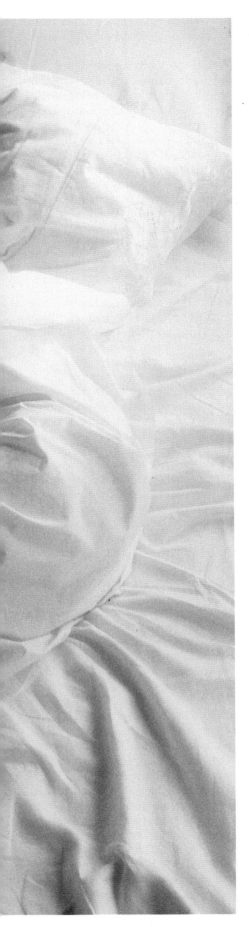

mostly to women. After all, if men were equally disinterested there would be no problem. The reason probably is that libido cannot easily be *reduced* by other than chemical or surgical means, whereas an interest can be *increased* by use of erotica, fantasy, foreplay, role-playing, etc. Thus the partner with the lower level of sexual appetite is more often seen as the suitable case for treatment.

One 'disorder of desire' that probably affects men more than women is the resistance that arises from repeated sex with the same partner. In laboratory animals this is called the Coolidge Effect, after a story about President and Mrs Coolidge. During a guided tour of a US government farm, Mrs Coolidge expressed curiosity about how often a rooster performed his duty. 'Dozens of times a day,' she was told. 'Tell that to the president,' she said.

On being told of this feat, President Coolidge was initially dismayed; then a thought occurred to him. 'Wait a minute,' he said. 'Is that with the same hen each time?'

'Oh no, Mr President, a different hen each time.'

'Tell that to Mrs Coolidge.'

A tendency for males to be sexually recharged by novel females is observed in most mammals (farmers need only one bull or ram to service all the females). Although not so striking in the human case, a residual of this exploratory drive remains, and it gets men into a lot of trouble with their wives. In the sex clinic, it appears as a specific loss of appetite for the wife – even though the man may still love her in more general terms.

The last category of problem, that of the orientation or 'target' of sexual interest, is much more common in men. Homosexual orientation (as opposed to occasional behaviour) occurs in something like five per cent

Case study 1

Jeremy was a good-looking and successful 30-year-old businessman. His wife had left him two years earlier because she had fallen in love with a close mutual friend. The divorce upset him deeply, leaving him depressed, insecure and ruminating about whether he was inferior to the other man.

Some months after the separation he went to a party where he met an assertive woman who wanted to have sex with him immediately. On her urging they went upstairs and attempted intercourse on the floor of an unlocked bedroom. Initially he was very excited, but he soon lost his erection and was unable to perform.

He reacted with alarm to this experience, feeling embarrassed and humiliated. He never saw the woman again, but a month later when he tried to make love to another woman he again lost his erection when the memory of his previous failure intruded. Thereafter the problem escalated, and he presented himself for treatment after falling in love with a woman whom he would like to marry but was afraid would leave him as soon as she discovered his problem.

The therapist explained to Jeremy that his impotence had been caused by a vicious spiral. The fear of failure had inhibited his sexual arousal, and this further reinforced his expectation that he would fail again next time. He was instructed not to attempt intercourse with his new partner but to engage in gentle caresses and foreplay when they both had plenty of time to relax. On the second such session Jeremy, freed of his performance anxiety, found himself possessed of such a firm erection that he ventured to break the no-intercourse rule. Reassured by his success, his confidence returned and the spiral of inhibition was quickly reversed.

of men and one per cent of women, while fetishism, transvestism, sado-masochism, paedophilia, zoophilia and other unusual preferences are almost exclusively male. Their causes are very complex, beginning early in life (if not before birth) and they are generally not amenable to alteration by any current therapeutic procedures. With a shift towards greater social acceptance (particularly of homosexuality), treatment is much less often sought.

The most widely-used methods of sex therapy are derived from techniques pioneered in the USA by William Masters and Virginia Johnson. There is a strong preference for treating couples as a unit whenever possible, though individuals may be seen if they have no partner, or if their partner refuses to co-operate. Some therapists provide patients with 'surrogate' partners who help train them in sexual competence, though the ethics of this are hotly debated.

Just as couples are usually seen together, so there are usually two therapists, one male and one female, to provide equity with respect to empathy and embarrassment. Masters and Johnson favour a residential 'crash course' in which the couple book into a hotel for about two weeks to concentrate on the exercises that are prescribed for them, but not all therapists require such intensive sessions. The main elements of treatment are:

● **Education** about sexual anatomy and physiology, hygiene, etiquette and love-making techniques.

● **Permission-giving** necessarily reviewed when a couple's background has been unduly repressive.

● **Encouragement** of open communication between the partners, so they can tell each other in non-accusatory ways about their feelings, needs and preferences.

● **Exercises** intended to slow down the love-making process and introduce a greater amount of foreplay, thus allowing sufficient time for each partner to achieve satisfaction.

● **Exercises** to increase clitoral stimulation and to give the woman a more active participation in love-making – most notably in the female-superior position.

One favourite technique of sex therapists is to ban all attempts at intercourse in the early stages of treatment. Instead the couple are instructed to take turns at gently touching and massaging ('pleasuring') each other while lying naked together. This has the dual purpose of slowing things down and reducing performance anxiety (where, for instance, the man's impotence is made worse by fear of failure). In practice many couples report breaching the non-intercourse rule, to their own surprise and delight.

A specific technique that is often prescribed for premature ejaculation is 'the squeeze'. The woman stimulates her partner until he signals that he is close to the 'point of inevitability', at which moment she gently squeezes the end of his penis (especially the underside where the head joins the shaft). This usually inhibits the ejaculation, and after a short rest the exercise is repeated. The idea is that the man will eventually learn conscious control of his own excitement.

Not all therapists follow the Masters and Johnson model. Coming from a medical background, they were very concerned about the respectability of their treatment programmes (hence their emphasis on treating married couples), and they tended to overestimate the importance of pathological factors such as anxiety and childhood trauma. But they probably underestimated the role of 'normal' processes such as boredom and hostility within a long-term relationship.

Another approach that has become popular in recent years is group therapy for women with orgasm difficulty. This is likely to include instruction in self-examination, obtaining satisfaction through masturbation, and training in control of vaginal muscles (Kegel exercises).

There is also a method called 'Sexual Attitude Restructuring' which involves meeting in a group over a weekend for brain-storming sessions of explicit films and discussion. This combines sex education with a breaking down of embarrassment and inhibition and is, not surprisingly, an import from California.

HOW DID YOU SCORE?

Check your answers from pages 84-5

1 Manipulativeness

Score 2 points for each statement you agree with. The higher your score, the more Machiavellian your personality. A score of 8 or more suggests you may be too calculating for your own good; a score of 4 or less indicates a level of gullibility which may sometimes get you into trouble.

2 Shyness

For questions 2, 3, 5, 8 and 9, score 2 points for each TRUE answer, and zero for every FALSE. For questions 1, 4, 6, 7 and 10, score 2 points for each FALSE and zero for each TRUE. The higher your score, the more shy you are. A score of 12 or more suggests you are ill-at-ease in the presence of others, and self-conscious even when you are alone. A score of 6 or less indicates that you rarely find other people intimidating, though it may be that you do not find them very interesting either.

3 Running your own life

For questions 2, 4, 6, 9 and 10, score 2 points for each YES answer and zero for every NO. For questions 1, 3, 5, 7 and 8, score 2 points for each NO, and zero for each YES. The higher your score, the more in control of your life you are. A score of 14 or more suggests you have a healthy degree of autonomy, while a score of 10 or less implies you should be taking steps to get a firmer grip on things.

4 Relationships

Give yourself 2 points for each time you answered TRUE to the odd-numbered questions (1, 3, 5, 7 and 9), and 2 points for each time you answered FALSE to the even-numbered questions (2, 4, 6, 8 and 10). The higher your score, the better you are at getting on with new people. A score of 12 or more suggests you are an accomplished social operator; a score of 6 or less indicates you are not at ease with strangers.

5 Getting on with your partner

A positive answer to any of these questions identifies a problem area in arguably the most important relationship of your private life. While a couple of TRUE responses are probably par for the course in most long-term relationships, any more than this may spell trouble, unless you are both prepared to re-examine the relationship – and yourselves.

6 Sexual maturity

Give yourself 1 point for each even-numbered statement you agreed with, and 1 for each odd-numbered statement you disagreed with. This will give you a 'sexual maturity' rating out of 20 that may be interpreted as follows: 16 – 20: congratulations, you are an A-Grade student of contemporary sexual attitudes and beliefs (which is to say that you agree with the authors of this questionnaire). 11 – 15: you have a reasonable understanding of the opposite sex, but also a few blind spots. In certain respects your attitudes lag behind those of expert opinion and society at large. 6 – 10: you could definitely benefit from greater information about sex, and a broader outlook. Either you have not 'grown up' sexually or you have rather slipped out of touch. 0 – 5: you can only be described as a sexual dinosaur whose attitudes and beliefs are completely out-moded. In another century you may turn out to be right, but from today's perspective your ideas are naïve and immature.

7 Emotional versatility

There are two separate scores to be obtained from this test. First calculate your *femininity* rating by scoring ONE point for each of the listed alternatives you ticked. Then calculate your *masculinity* rating in the same way, and add up the total for each list. Femininity rating: question 1, false; 3, true; 5, false; 7, false; 9, false; 11, true; 13, false; 15, true; 17, true.

Masculinity rating: question 2, true; 4, false; 6, true; 8, true; 10, false; 12, true; 16, true; 18, false; 20, false.

Now subtract your masculinity score from your femininity score. If the resulting total is positive, you show a predominance of behaviour associated with the traditional feminine stereotype; if it's negative, you show more of the attributes which traditionalists would call 'masculine'. The possible range of scores is −10 to +10. A score of 0 indicates a perfect balance between the two traditional gender roles; in other words, you are truly emotionally versatile. In fact a score of −1, 0 or +1 counts as versatile, with −2 or +2 showing a fair degree of flexibility between the masculine and feminine roles. A score of 3 or 4 suggests you are firmly predisposed towards behaving in either the feminine (if your score is positive) or the masculine (if it's negative) way. These observations apply regardless of the sex of the person completing the test.

MAKING IT WORK

1 Health/fitness

1 Have you walked a mile at any time in the last week?

2 Would you usually take the lift rather than the stairs to go up two floors?

3 Do you take some form of fairly vigorous exercise (enough to make you a bit breathless) lasting at least 20 minutes, at least twice a week?

4 Is your pulse rate *at rest*:

a for men aged under 40, less than 70 per minute?

b for men aged 40 or over, less than 75 per minute?

c for women aged under 40, less than 80 per minute?

d for women aged 40 or over, less than 85 per minute?

5 Step test: this is moderately vigorous and quite safe for most people, but you should not attempt it if your resting pulse rate exceeds 100. If it starts to make you feel at all uncomfortable or dizzy, stop the test. Using one step on a staircase, or an 8in high box, step up and down, changing feet each time. Continue at the rate of about 25 step-ups a minute for three minutes, rest for 30 seconds and take your pulse. Is your pulse rate now:

a for men aged under 40, less than 85 per minute?

b for men aged 40 or over, less than 90 per minute?

c for women aged under 40, less than 95 per minute?

d for women aged 40 or over, less than 100 per minute?

6 Men: breathe out and measure your waist; breathe in and measure your chest. Is your waist measurement greater than your chest?

7 Women: can you pinch at least an inch of fat from the back of your upper arm?

8 Do you try to limit your intake of sugary, salty or fatty food?

9 Do you usually grill rather than fry?

10 Do you usually use silver or gold topped milk rather than skimmed/semi-skimmed?

11 Do you eat some fresh fruit most days?

12 Do you eat wholemeal bread or wholemeal chapattis most days?

13 Do you have a breakfast cereal most mornings?

There is no universal panacea, and no magic wand. You should be a wiser person for having read this book, but you will be a better one only if you put its precepts into practice. This takes commitment. In some cases, depending on the goals you have set yourself, it may take considerable feats of willpower. Easy for us, you may say, to argue that you should give up smoking, but in the end only you can provide the impulse to do it. But not everything is so difficult, and there is very little in the Lifeplan programme that demands the sacrifice of pleasure. More often, the reverse is true. Making better use of your mind; taking regular exercise; eating sensibly (but not faddishly); reorganizing your sleeping patterns to match your needs more closely. All these things will enhance the enjoyment of your daily life.

See page 133 for interpretation of your answers

14a Do you usually drink more than five cups of coffee (or 10 cups of tea) a day?

b If No, is it 3-5 cups of coffee (6-10 cups of tea)?

15 What's your cigarette habit? (Tick one)
a More than 40 a day
b 21-40 a day
c 11-20 a day
d 10 a day
e Ex-smoker
f Never smoked

16 Do you sometimes miss work because of a hangover?

17 Do your gums often bleed when you brush your teeth?

18 Do you often take work home with you?

19 Do you often fall asleep in front of the television?

20 Do you usually wake up looking forward to the day?

2 Stress

In each of the following questions you must decide which of the alternatives, a or b, is more true for you. There is no inbetween category. Just tick whichever statement seems to apply more accurately.

1 Are you **a** casual about appointments or
b never late?

2 Are you **a** very competitive or
b not competitive?

3 Are you **a** a good listener or
b do you often interrupt?

4 Are you **a** always rushed or
b never rushed?

5 Can you **a** wait patiently or
b are you impatient?

6 Do you **a** tend to hide your feelings or
b usually express what you feel?

7 Do you **a** take things one at a time or
b do lots of things at once?

8 Would you describe yourself as
a hard-driving or
b easy going?

9 Do you tend to
a do things slowly (eg eating or walking) or
b do things fast?

10 Do you **a** have few interests outside work or
b lots of outside interests?

3 Reading the signs

1 Do you often feel you want to burst into tears?

2 Do you bite your nails or have any nervous tics?

3 Do you find it hard to concentrate and make decisions?

4 Do you often feel irritable, snappy and unsociable?

5 Do you often find yourself eating when you're not hungry?

6 Do you sometimes feel you're going to explode?

7 Do you regularly drink or smoke to calm your nerves?

8 Do you sleep badly?
9 Have you lost interest in sex?

10 Do you feel increasingly gloomy and suspicious of others?

4 Logical reasoning

In the following test there are 10 short sentences, each followed by a pair of letters (AB or BA). The sentences purport to describe the order of the two letters – ie to say which comes first. They can do this in several different ways. Thus the order AB can be correctly described by saying either (1) A precedes B, or (2) B follows A, or (3) B does not precede A, or (4) A does not folllow B. All these are correct descriptions of the pair AB but are incorrect when applied to the other pair, BA.

Your job is to read each sentence below and to decide whether it is a true or false description of the letters following it. Work as quickly as you can without making mistakes. Start with sentence 1, then work systematically through the test leaving no blank spaces. Time yourself, so that your logical efficiency measure reflects both how accurately and how quickly you are thinking.

1 A is preceded by B – BA.

2 B does not precede A – AB.

3 A is not followed by B – BA.

4 B is preceded by A – BA.

5 A is followed by B – AB.

6 A does not follow B – AB.

7 B is not preceded by A – AB.

8 B follows A – AB.

9 A precedes B – BA.

10 B does not follow A – BA.

MAKE THE MOST OF YOUR MIND

Other people can provide you with information, but only you can learn it. How can you improve your mental efficiency and reveal its full potential?

Psychological research shows we consistently underestimate our mental powers. If you think this does not apply to you, then here is a simple test to show you are wrong.

Write down the names of all the English counties you can remember. Put the list away and then set yourself the same task in a week's time. Provided you have not cheated by consulting an atlas you will notice something rather surprising. The two lists will contain roughly the same number of counties, but they will not be identical. Some names will have slipped away, but others will have replaced them. This suggests that somewhere in your mind you may well have a record of virtually every county. So it is not really your *memory* letting you down; just your ability to retrieve information from it.

The tip-of-the-tongue phenomenon makes the same point. Next time you are in the position of almost but not quite being able to remember a word, control your rage and write down all the alternatives that are blocking out the word you want. When you eventually remember it, the chances are you will find it has something in common with all the other words you have written down. Perhaps they all start with the same letter, or maybe they have the same number of syllables. But you have not really *forgotten* the word: it obviously exerted an influence on the other words that came into your head.

We would remember a lot more if we had more confidence in our memories and knew how to use them properly. One useful tip is that things are more likely to be remembered if you are in exactly the same state and place as you were when you learnt

them. That is why alcoholics often forget where their bottle is hidden once they have sobered up, and yet go straight to it next time they are drunk. Similarly, when divers return to the surface they sometimes forget information they have absorbed underwater, but they remember it next time they are 40 feet down.

So if you are a student who always revises on black coffee, perhaps it is sensible to prime yourself with a cup before going into the exam. If possible, you should also try to learn information in the room where it is going to be tested. Exactly the same principle applies to your emotional state. You should aim to take a test, *any* test, in the same frame of mind as you were in when revising for it. This is one reason why people who get nervous in exams sometimes find it helpful to frighten themselves.

First absorb, then consolidate

When you learn is also important. Lots of people swear they can absorb new information more efficiently at some times of day than at others. Research shows that this is not just imagination. There is a biological rhythm for learning, although it affects different people in different ways. For most of us, the best plan is to absorb new information in the morning, and then try to consolidate it into memory during the afternoon. But this does not apply to everyone, so it is essential to establish your own rhythm. You can do this by learning a set number of lines of poetry at different times of the day, and seeing when most lines stick. When you have done this, try to organize your life so that the time set aside for learning coincides with the time when your

memory is at its best.

You should also be sensible about organizing what you have to learn. Trying to memorize too much similar information at the same time can lead to confusion. If you are preparing for several different exams, do not spend a whole learning period on any one of them. A switch of material is more likely to be a help than a hindrance. It also enables you to exploit what psychologists call primacy and recency effects. What you learn when you first sit down, and the last thing you read before taking a break, tend to be remembered better than the material your eye passes over in between. The same applies to material you hear, which is why good lecturers make their really important points at the beginning of the talk and repeat them at the end. Avoid learning marathons, because they do not make the best use of your mind. Take plenty of breaks. They offer a double bonus: the time off gives your mind a chance to do some preliminary consolidation, and it also gives a memory boost to the learning which occurs on either side of it.

Tricks of association

Then there are the 'revolutionary' tricks and systems offered in all those *How To Improve Your Memory* advertisements. The techniques on which they are based are actually more than 2,000 years old. They advise you to reduce any information you want to remember to a small number of key words – preferably not more than seven – each of which should trigger off a strand of related but more detailed facts or figures. The key words themselves are remembered by first memorizing a sequence of locations – for example, the rooms and cupboards in your home – and then visualizing in turn each of the things you want to remember (or a particularly memorable object you associate with them), sitting in each of these locations. So, an aspiring Labour MP who wanted to make a speech without notes which consisted of (a) an attack on Tory defence policy, (b) the decline of the National Health Service and (c) Mrs Thatcher's personality, could memorize it by imagining a cruise missile in his bedroom, an ambulance in his living room and the Prime Minister locked in his wardrobe.

But this example makes two important points about artificial memory aids. The first is that they really work only if you are a visualizer – i.e. if you find it easy to conjure up vivid mental pictures. For reasons we do not understand, some people are happier with verbal than with visual material. The difference between a verbalizer and a visualizer is the difference between a Scrabble and a chess player. If you are in any doubt which is your strength, go through the alphabet in your head, working out first how many letters contain an E sound; and then how many curves in their shapes when typewritten in capitals. The correct answers are eight and 11. Most people find the first task easier, but the smaller the discrepancy between the time it took you to carry out the two tasks, the more likely it is that you are a visualizer.

If you are a verbalizer, do not worry. You may not need to boost your memory by using party tricks. And if you really do have a poor memory, here are two thoughts to console you. The first is that the

importance of memory declines with the invention of every new external information storing device – from the address book to the computer. Schools now recognize this by encouraging children to think *about* things, rather than by forcing them to remember information they can perfectly well look up in a book. There is also a lot of truth in the old saying that a great memory does not make a mind, any more than a dictionary is a piece of literature.

Mental activity is not just about remembering things, however. You also have to *learn* them. Here, too, research suggests that we tend to be unnecessarily pessimistic both on our own behalf and about other people – particularly the very young and the very old. Babies, for example, are a lot smarter than we sometimes realize. Far from being wrapped up in their own little worlds, most babies are desperately eager to make sense of what is going on around them, not just by watching but by active experiment. These experiments include imitating the sounds and gestures that adults

make, and throwing things from their high chairs to the floor. Adults too often misinterpret this as simple *joie de vivre* or bloody-mindedness.

Young children, too, are not only anxious to learn but capable of quite sophisticated logical reasoning – provided that the problems are presented in a way which is interesting to *them* rather than to the adult posing the problem. Unfortunately many teachers not only fail to exploit children's natural curiosity, but also create learning difficulties which can last a lifetime.

Perhaps the most dramatic example of this is seen with rather older children: specifically, girls in science lessons at mixed schools. Studies of classroom behaviour show that when a boy gives a wrong answer the teacher usually stays with him to suggest new approaches to the problem until he gets it right. So the boy comes to *expect* to give right answers if he tries hard enough, and learns to regard an initial failure as a challenge. Girls, on the other hand, are not encouraged to keep trying. When they give the

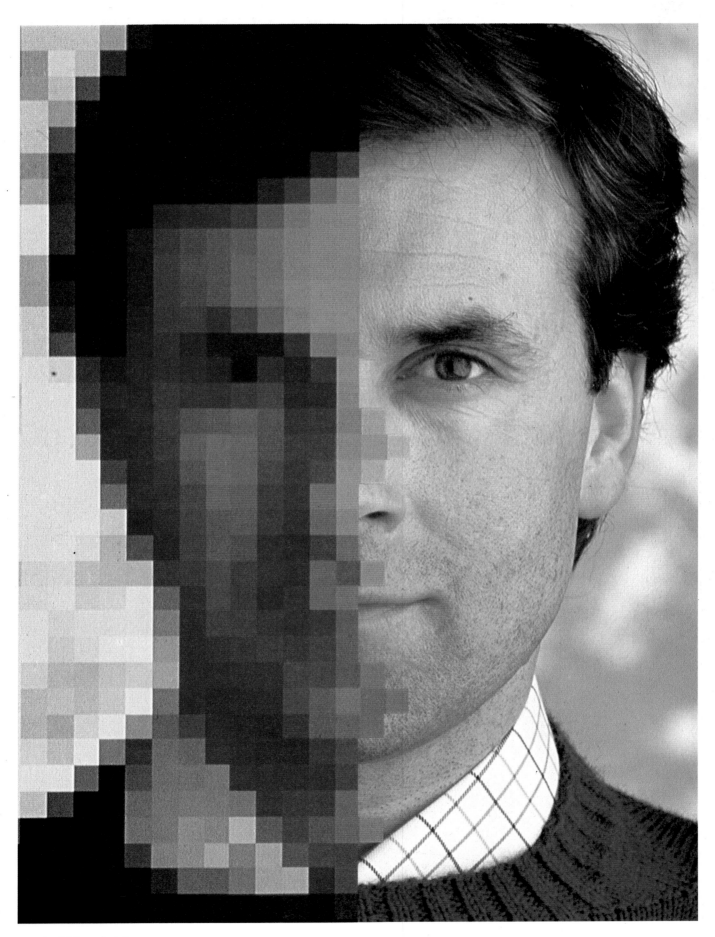

wrong answer, the teacher tends to move on to another pupil. Both sexes can become 'infected' with the fear of failure at school. They retain this fear in adult life, so that their willingness to take the risks that learning involves is permanently crippled and they are condemned to a life of playing it safe.

At the other end of life, old people are often reluctant to take the risk of learning the new skills they need to take up new interests. Perhaps they have been brainwashed into believing that old dogs cannot learn new tricks. But if that were the case, how can we explain the results of an Australian experiment in which 80 volunteers aged between 63 and 90 were taught German by methods specially devised to draw on their experiences of life? None of the 'students' had been to university. In fact most of them had received no more than eight years' schooling before starting work. And yet within six months half the group had reached the equivalent of O-level standard.

Anxiety and learning

Popular fears about the effects of ageing on intelligence are based on a misconception. Research shows that although we *do* slow down mentally as we approach the end of life, becoming stupid or losing your grip on the world is not an inevitable consequence of the ageing process. On some measures – vocabulary, for example – we actually improve in the second half of life. In old age, intellectual functioning is closely related to physical health. But there is also a lot of truth in the old adage: If you don't want to lose it, use it.

Learning goes well when people feel challenged, and badly when they feel threatened. Whenever a learning task becomes threatening, both adults and children feel anxious. Anxiety interferes with the process of learning because it is distracting. In order to learn effectively, you have to be attending closely to the task. An anxious person is likely to be worrying about what will happen if he fails, to the detriment of his attempts to succeed. If his mind is full of thoughts such as 'I'm sure I'm going to fail this test,' or 'What are my parents going to say?', he will not do as well as he should.

Anxiety also interferes with the learning process directly. An anxious learner is less good at concentrating on what is relevant and shutting out what is not. Every student knows the difficulty of 'getting down to it', and the sudden attraction of tidying up or making a cup of tea. For the apprehensive learner this problem is magnified. Anxiety also seems to affect short-term memory, and when the material to be learned is difficult this effect is particularly marked. Anxiety therefore does not just make us less confident; it actually makes our minds work less efficiently.

Learning is an active process. Despite claims to the contrary, you cannot learn when you are asleep. 'Sleep learning' – a tape recorder under your pillow playing soothing but improving messages while you are recharging your tissues – is unfortunately a myth. Any learning that seems to have occurred in this situation will actually have been done after you woke up but were still drowsy. Other people can provide you with information, but only *you* can learn it. It also has to be 'chewed

over' before it can be integrated into your body of knowledge. That is why just reading a book is no way to acquire information unless you happen to possess a photographic memory. Repeating the author's words like a parrot is not much better. You have to make your own notes, because this obliges you to apply an extra stage of processing to the information before committing it to memory. Effective revision always involves reworking material, making notes on notes, and perhaps re-ordering information in the light of newly-observed connections.

As a general rule, the greater your brain's investment in a body of information, the better its chances of reproducing it accurately and effectively when you need it. As in so many other aspects of Life Planning, the secret of making the most of your mind is to understand the mechanisms involved, to draw up a realistic shopping list of specific changes you want to make, and then set to work on the assumption that you will succeed in achieving at least a substantial proportion of your goals.

ENJOY BETTER HEALTH

Can you touch your toes? Do you get out of breath when you run for the bus? Exercise can and should be fun. Make it a daily habit, find a sport you enjoy — and wonder why you ever lived without it

Take a step back and ask yourself: 'How fit am I?' If you were to take a fitness test you would probably be surprised at the results unless you exercise regularly three or four times a week. Our attitudes to exercise, sport and fitness have undergone a revolution during the past decade, and many previously armchair only sports enthusiasts are now out jogging, cycling, swimming, dancing, walking or bouncing across the tennis and squash courts. They are not necessarily young – many are in their forties, fifties or even their sixties – but they all share a new-found enjoyment of exercise and the sense of physical fitness and emotional well-being that it brings. For them, exercise has become an indispensable part of their lives.

Why should you exercise?
People exercise for many different reasons – to lose weight and tone up muscle; to stay strong and youthful; to reduce the risk of heart disease; to socialize and make new friends; to deal with the stress factor in their lives and release tension; and to feel fit and enjoy themselves. Whatever your reason for taking up exercise, it is important that you *enjoy* doing the sport you choose. Then you will stick with it and make it an essential part of your life. If you do not enjoy it, you will forever be making excuses not to go out, instead of a positive commitment to follow an exercise programme of your own design.

When you find the exercise you enjoy, try to build it into your daily or weekly routine. Do not overdo it initially and practise hard every day to get fitter, better, faster, stronger... This is the time-honoured route to injury – not fitness. Exercise should be fun, not painful. It should make you feel good as well as doing you good. The old

saying goes, 'Train, don't strain', and you must start off gradually and build in the pleasure principle if you can. As the initial aches, pain and stiffness fade away and you feel fitter and more proficient, you will enjoy it more.

How fit are you?
If you fear that you are very unfit or overweight, then you should consult your doctor before embarking on any kind of exercise programme or a new sport. Ask yourself the following questions and answer them honestly. You may be surprised at the responses:
● Do you get out of breath running upstairs or to catch a train or a bus?
● Can you run one mile or walk four without feeling breathless or any pain or discomfort?
● Can you touch your toes?
● Do you tire easily?
● Are you more than 3.5kg/7lb overweight?
● Can you do 10 sit-ups or press-ups without cheating?

You will know when you are getting fit because you will tire less easily, have greater stamina and endurance, your body will feel lighter and more flexible, and you will breathe more naturally during exercise. You will feel slimmer and firmer, and people may comment on how well and healthy you look.

You will also feel more energetic, you may find that you sleep better, that your powers of concentration are increased and that you are better equipped to cope with stress. As you can see, the benefits are far-reaching.

Exercise safely
Here are some guidelines for safe, injury-free exercise. Many people are frustrated initially by unnecessary stiffness and injury. Although some persevere regardless, others are put off and give up. Most injuries occur as a result of over-zealous exercise or thoughtlessness, so exercise a little caution and follow our guide:

1 Have a medical check: especially if you are overweight, have a history of high blood pressure, diabetes or heart disease, or are over 35 years old. Do this if you are a sedentary person taking up exercise for the first time in many years.

2 Don't exercise after eating: wait at least two hours to avoid stomach ache and cramps.

3 Wear the right clothing: choose something loose and comfortable. Tracksuits, shorts, T-shirts and sweatshirts do not inhibit movement. Wrap up warmly in cold weather to prevent

muscle cramp. And invest in some good footwear.

4 Do not exercise if you have a fever: it will affect your performance and may inflame muscles and joints and cause the condition to worsen. Wait until you have recovered from any infections, fevers and viruses.

5 Do not exercise in hot weather: you may become dehydrated. Wait for the cool of early morning or evening or exercise inside.

6 Always warm-up before exercise: stretching exercises will accustom your muscles to increased activity and reduce the likelihood of injury and stiffness. Include some jogging on the sport to get your heart beating faster and prepare your body for action.

7 Build up gradually and slowly: do listen to your body and do not push it beyond its limits. Exercise every other day or three times a week only. Do not try to achieve too much too soon.

8 Stop if you feel any pain: stretch gently and slowly to ease out pain and tension. If you feel faint, sick or giddy, stop immediately and rest.

9 Cool down afterwards: stretch out your muscles gently after exercise to prevent stiffness. Shake out your legs and arms and bend over from the hips with your arms hanging loosely. This helps you to relax and allows your pulse rate to return to normal.

10 Relax in a bath or shower: feel refreshed, clean and warm up your tired muscles. Massage your legs to ease out any stiffness.

Choose the right sport

It is best to choose a sport that you enjoy and that is accessible. It is no good taking up swimming if there are no swimming baths in your area, or playing tennis if the courts are fully booked for weeks ahead at your local club. Team games may be difficult, too, as they demand a full quota of players at a predetermined time on a regular basis. Most people find that the best sport or exercise is the one that they can fit in easily and regularly without being dependent on other people for co-operation, partners and support. This is part of the attraction of running, walking and cycling. You can practise them anywhere anytime.

You can consult Tom McNab's chart overleaf to discover the benefits of different sports and activities and what

they can offer you. One of the most popular sports in recent years has been running. Its appeal lies in that it can be as individual or competitive as you make it, and anyone can run – no matter what their age. It is easy, cheap, available, can be practised all the year round and does not require any special facilities. All you need is a pair of running shoes and away you go. Unfortunately, a lot of new runners do just that and go too far too fast and too often. Here is a basic running programme to get you started slowly and sensibly so that you can build up gradually.

Beginner's running programme

Weeks 1-4
Run/walk alternately for 15 minutes, three times a week, gradually stepping up the running until you can run non-stop.

Weeks 5-8
Weekdays: run/walk for 20 minutes, three times a week.
Weekends: run/walk for 30 minutes on either Saturday or Sunday. Do this until you can run non-stop.

Weeks 9-12
Weekdays: slow, steady run for 20 minutes three times a week.

Weekends: slow run for 45 minutes on either Saturday or Sunday.

Swimming
This is probably the best kind of all-over-conditioning exercise you can take. It gives you a complete work-out, firms and strengthens muscles and reshapes and streamlines your body. To benefit from swimming, you should try to swim at least three times a week. Start with 15 minutes non-stop swimming backwards and forwards along the length of the pool and gradually work up to 30 minutes or more. Stop for a rest if you feel tired.

Cycling
This ranks among the best cardio-respiratory exercises and is an enjoyable way to get fit. It is also a cheap way to travel and so you can try cycling to work or the shops instead of taking the car. You should go out at least three times a week or cycle on alternate days for about 30 minutes per session, and then gradually build up your time and distance. Have a longer bike ride at the weekends. Be aware of road safety – cyclists are especially vulnerable on busy roads. Make sure also that your bike is in good working order, and pay particular attention to brakes and lights.

DO AS YOU THINK FIT

Whatever your age, sex or fitness, lack of opportunity can no longer be an excuse for not taking regular exercise

The good news is that sport is going open. This does not mean that professionals will mix with amateurs at every level. It means everyone can have a go.

Gone is the old image of sport as something to be watched from an armchair in front of the television. Indeed, a new survey of sporting trends indicates that those who take part in sport outnumber those who watch it by five to one. Gone, too, is the old image of the 'veteran' sportsman who pedalled a bicycle or swam all year round and was assumed to belong to a semi-monastic fitness cult.

NOW CHOOSE THE SPORT FOR YOU

The sports shown right, are scored on a scale of 10, according to their potential to improve your general physical endurance (increasing capacity to exercise, or work longer); specific muscle endurance (increasing the ability of a particular muscle group, eg biceps, to work longer); body shaping (giving you a better muscle tone and shape), strength and suppleness. There is a rating, too, for the degree to which each activity can also be pursued as a competitive sport, under the heading of 'Recreational sports potential for adults'

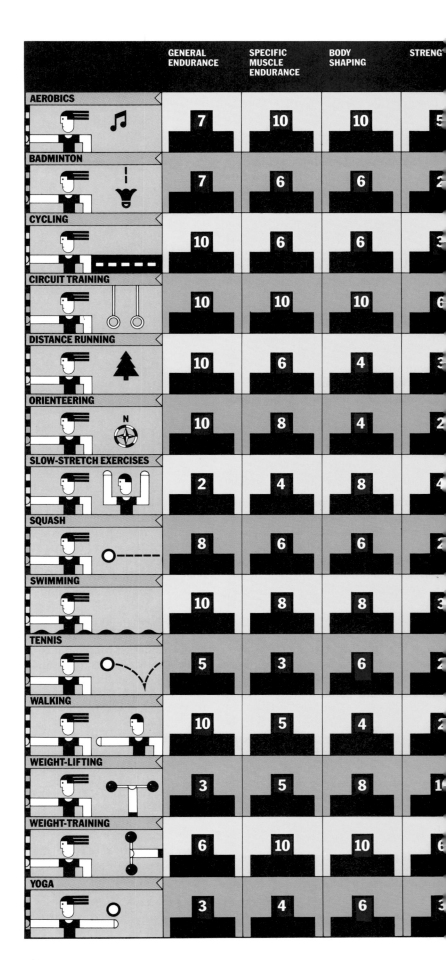

	GENERAL ENDURANCE	SPECIFIC MUSCLE ENDURANCE	BODY SHAPING	STRENG
AEROBICS	7	10	10	5
BADMINTON	7	6	6	2
CYCLING	10	6	6	3
CIRCUIT TRAINING	10	10	10	6
DISTANCE RUNNING	10	6	4	3
ORIENTEERING	10	8	4	2
SLOW-STRETCH EXERCISES	2	4	8	4
SQUASH	8	6	6	2
SWIMMING	10	8	8	3
TENNIS	5	3	6	2
WALKING	10	5	4	2
WEIGHT-LIFTING	3	5	8	10
WEIGHT-TRAINING	6	10	10	6
YOGA	3	4	6	3

...ENESS	IS THERE AN AGE LIMITATION?	RISK OF SELF-INDUCED INJURY	RECREATIONAL SPORTS POTENTIAL FOR ADULTS	ACCESSIBILITY	COMMENT
0	YES	LOW	0	Excellent — mainly through private teachers	Though aerobics has lost much of its initial appeal, there is now more formal training for teachers. Low-impact aerobics has cut out much of the bouncing about on hard floors, and the sport now provides better value than in the Jane Fonda years.
6	NO	LOW	10	Excellent — through clubs and sports centres	The slowness of the shuttle makes badminton a game which can be played and enjoyed by a couple of maiden aunts — or by the young and very fit. A wonderful game for life.
2	NO	LOW	10	Very good — through cycling and touring clubs	Big business in the USA, but it has not yet caught on here. Its fluid, non-weight-bearing movements make it ideal for the fitness-seeking adult — although the competitive scene is not as well suited to the novice as it is in running.
5	YES	LOW	0	Good — through local authorities	Circuit training involves a wide range of exercises using your bodyweight or light weights, with one exercise flowing into the next. Because of the short bursts of exercise, it can have a great endurance effect — but you should build up to it gradually.
2	NO	MEDIUM	10	Excellent — through athletics/jogging clubs	The marathon-running boom has flattened out, leaving many shorter distance road events that are suitable for the fitness runner. These are well-organized, regularly spaced through the calendar, and offer plenty of challenge to any runner.
2	NO	LOW	10	Very good — through clubs	Cunning running! A marvellous sport combining cross-country running and map-reading, with great family potential and on-the-day entry to most events.
0	NO	LOW	0	Fair — mainly through private teachers and aerobic clubs	A spin-off from aerobics, slow-stretch involves gently-paced mobility exercises with no stress on the heart-rate. It has great application through all age ranges.
6	YES	MEDIUM	10	Very good — through local authorities and clubs	Best not to take up squash in middle age, particularly if you are ultra competitive. The high temperatures and pulse rates achieved on squash courts can be dangerous for the unfit.
5	NO	LOW	6	Excellent — through municipal pools and clubs	The best exercise for the elderly and the obese. Many local authority pools have opened 'jogger-lanes' for adult fitness swimmers. Adult competitive swimming does not yet compare with athletics or cycling.
5	NO	LOW	10	Very good — through local authority courts and clubs	Easy to play at low speeds well into your 60s though more difficult to pick up as an adult than badminton or squash. It is worth considering starting with short tennis — played with sponge balls and short-handled rackets.
2	NO	LOW	10	Excellent — informally, or through walking/athletics clubs	Marvellous exercise for the elderly. Race-walking is a friendly and well-organized sport but the standard is high, with 10-minute-a-mile pace (a running pace for many adults) reeled off easily, even by veterans.
2	NO	MEDIUM	6	Very good — through local authorities and clubs	Weight-lifting is not a sport to be entered lightly, but it does attract many adults of all ages, and generates a great deal of camaraderie. Weight training involves lighter weights and many repetitions with shorter rests, and has a very big following.
4	YES	LOW	0		
0	NO	LOW	0	Very good — through local groups, often arranged by local authorities	Excellent exercise for all ages, having great potential for the relief of stress. Note the relatively low exercise value in most elements.

Now local sports centres, encouraged by publicly-funded bodies like the Sports Council, are selling Sport For All. Events are being staged specifically to urge people to 'Come and Try It'. Public swimming pools are catering for fitness swimming. And the GP who frowns at the idea of your taking up sport 'at your age' has become an anachronism.

It started with aerobics, and, especially, with the idea of jogging as a way to fitness. Running events now attract around a million competitors a year, many of them unattached to clubs and spanning a wide range of ages and abilities. Each year *The Sunday Times* National Fun Run, a distance of two and a half miles, draws 30,000 entrants with an age range of four to 80. And the annual London Marathon whittles 60,000 applicants down to a manageable 20,000.

People have turned to running in their 40s, 50s and even 60s. Many say that they have 'never done anything sporting before', and gain immense satisfaction not only from feeling fitter and stronger but in giving new focus to their lives.

Fading, too, is the image of sport as something organized exclusively for the benefit of men, with wives there only to make afternoon tea. Even the traditionalist game of rugby has encouraged the establishment of a women's branch. And at Twickenham they have staged 'New Image' rugby, a non-tackling form played by boys and girls together.

For all people, sport has become much more accessible and is now organized by a small but enthusiastic number of officials in tracksuits rather than a large number of officials in blazers.

Out of the marathon boom the sport of triathlon has mushroomed – with more people swimming, cycling and running in triathlon competitions than ever took part in conventional swimming events. In orienteering, all members of the family can take part in their various age classes. Some 3500 people compete in orienteering's biggest event each Easter, while small children are led around a separate course enlivened by 'Mr Men' pictures.

Conventional team sports like cricket may mourn the dwindling support by schools, but the fact is that today's youngsters are more likely to be introduced to a sport they can follow throughout their adult years.

ONE FOR THE ROAD

Dr Hugh Bethell, right, is a coronary rehabilitation specialist whose faith in the value of exercise led him to found a jogging club. Here he explains why fitness can mean longer life

Dr Hugh Bethell, a coronary rehabilitation specialist, has such faith in the value of exercise that he founded a jogging club. Its appearance, in the 1981 *Sunday Times* National Fun Run, was not, by any standards, a competitive triumph. Out of 1350 teams they came 1345th, beating the Worcester College for the Blind C and D teams, the Frog Lovers Appreciation Society and the Islington CHE Gay Runners.

In a way, it was the most symbolically perfect thing they ever did. By 1984 they had hauled themselves all the way up to 14th place – which was gratifying to a degree, but rather beside the point. The strength of a jogging club, is not in athletic excellence but simply in encouraging a little physical activity to enliven otherwise sedentary lives. Judged by this criterion, their real success lay in having recruited 200 active members.

They *do* try to enjoy their jogging. They *do not* try to look threatening or even offensively self-satisfied. Yet it is clear that the non-exercising mass *does* feel threatened by them – or, at least, by what it thinks they represent – and has put itself on the defensive, with a litany of well-worn assertions and excuses. These are some of the most common arguments:

Exercise is boring
Well, it certainly can be, and those who take up a form of exercise they do not enjoy nearly always give it up. However, the wealth of choice now available (see, for example, our chart on pages 116-7) ensures that very few people should be unable to find something they will like.

Exercise does not do you any good
As a general practitioner Dr Bethell is all too familiar with the consequences

of long-term inactivity. From the 40-year-old breadwinner struck down by a heart attack to the fat old lady who cannot heave herself on to a bus, the penalties of physical idleness permeate our society. Obesity, diabetes, arthritis, heart disease, hypertension, osteoporosis and constipation are all diseases of a chairbound culture.

Exercise is dangerous

This is demonstrable nonsense. A survey of exercise programmes of patients with *known heart disease* found the death rate to be one per 116,402 man hours of exercise (about 13 years). Musculo-skeletal injuries are the penalty of injudicious or irregular exercise when the untrained sportsman tries to do more than his body is prepared for, or when the struggle for excellence drives him to do more than his body can manage. It is good to see that, sensibly, marathon running is now giving way to the much more manageable 5-mile, 10-kilometre and 10-mile races.

I have no time

Well, you *have* got time to go to the pub, watch *Dynasty*, lie in on a Sunday morning. If you cannot find time be-cause your work is so arduous, maybe you should re-examine your life style.

My job keeps me fit

Being on your feet all day is no guarantee of fitness. None but the most strenuous jobs make any difference to measurable physical fitness. The fitness level of manual workers is no different from that of office workers, and the average exercise capacity is abysmally low. A recent study of middle-aged factory workers concluded that only 15.6 per cent of 35 to 39-year-olds are capable of sustained running, even at minimal speed. For those aged 55 to 59, the figure is 1.4 per cent.

I garden and play golf regularly

Such activities do not raise the pulse rate to the levels necessary to improve fitness.

No one should be surprised that exercise is good for us, or that inertia is bad. Our bodies evolved as machines for moving about, and machines deteriorate if they are not properly used. Our muscles weaken and waste if they are left inactive. Our circulation relies on exercise to keep it efficient. The unfit individual has 30 per cent less ability to feed oxygen to his muscles than his fit counterpart. Our reaction to stress results in increased heart rate, blood pressure, blood fat and blood sugar, to prepare us for exertion – the fright, flight, or fight response. Modern man retains this primitive response, but can no longer dissipate its effects by combat or by running away, so that the blood pressure, blood fat and blood sugar levels remain raised and damage the arterial tree. This damage eventually leads to heart disease.

So what guidelines should the born-again exerciser follow? You must find a game or a sport which you enjoy. If necessary, try several. Those which bring most benefit are the dynamic (aerobic) ones like running, swimming, cycling, circuit training, dancing, foot-ball and hockey. But beware those like squash which involve bursts of intense effort. Start at a low level and build up gradually. You should aim to do your chosen activity three or four times weekly, for at least 20 to 30 minutes, sufficiently vigorously to keep you short of breath. You will be gratified by how good you feel within a few weeks and how pleased you will feel at your own active achievements.

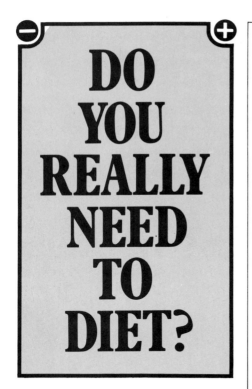

DO YOU REALLY NEED TO DIET?

For many people on fitness and diet programmes, weight-loss is the major objective

What is an ideal weight?

It is difficult to decide what constitutes your ideal weight on the basis of weight-tables alone. Differences in body-build mean that a woman 1.6m/5ft 3in tall can have an ideal weight varying between 47.5kg/7st 7lb and 60kg/9st 7lb depending on her build and body shape. Therefore some people who embark on a slimming regime are aiming at too low an ideal weight.

Endomorphic individuals with a broad, bony framework are usually stocky with broad shoulders and hips, and round heads; they are naturally heavy for their height. At the opposite end of the spectrum are the narrow-framed, slim-built ectomorphics who are naturally light for their height and who tend to have narrow shoulders and hips, and long heads. However, most people fall somewhere between these extremes. Charlotte Fleming was anorexic at 60kg/9½ stone, as she had ceased to menstruate. She is likely therefore to be of endomorphic build with an ideal weight of 66.5-70kg/10½-11 stone, towards the top end of the range for her height.

A better estimate of overweight is the 'pinch an inch' test – i.e. if you can

Charlotte Fleming

Charlotte Fleming started her love-hate relationship with eating seven years ago. She was 76kg/12 stone, (height 1.7/m 5ft 8 1/2in) and working as a stage manager with a ballet company. She was under stress – 'people kept telling me what a lousy job I was doing' – and she wanted to be slim like the dancers. For a year she followed a diet of a half-pound (225g) of cheese and a pound (450g) of fruit a day.

Her weight dropped to 60kg/9 1/2 stone but she felt ill and suffered amenorrhea (loss of periods). Then she started eating compulsively – 'anything I could get my hands on'. To offset the effects of this she took laxatives and made herself vomit. It was a condition she soon diagnosed as bulimia.

She tried hard to bring things under control, and to find a more balanced diet which would still help her to lose weight – first by eating salads for lunch and supper, and later by adding carbohydrates. She also worked for a year as a bicycle dispatch rider, which involved cycling up to eight hours a day; and she trained as a ice dancer. However, despite all this activity and her low-calorie diet, her weight continued to increase.

Charlotte also changed her work. She gained a diploma in wines and spirits, and set up as wine merchant in Ely in East Anglia. This has meant less time for exercise. She walks her dog for two hours a day, but her ice dancing has to be limited to two visits a week to a rink 36 miles away. In a sport based mainly on pairs skating, her motivation has to be individual qualifications. However, starting her own business has been satisfying, and good for her self-esteem.

Since August 1986 Charlotte has decided to 'not even try to lose weight, and to let my metabolism have a rest'. She says that she is 'not even counting calories, and it's wonderful'. Her current diet would, however, seem to be a model. On a typical day her breakfast is muesli and herb tea; lunch is simply cheese and bread; dinner consist of spaghetti or rice, cooked vegetables, and fruit, with half a bottle of wine.

So now she is around 76kg/12 stone again. She would prefer to be about 65kg/10st 4lb and her skating teacher would like it to be even less. She says that she does not find herself appealing, but appears to be less unhappy about it than she once was.

Readers working with the Lifeplan Scorechart might like to know that her mark in the health/fitness section was extremely high: 240 out of a maximum 280. She also noted that her scores for aggression and manipulativeness were very low (4 and 2).

Bill Jones

Bill Jones, Cardiff travel agent, is 43. It is the sort of age at which many men question their fitness, their motivation and, indeed, their longevity. The thought that 'you're playing the second half', as Bill Jones says, was underlined when his doctor told him that his blood pressure was high. For him, this was significant: his father had died at 57 of hypertensive heart disease.

Bill knew that stress was to blame – not just the pressure of a job which involves meeting deadlines but the worry, at that time, of having a new house built while living with his family in a small flat, and also trying to tackle an Open University course. Fourteen months later, with the help of medication, his blood pressure is back to normal, but the experience has made him critically examine his lifestyle.

Dietary changes came first: he cut out salt and crisps, of which he used to eat a great deal, and replaced them with healthier jacket-baked potatoes. Bill hopes that getting fitter will be the key to other changes. His first thought was to try one of the martial arts, since a colleague is involved in Tae Kwondo, and he liked the idea of training for self-discipline as well as pure fitness. But initially he will try to improve his basic fitness. His first move has been to join a health club/gymnasium.

Bill Jones's mark for Fitness/Health in the Lifeplan Scorechart was a modest +20.

pinch an inch (2.5cm) or more of fat between your finger and thumb anywhere on your body, then you are likely to have some unnecessary fat which you could well do without. There is an even easier guide, of course, for older people who used to be slim and fit when they were young: their weight in early adult life is probably their ideal.

What physical harm results from being overweight?

The dangers of obesity have been overestimated in the past, and most women will come to no appreciable harm from being up to 30 per cent overweight. However, this rule does not apply if there are (or have been) close blood relatives who have suffered heart attacks, coronary artery disease, high blood pressure, strokes or diabetes. If Charlotte's ideal weight is 66.5kg/10½ stone, she is unlikely to come to any harm unless she weighs appreciably more than 82.5kg/13 stone.

Why do some people have greater difficulty in losing weight than others?

Inherited body-build is a major factor in whether you lose weight easily and successfully. Broadly-built individuals cannot burn off unwanted calories as heat in the same way that slim-built people can. In particular, they cannot burn off the excess fat they eat, and it is therefore added to the fat they have already stored around the body. Unfortunately, this inherited tendency to lay down fat easily and lose it with difficulty cannot be altered. People like Charlotte must accept that they are permanently disadvantaged in this respect. In addition, many people with difficult weight problems may be going through periods of stress in their lives that trigger off a need to eat for comfort.

People with this kind of problem are usually sensitive individuals with low self-esteem or an inferiority complex.

Charlotte begins by telling us about her 'lousy job', involving 'mental stress'. No wonder she became anorexic and followed this with an episode of bulimia. She was not able to be in control at her job, and therefore she tried to gain satisfaction by achieving strict control over her food intake – with potentially dangerous results.

How easy is it to count calories?

The simple answer is that it is very difficult indeed. One apple, for instance, can provide fewer than 30 calories or more than 100 calories, depending on its size and variety. As food tables give only average figures, 50g/2oz of ordinary hard cheese may provide between 140 and 280 calories; and a person who does not actualy weigh the cheese may dis-

The Richards Family

Moving from a village in Herefordshire to the city of Shrewsbury was the catalyst which made the Richards family search for new interests. Anne, 44, and Brian, a 43-year-old police inspector, both wanted to get fitter and also to find activities they could share with their 18-year-old son Paul.

Since Lifeplan started they have been busy. Mrs Richards first tried the Trimnasium – a multi-exercise programme at a local gym – and when she troubled her weak back she switched to swimming. She was pleasantly surprised at how quickly she improved and also at how much better she felt for it. Soon, Brian and Paul were coming too.

The idea was to build up fitness to the point where they might tackle an outdoor sport. Anne had rambling vaguely in mind, though the distances and climbs seemed daunting. Then they heard about orienteering, and were persuaded that they did not need to be fit athletes to try it: as long as they could walk and read a map, there would be a course suitable for them.

Only days after hearing about an event in their area, they drove to Brompton Bryan, near Ludlow. Together with their 20-year-old daughter Suzanne, a nurse who lives away from home, they walked around a 'course', in well-coloured and partially wooded terrain – about 4km/ 2.5 miles, with 10 check-points. It took them two hours, and they finished the day 'nicely tired'.

They enjoyed it so much that they will go again. 'I wouldn't have thought,' said Brian, 'that you could take up a sport quite so easily. One of the nice things is that it seems to attract such a mixed bag of people. Another time, one of us could do it at a walk, and another at a run, and you'd still feel you'd had a day out together.'

In the Lifepaln Scorechart, Anne had a fitness/health score of 60, Brian 90 and Paul 200.

cover that the estimated 50g/2oz turns out to be 65g/2½ or even 75g/3oz. People who genuinely feel that they cannot lose weight on 1,000 calories per day are probably victims of inaccuracies in calorie counting, possibly compounded by a failure to count the calorie content of their drinks properly. When a group of women were isolated in a country house in a controlled experiment and given a strictly-measured 1,000 calories daily, they all lost weight – though some reduced much more slowly than others.

Charlotte Fleming's current overweight probably represents a reasonable compromise with her life situation. She has control of conditions in her job; she is increasing in confidence and should carry on enjoying her sensible nutritional diet with possibly minor modifications. For instance, as muesli is high in calories for its bulk, it could be replaced by a high-fibre cereal. She might try cottage cheese with some of the various added flavourings (herbs, pineapple etc) which are in most health stores and super-markets to make it more palatable; and she might reduce her wine intake a little. She can make a few more modifications in her diet when she is more settled in her way of life, or she might fast on one day a week. However, with any luck she will not have to return to the tedium of counting calories, which tends to allow the mind to dwell on food over-much. Good eating habits and a healthy diet are the only means to long-term weight control, and an end to the vicious cycle of slimming and bingeing.

HEALTHY EATING

At every turn we are besieged by advice on what to eat. What is the healthy answer?

Healthy eating does not actually make you live longer. It just *feels* longer. Wry grins all round.

The sad thing is that a great many people really believe, in the spirit of this old joke, that a 'healthy' diet is not only ineffective but also dreadfully dull. In fact they are wrong on both counts, although the myths remain hard to dispel. Lounge bar nutritionists pursue a fairly predictable pattern of argument. Thus:

What is the point, the doctors cannot agree?
Wrong. The great majority of experts in nutrition and diet-related diseases have reached a consensus on what constitutes a healthy diet. The guidelines they lay down are based on very precise scientific and epidemiological research, and have the backing of the World Health Organization. Inevitably there are some disagreements, particularly from those associated with particular interests in the food industry – meat production, milk marketing and sweet manufacture, for example. Even this opposition is now fading as consumer demand for healthier products leads the food trade to explore new marketing opportunities.

If it looks good and tastes good, it cannot be bad.
Britain is at the top of the international league for heart disease, with Scotland and Northern Ireland vying for the distinction of having the highest related death rate in the western world. More and more evidence indicates that one of the chief culprits is our high fat diet.

There is a strong correlation be-

tween susceptibility to heart disease and cholesterol levels in the blood. High levels of blood cholesterol result from eating fatty foods – particularly saturated fats, found mainly but not exclusively in meat and dairy products. The link is direct: the higher the proportion of saturated fatty foods, the higher the blood cholesterol level; the higher the blood cholesterol level, the higher the risk of heart disease.

And it does not end with heart disease. There are many other diseases and disorders with dietary links, ranging from toothache to bowel cancer. The good news is that we do not need a different diet to avoid each one. It is probably no accident that the diet that is healthy for our hearts is also healthy for our teeth, bowels, and most of the bits in between.

Diets are all phoney, they are not real eating.

It is true that a lot of *slimming* diets can hardly be thought of as natural, which is why they usually do not last more than a few weeks. But a truly *healthy* diet could not be further from the semi-starvation, grapefruit-with-everything and bran-on-the-top sort of diet that so many women seem to find so persuasive. And yet a healthy diet *can* help you to lose weight or stay slim.

But it is all muesli, lentils and yoghurt, strictly for fruit-and-nut-cases.

Wrong! You can eat a perfectly healthy diet without going anywhere near a health food shop. It need consist of nothing more than the ordinary everyday foods you can buy in any supermarket. The difference is in the *balance* between the things you eat. Nutritionally speaking, there is no such thing as a 'healthy food' or an 'unhealthy meal'. What matters is the mixture of all the different sorts of food you eat over a period of days, weeks, months, years and even decades. Your diet is healthy if that mixture, that balance, is right *for you*.

How can I know what is right for me?

Of course it is true that everybody is different and that we all have different dietary needs depending on our sex, age, activity level, body-weight, etc. Broadly speaking, however, the average person in the UK eats too much fatty food, too much sugar, too much salt, and not enough fibre.

The main difference between individuals is in their need for calories. Women have a lower calorie requirement than men, older people lower than younger, sedentary lower than active. If you take in more calories than your body can use, then you put on weight. One adult in three in the UK is either overweight or obese.

But there are other differences too. Some people need more protein than others, or more vitamins or minerals. Calculating your precise requirements is well-nigh impossible, but fortunately it is not necessary.

Take your energy needs, for example. There is a very simple way of checking your calorie balance – a weekly walk to the weighing machine. As for the other components – protein, vitamins and minerals – if you follow the basic guidelines for healthy eating, then you will be getting more than enough of these. It is only people in special circumstances – pregnant women, for example – who may need supplements.

So how do I cut down on fat, sugar, and salt, and eat more fibre without ruining the quality of my life?

Let us start with fat. In many ways this is the most important – not only because of the link with blood cholesterol but also because it is crammed with calories.

The first thing is to become fat-conscious. You have got to think fat. Whereabouts in your food is it? As a rule of thumb for the average adult, about one third of the daily fat intake is in the form of milk, butter and other dairy products; one third in meat and meat products; and a third in margarine, cooking oil and a long list of other minor sources. *Saturated* fat is mainly in the first two groups, but also in harder margarines and some blended vegetable oils.

Next, you find ways to cut down. A

little less here, a swap there, a new idea somewhere else.

Surely it takes a lot of getting used to?

Not at all. You can do it in easy stages. For instance, you could start by making just a single change to your usual eating habits. Let us say you decide to use a soft, polyunsaturated margarine, like sunflower margarine, instead of butter. That does not mean you never have butter again – simply that you spread or cook with the margarine for routine meals, and save the butter for treats. Once you have got used to that simple substitute, you make another switch – let us say semi-skimmed instead of full cream milk. Let yourself get used to that, then move on to another change – perhaps grilling rather than frying. Gradually, step by step, you are moving towards a healthier way of eating.

The same goes for sugar and salt, but here your taste buds can be a useful guide – and so can the labels on

tins and packaging. Once you start to wean yourself away from these very strong flavours – again by making small, gradual changes – your taste buds will become increasingly sensitive to them. You will need less and less for the same sensation, and you will start to notice many more subtle, aromatic flavours, (in herbs, for example). Incidentally, two more myths while we are dispelling them – honey and sea-salt are no more 'healthy' than their mundane equivalents.

But what about fibre? Isn't it all chew, chew, chew?

What is wrong with that if it is tasty? Delicious fillings between slices of nutty wholemeal bread; stuffed jacket potatoes; fresh fruit sliced on to wholegrain cereals; vegetables lightly cooked to bring out their flavour; a dozen different kinds of bean served in scores of different ways; any number of exciting dishes with brown rice or wholewheat pasta . . . the permutations are endless.

Right, so I cut down on fat, sugar and salt and eat more fibre. How do I know when enough is enough?

It depends on how much of these you usually eat compared with the average, and there is no simple way of calculating this. But on the assumption that your diet *is* about average, medical experts recommend that you should reduce your saturated fat intake by nearly half, sugar by half, and salt by a quarter. Increase fibre by half as much again. But not all at once – easy stages, remember.

Does it cost more to eat a healthy diet?

No, it does not have to. Certainly, leaner cuts of meat cost more than fattier cuts, but you can offset that by eating rather less meat, and more vegetables, pulses, rice or pasta. Or you can choose more polyunsaturated meats such as chicken and turkey, which are usually cheaper than red meat. Fish is also an excellent substitute (white fish are very low fat, and oily fish are highly polyunsaturated), and need not be more expensive. By cutting down on processed foods and made-up meals, which are often high in fat and salt, you can save the money for more fresh fruit and vegetables, and the occasional wicked cream cake.

SLEEP: HOW MUCH YOU NEED

Although many of its processes remain a mystery, we do know that sleep provides essential restorative powers. The mind slows down when the body needs rest. Test your own reactions

Were there a lullaby guaranteed to prompt sleep in adults, the record would out-sell the Beatles overnight. Sadly, in its absence, too many of us opt for sleep-inducing drugs and tranquillizers (known medically as hypnotics), with 16 million prescriptions a year costing the state £30 million.

The popular belief is that we need to spend a third of our lives asleep. In restoring our generosity, our sense of order and concentration, sleep is far more efficient than a game of squash, a jog or a swim. Yet it has not engaged the attention of the health-fanatic with anything like the same intensity as exercise or diet.

What *does* sleep actually do for you?

Dr Jim Horne, director of the Sleep Research Laboratory at Loughborough University, has found that all the organs of the body (except the brain) can cope surprisingly well without sleep for between eight and eleven days. They are sufficiently repaired and restored by rest and food alone.

The brain, by contrast, does not rest properly, even in a darkened room, unless it shuts down completely. Prolonged sleeplessness induces irrational behaviour and hallucinations (a phenomenon frequently reported by lone yatchsmen) and is commonly used as a form of torture. In experiments, small animals die after a few days without sleep.

At a more mundane level, one lost night of sleep is enough to slow us down and provoke mistakes in our everyday activities, although we can still use the creative part (the cerebral cortex) of our brains to accomplish challenging tasks – providing that we are sufficiently motivated or have enough adrenalin in our veins.

Horne says most people need seven to eight hours sleep a night; some need five to seven hours; and a few (in the Margaret Thatcher mould) need five hours or less. In old age our internal clocks wear out and we wake early in the morning and nap in the afternoon.

Worrying about sleeplessness, says Horne, is itself often the cause of insomnia – although the symptoms (lack of motivation, listlessness) for depression and insomnia are often indistinguishable and inseparable. Both, incidentally, rank high among the most common reasons for visiting a doctor.

Michael Crawford

Michael Crawford, 46, television and stage actor who played the leading roles in Barnum **and** The Phantom of the Opera. **Test scores: alert, 1 min 05sec (2 mistakes); tired, 1min 45sec (no mistakes).**

He is a great enthusiast for the afternoon nap. And just before a performance he sneaks 40 minutes of quiet in a chair to put a brake on his adrenalin flow. The actor Frank Finlay taught him this in repertory theatre 30 years ago.

Crawford values his sleep enormously. Without it, he feels he cannot cope. Ironically, in view of his flair for stunts, his childhood nightmares were of hanging off cliffs and being chased. These have faded now, and he is altogether less anxious in his adult life.

Inevitably, while a show is running, his life is more nocturnal than most people's. He does not reach home in Wapping, East London until around midnight, then goes to bed and watches television to unwind before switching out the light at 1.30am. He wakes between 7.30 and 8am.

His mornings are relatively relaxed, spent dealing with mountains of post; then he always sleeps between two and three o'clock in the afternoon. This sets him up for the elaborate two-hour make-up session he needs for The Phantom of the Opera. He says that his performance in the 'tired' test was boosted by adrenalin, still running high at the end of a show.

THE LOGICAL REASONING TEST

THIS IS an extended version of the logical reasoning test from the Lifeplan Scorechart. It consists of 20 short sentences, each followed by a pair of letters (AB or BA). The sentences purport to describe the order of the two letters – i.e. to say which comes first. They can do this in several ways. Thus the order AB can be correctly described by saying either (1) A precedes B, or (2) B follows A, or (3) B does not precede A, or (4) A does not follow B. All these are correct descriptions of the pair AB but are incorrect when applied to the other pair, BA.

Your job is to read each sentence and to decide whether it is a true or false description of the letters following it. Using a blank sheet of paper make a tick for each statement you think is true, a cross for each one you think is false. Work as quickly as you can without making mistakes. Start with sentence 1, then work systematically through the test to the end. Time yourself and then re-check your answers, so that your logical efficiency measure reflects both how accurately and how quickly you are thinking.

1 B precedes A – AB
2 B is followed by A – AB
3 B is not followed by A – BA
4 B is preceded by A – AB
5 B is followed by A – BA
6 B precedes A – BA
7 A is not followed by B – AB
8 A is followed by B – BA
9 B is not preceded by A – BA
10 B is followed by A – AB
11 A does not follow B – BA
12 A is preceded by B – AB
13 B does not follow A – AB
14 A is not preceded by B – BA
15 A follows B – BA
16 A is not preceded by B – AB
17 A follows B – AB
18 A does not precede B – AB
19 A precedes B – AB
20 B follows A – BA

Research nevertheless shows that insomniacs overestimate threefold the amount of time they spend tossing and turning. Most of them actually spend about 30 minutes getting to sleep but worry about it so much that they think they have taken longer.

Usually, a good night's sleep naturally follows a bad one, and often, if a person has taken a sleeping pill on the second night, he is convinced it has worked. In this way he may develop an unfounded faith in drugs, then take too many of them and suffer withdrawal, insomnia and nightmares when he comes off them. Horne believes nobody should take sleeping pills for longer than a fortnight, though a single pack usually lasts a month.

By far the best way of overcoming insomnia is to use what Horne calls 'sleep hygiene'. This means avoiding daytime naps, getting up at the same time every day and going to bed only when you are exhausted, so that you associate bed with sleep rather than tossing around. There is no evidence to show that extra exercise makes it easier to sleep. The best thing is to give yourself hot drinks and good books – and lower your expectations. Five solid hours of sleep will probably do as much, if not more, good than eight broken hours.

The first part of your night's sleep is the most useful, for then you spend more time sleeping deeply and dreamlessly. Sleep occurs in cycles, with deep sleep alternating with lighter, less restful dreaming sleep (also known as Rapid Eye Movement or REM sleep). The proportion of REM increases as the night wears on.

If you like lots of sleep and have access to a pillow after lunch, an afternoon nap is very good for you (although see the reservation about insomniacs, above). There is an inevitable post-lunch dip in your levels of efficiency and concentration. Experimental measurements taken at 5pm have shown that people who nap not only speed up their reactions but also improve their moods. The results are equally beneficial whether you nap for two hours or only 30 minutes.

John Humphrys

John Humphrys, 46, presenter of BBC Radio 4's Today programme. Test scores: alert, 1min 17sec (2 mistakes); tired, 1min 30sec (4 mistakes).

Since he started his new job in January 1987, Humphrys has been sleep-obsessed. Four days a week he plucks himself out of bed at 3.30am and is on the air from 6.30 to 9am. While most of us are just un-gumming our eyelids, his heartbeat is going at such a rate that he says, it ought to kill him.

His self-confessed exaggerated sense of duty gives him the occasional nightmare. He used to wake up sweating with the fear that he might have taken up smoking again. His new nightmare, however, sees him chasing through the streets and buildings from his home in Henley, trying to reach the Today studio on time. When at last he finds a microphone to sit in front of, he picks up his script – beautifully written and left in readiness the night before – to find it

has translated itself into shaming gibberish.

Twice he has gone on air at dawn after being out for supper and wine the night before, and survived shakily on adrenalin. He needs his routine of an hour or two of Mozart and reading at night, followed by the Nine O'Clock News headlines and bed. He relaxes only a little at weekends, remaining busy remote-controlling his organic farm in Wales, or doing charity work.

Nicholas Scott

Nicholas Scott, 53, Government Minister. Test scores: alert, 1min, 54sec (2 mistakes); tired, 2min 06sec (1 mistake).

Scott has a tough-guy approach to sleep, which Mrs Thatcher will doubtless be pleased to hear. Being a member of Parliament and surviving all-night sittings, he says, have hardened him wonderfully to survive without much sleep.

He feels refreshed after a five-hour night, though at least once a week he treats himself to a full eight-hour stretch. His stress loading is well under control since he has no trouble nodding off, but he never reads in bed.

However, his Northern Ireland posting imposed a slight extra strain. His body had become accustomed to busy nights and relaxed mornings, but he had to change gear for early starts at Stormont, ministerial paperwork or dashes to the airport – he flew the Irish Sea 200 times a year.

His Westminster routine also allowed him to use the House of Commons gym twice a week. In Ireland he tries to play a game of tennis, golf or cricket whenever he can. He says a good dose of exercise is more refreshing than sleep.

Caroline Dale

Caroline Dale, 22, classical cellist. Test scores: alert, 1min 30sec (no mistakes); tired, 2min 38sec (1 mistake)

The problem for a performing cellist is that she must peak at eight o'clock at night when most other people start to wilt. Caroline says that she has to remember not to expect herself to live a normal day and then pile a night's work on top of it.

She is self-disciplined, and survives the lack of routine in her life as long as she sleeps until the magic hour of 10 o'clock each morning. Sometimes she may remain in her flat at Kensal Rise, in London, for five hours of rehearsal. In winter she may perform every night, and travel around the country between venues by day.

It is a debilitating routine, and after a tour of more than a few days she invariably catches a cold as soon as she returns home. She has started running four miles after dark every evening to improve her preparation for sleep, but she is thinking of abanding this routine because she is afraid of being mugged.

Fatima Whitbread

Fatima Whitbread, 26, European champion and women's world record holder for the javelin. Test scores: alert, 4min 49sec (1 mistake); tired, 5min 07sec (1 mistake).

When Fatima flew out for a month's training in Lanzarote, she took two essential sleeping aids: cassette tapes of Joseph Heller's novel Catch 22 and Charlotte Bronte's Jane Eyre. In the past she has listened to music or watched television in bed, but she thinks that a bedtime story might be more effective.

Her demanding physical routine – even at home in Tilbury she does two to three training sessions a day after taking her young brother to school – is fuelled by eight-and-a-half hours' sleep each night. If it drops to seven hours she feels less able to concentrate on her throwing, which is as much a matter of balance and technique as it is of sheer strength.

Nervous anticipation means that her sleep is often broken on the night before a major competition, but then she compensates by having a nap before she performs. Her philosophy is to accept every stumbling block as a stepping stone. Hence, when she was 20, she competed after a 16-hour sleepless journey to East Germany and threw a personal best. These days she would rather not take such risks.

HOW DID YOU SCORE?

Check your answers from pages 108-9

1 Health and fitness

For question:

1 YES, +10 NO, −10	11 YES, +20 NO, −20
2 YES, −10 NO, +10	12 YES, +20 NO, −20
3 YES, +40 NO, −10	13 YES, +20 NO, −20
4a YES, +20 NO, −20	14a YES, −20 NO, 0
4b YES, +20 NO, −20	14b YES, −10 NO, 0
4c YES, +20 NO, −20	15a −40
4d YES, +20 NO, −20	15b −30
5a YES, +20 NO, −20	15c −20
5b YES, +20 NO, −20	15d −10
5c YES, +20 NO, −20	15e +10
5d YES, +20 NO, −20	15f +40
6 YES, −40 NO, 0	16 YES, −20 NO, 0
7 YES, −20 NO, 0	17 YES, −20 NO, 0
8 YES, +20 NO, −20	18 YES, −20 NO, 0
9 YES, +20 NO, −20	19 YES, −10 NO, 0
10 YES, −20 NO, +20	20 YES, +20 NO, −20

Do your points add up to a plus (more healthy) or minus (less healthy) score overall? If you scored +200 or more, you are already taking most of the right steps for health and fitness. If you scored −200 or worse, you have defied medical theory so far, but don't count on it. All those in between, read on.

2 Stress

For the odd-numbered questions (1, 3, etc.) score 2 points for every tick you have in a B box. For the even-numbered questions, score 2 points for every A answer. The higher your score, the more stress you are imposing on yourself. If you have a score of 16 or more, you really need to take active steps to reduce the burden you are imposing on yourself. A score in the 12 – 16 range indicates a fair degree of ambitiousness and concern with time. A score of 5 – 11 suggests that you are fairly relaxed in your approach to life. A score of 4 or less means that you are not merely 'laid-back' but almost horizontal.

3 Reading the signs

If you answered YES to more than four of the questions, you should take active steps to reduce the stress in your life.

4 Logical reasoning

Unlike the other tests, there are right and wrong answers here. The correct ones are:

1 TRUE	6 TRUE
2 TRUE	7 FALSE
3 TRUE	8 TRUE
4 FALSE	9 FALSE
5 TRUE	10 TRUE

The object of this test is to allow you to measure change in your own performance rather than to compare yourself with other people. It is connected with IQ, and it will enable you to judge whether or not you are in a fit state to make decisions. If you are very tired, or under the weather for some other reason, you will take longer to complete the test than usual, and will probably make errors.

THE PROJECT: YOUR RESPONSE

The statistical evidence of the Lifeplan questionnaire and score-chart was sorted and sifted. Although it revealed that readers were not unusually dissatisfied with their lives, most seemed to need further mental stimulation. They also wanted to improve their physical fitness – and needed to drink a little less

At the planning stage of the Lifeplan project readers were invited to complete a questionnaire designed to reveal those areas of their lives they would most like to improve. They were free to choose as many areas as they wished, although we gave them a checklist of 20. The first 375 replies were analysed by computer – overall at first, then categorized by age and sex.

The first surprise came in the sex breakdown. There is a strongly-held belief that women are most drawn to features on psychology and self-improvement. Yet 61 per cent of our early responders were male. We also expected, although with less certainty, that Lifeplan would appeal most strongly to younger readers. In the event, only 28 per cent of our responders were aged under 35. Twenty-eight per cent were over 50, and 44 per cent were between 35 and 50.

Two ambitions dominated our sample: to increase mental stimulation and to improve physical fitness. The first concerned both sexes and all ages equally; the second held most appeal for the younger group. Neck-and-neck with each other, although some way behind the first two, came acquiring new skills and thinking more positively. Here older readers were slightly less interested than the younger ones, and women showed significantly more interest than men in expanding their range of skills. Close behind came the more general headings of enhancing lifestyle, which appealed slightly more to men and more to middle-aged readers than to younger or older ones,

and enjoying life more – an invitation which seemed to have particular relevance to men.

Next in order of preferred interest came eating more healthily (especially among the under 35s) and improving appearance (although only 42 per cent of males showed any interest here). The top ten self-improvement areas were completed by financial security (a concern of most importance to younger males) and better health (interestingly, an area targetted by 50 per cent of men but only 37 per cent of women). Enjoying work more, losing weight and worrying less came just outside the top ten (all three seemed equally important to both sexes), while interest in improving relationships and enjoying sex more were both lower than had been anticipated. The areas which attracted least interest were coping better at home, feeling safer and overcoming fears.

In addition to establishing general interest in the different areas of self-improvement, we also asked which areas readers felt were most important. Here there was a clear winner. Getting fitter was the number-one choice for one person in five, regardless of age, although apparently more important to men than to women. The reverse applied to the second choice, stimulating the mind, which was mentioned by three times as many women as men, and by significantly more older than younger readers. The less specific category, enjoying life more, was the third most popular choice as primary target for action, appealing equally to all groups. Fourth in the list came

thinking positively, an area particularly interesting to women under 35, with better health, financial security and enhancing lifestyle clustered together at the back of the leading group. The remaining categories attracted significantly less interest. Only one per cent of respondents mentioned enjoying sex more, and no one at all described feeling safe or coping better at home as the areas they would most like to improve.

The panel of early responders were invited to send in their completed Lifeplan Scorecharts. The instructions to this huge questionnaire (it contained more than 300 questions) made it clear that there were no right or wrong answers, and that the main purpose of completing the questionnaire was not to obtain

absolute values. The number of questions in individual categories was too small for these to have real significance. The objective was to identify points of comparison which readers could use to measure changes in themselves over a period of time. To this end, the questionnaire was designed so that readers could take two separate tests – ideally before and after they had attempted some programme of change.

No objective measurement of changes that have been achieved has yet been received. However, a report can be made on a number of interesting trends which emerged from the early responders. Although absolute individual scores are difficult to interpret, overall the sample seems gratifyingly content (especially the over 50s), low on anxiety (no differences here between ages or between men and women), quite pleased with their jobs and relationships, more assertive than aggressive (a healthy state of affairs), and in average physical shape – although not a single responder obtained an entirely clean bill of health in his or her drinking habits.

The interesting results lie in differences between the sexes and age groups. The men emerged as more assertive, aggressive and much more manipulative than the women. They also tended to score higher on sensation-seeking, although not on risk-taking. Women were more prone to technophobia, cared more about their appearance (little sign here of the Peacock Male), were much more confident about their relationship skills and less prone to problem drinking.

Growing older clearly has its consolations. Compared with younger respondents, the over-50s group were generally happier, much less aggressive, less shy, more in control of their lives, better at relationships, more satisfied with their jobs, much better at household management, more financially secure and much less affected by drink-related problems. The only problem for them lay in a slight tendency to be less adaptable. Not unexpectedly they were also slightly more likely to take a traditional rather than a progressive approach to sexual matters, although there was little evidence that this caused them much concern.

THE VOLUNTEERS: HOW THEY COPED

Here we reflect on the progress of some individuals who pinned their faith on the Lifeplan programme. Some experienced a complete change in life style; some became happier and more confident; some resigned themselves, contentedly, to their lot

Joan Lee had always held a child-like conviction that she would become rich and famous. She had no idea how it would happen – only that, some day, somehow it must.

At the age of 45, with two marriages behind her and a job as an office manager in a small London publishing house, what she got instead was *The Sunday Times* Lifeplan Questionnaire. The view she held of herself as a mature, competent but as yet undiscovered talent was delivered a mortal blow.

'It told me I did not really look after myself. It said I was not taking my responsibilities seriously, and it made me feel frightened that somebody so adult was actually not in control. I had always felt financially terribly insecure, and that was why.'

From that moment she began to mould her own future into a more attractive shape. She is becoming a property owner by buying not only a scruffy cut-price flat from Wandsworth council but also a glitzy timeshare near Marbella with a sun terrace, tropical garden and jacuzzi. She has also organized career consultations to help assess her strengths and weaknesses.

She believes her relationships may become more vigorous now that her powerful personality has found a creative outlet. 'I wanted a sort of daddy to find all the solutions for me but I was also rather aggressive. Now I should hate to burden any man with all that,' she said.

Joan Lee's extraordinary story has all the ingredients of the American Dream – the belief that no matter where you were born, who your parents were, or how you were educated, you can salmon-leap upstream to your chosen goal. In old Hollywood movies, they did it all the time.

Lifeplan has tried to introduce people to the idea that there *are* immense possibilities in their lives. With high unemployment on one hand, and big-bang profits on the other, the 'Go for it' philosophy might seem to have limited application. But in reality its appeal is universal. *Everybody* has it in his power to organize his time more efficiently, enjoy himself more, and methodically set about achieving his ambitions.

Positive attitudes cost nothing, whereas negative ones can cost a great deal in wasted energy, emotion, anxiety, work-time and consequently money. *The Sunday Times* has been the first newspaper in this country to analyse people's everyday (sometimes entrenched) attitudes in such breadth and depth *and* give basic advice on how to change.

Many readers volunteered to help and enabled us to identify people's worries and blind spots. And Lifeplan in return has given them the knowledge and energy they needed to make the salmon leaps. It did not, and could not do the leaping *for* them.

Elizabeth Unger, a 70-year-old widow of a professor of international law, began with the hope that Lifeplan would put old people in touch with the young, and rich people in touch with the poor. This, she felt, would give her an opportunity to involve herself in helping others, and to feel she was using her life more constructively. She was disappointed that Lifeplan did not do this, but now that she has made her own imaginative leap she should realize that it is within her own power to involve herself in voluntary work as much as she wants.

Judith McDonald was another who initially balked at taking too drastic a step. She told us she was extremely happy with her life as a science lecturer in Berkshire, but that she and her husband, a business studies lecturer, would like to enjoy sex more. With the help of Lifeplan she made an appointment to see a sex therapist but changed her mind at the last moment and did not turn up.

Instead, she and her husband took time to complete the entire Lifeplan Scorechart together, and found that it gave their marriage the touch on the tiller she had wanted.

'Our expectations did not fit in with each other. I had expected my husband to behave in the traditional way, but when we really thought about who was submissive and who was instigative, it was often more natural for it to be the other way around. It seemed quite logical when we looked at it in black and white, but we never would have thought it through on our own. Suddenly sex therapy did not seem necessary.'

Before Lifeplan they would travel to work together, share an office, come home together, go shopping together and, in their spare time, go sailing together. Now they try not to shadow each other quite so doggedly.

Some of the volunteers felt socially at odds with life – unable to make or

Doug Stewart, better organized

maintain contacts with their friends. Those whose cases have already been described on pages 94 and 95 are all more content now. Doug Stewart, a busy builder married to an even busier wife, then had a swimming pool turning green with neglect, and a house being extended that the family rarely seemed to be at home in. A course on time-management opened his eyes to 'pearl-fishing' – noticing and nurturing the special things in the fast currents of their lives. They have now acquired a housekeeper and recently had friends over for a poolside lunch at *their* home.

Sharon Faith, a solicitor who had given up work to have a baby, attacked post-natal isolation blues by organizing a three-day a week job for herself. 'It sounds terribly spoilt because you have to be able to afford it, but the answer is live-in help. My sense of freedom returned as soon as I went back to work and we could go out again in the evenings,' she said. Another baby is now on the way.

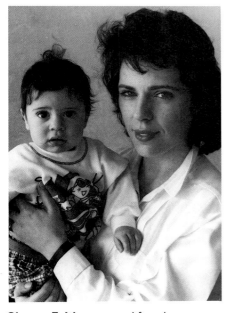

Sharon Faith, renewed freedom

The phobics described on pages 70-72 were all directed to appropriate therapists, and all have done well. Kelly Flynn's terror of snakes was so remarkable that the very mention of the word could induce panic. Now she has recovered to the point where she can at least look at a picture of one without trembling – a significant improvement for someone who works in publishing.

Alan Cooper, a sports marketing consultant with a fear of flying, has now booked seats for the entire family to fly to Portugal for a holiday. He has learned to kill his fear with the power of logic – although he does rather wish his therapist could come with him on the flight.

Smokers, on the other hand, have not all found it quite so easy to regain control. Carole Holt, a mother of five who smoked 30 a day, has been one of the most successful. Through

Alan Cooper, happy to fly

consulting a psychologist, Dr Alan Norris, she has been able to tackle the personal problems which were at the root of her addiction and plan a strategy for fighting the habit. She has not smoked for three months. Andrew Duncan has not been so fortunate. He went to an anti-smoking clinic but found that a combination of blandness at the clinic and stress at work soon put him back on the weed again.

James Peters' problem was that he drank a little too much, with a daily intake of four pints of beer and a few glasses of wine. His solution was to attend Drinkwatchers, whose aim is to help mild problem drinkers.

'I went four times,' he said. 'It gave me a direction, some encouragement and some goals. I may not always achieve them but my drinking is far more under control than at any time in the last 20 years. I now do not drink every day, and I never drink at lunch-times.' For some volunteers, the

Charlotte Fleming, came to terms

answer to their problems could be only patience and acceptance. Charlotte Fleming, a competitive ice-skater who became so obsessed with losing some of her 12-stone weight that she developed a vomiting illness called bulimia, has now become resigned to her shape. 'It is not damaging my health and I would rather be eating and drinking what I like than dieting, which I do not like,' she said.

One particularly moving and encouraging result of Lifeplan concerns a teenager called Adam who had become a video arcade gambler, getting into trouble with the police and regularly deceiving his family. His father, who had remarried and lived abroad, contacted us for advice on ways to repair their troubled relationship.

Lifeplan suggested family therapy. Adam went with his elder sister Jane but they both found the one-way mirror, concealing a team of therapists, rather sinister. Jane sent him instead to Gamblers Anonymous. Since then he has made new friends in a new job, and has found the confidence (and the money) to take a girl out for lunch. He is beginning to pay off his debts to his much-relieved father and hands over his wages to Jane, who redistributes them. He swears he is no longer gambling.

USEFUL ADDRESSES

Addictions

Accept Clinic(Tranquillizers)
200 Seagrave Road,
London SW6 1RQ
Tel: 01-381 3155

Alanon(Alcohol)
61 Great Dover Street,
London SE1 4YF
Tel: 01-403 0888

Alcoholics Anonymous(Alcohol)
General Services Office:
P O Box 1,
Stonebow House,
Stonebow, Yorks YO1 2NJ
Tel: 0904 644026
London Helpline:
1st Floor,
No. 11 Redcliffe Gardens,
London SW10 9BQ
Tel: 01-352 3001

ASH(Smoking)
5/11 Mortimer Street,
London W1N 7RH
Tel: 01-637 9843

Drinkwatchers(Alcohol)
200 Seagrave Road,
London SW6 1RQ
Tel: 01-381 2112

National Society of Non-Smokers(Smoking)
Latimer House,
40-48 Hanson Street,
London W1P 7DE
Tel: 01-636 9103

Relief(Drugs use)
169 Commercial Street,
London E1 6BW
Tel: 01-377 5905

TRANX(UK) Ltd(Tranquillizers)
25a Masons Avenue,
Wealdstone,
Harrow HA3 5AH
Tel: 01-427 2065
     01-427 2827

Phobias

The Maudsley Hospital,
Denmark Hill,
London SE5

Thanet Phobic Group
47 Orchard Road,
Westbrook,
Margate,
Kent CT9 5JS
Tel: 0843 33720 (except Wed.)
(Send sae for details)

Phobics Society
4 Cheltenham Road,
Chorlton-cum-Hardy,
Manchester M21 1QN
Tel: 061 881 1937
(send sae for details)

WASP
10 Silverknowes Bank,
Edinburgh EH4 5PB
(send sae for details)

Marriage and parenthood

The Association of Sexual and Marital Therapists
Whiteley Wood Clinic,
Woofinden Road,
Sheffield S10 3TL

Centre for Personal Construct Psychology
132 Warwick Way,
London SW1V 4JD
Tel: 01-834 8875

Exploring Parenthood
39-41 North Road,
London N7 9DP
Tel: 01-607 9647

The Mastery Workshop
The Actors Institute,
137 Goswell Road,
London EC1V 7ET
Tel: 01-251 8178

National Marriage Guidance Council
Herbert Gray College,
Little Church Street,
Rugby,
Warwicks CV21 3AP
Tel: 0788 73241

Relationships
74 Warwick Avenue,
London W9 2PU
Tel: 01-289 5742

Sexual problems

The Association of Sexual and Marital Therapists
Whiteley Wood Clinic,
Woofinden Road,
Sheffield S10 3TL

The British Association for Counselling
37a Sheep Street,
Rugby,
Warwicks CV21 3BX

Institute for Sex Education and Research
40 School Road,
Moseley,
Birmingham B13 9SN

The London Institute for the Study of Human Sexuality
10 Warwick Road,
London SW5 9UG

Shyness and loneliness

British Psychological Society
St Andrew's House,
48 Princess Road East,
Leicester LE1 7DR
Tel: 0533 549568

The Times Management Course
Information from TMI,
50 High Street,
Henley-in-Arden,
Solihull,
West Midlands B95 5AN
Tel: 05642 4100

Security

Neighourhood Watch Schemes
Information available from your
local police crime prevention officer
who will also advise on crime
prevention in the home.

Sport

Sports Council Offices
London: Sportsline 01-222 8000
East Midlands: 0602 821887
Eastern: 0234 45222
North-west: 061 834 0338
Northern: 0385 49595
South-west: 0460 73491
West Midlands: 021 454 3808
Yorks/Humberside: 0532 436443

Work courses

Understanding Business Finance course
Monadnock International,
2 The Chapel,
Royal Victoria Patriotic Building,
Fitzhugh Grove,
London SW18 3SX
Tel: 01-871 2546

Runge Effective Leadership course
Balliol College,
Oxford

Young People at Work course
The Industrial Society,
Wira House,
Clayton Wood Rise,
Leeds LS16 6RF
Tel: 0532 780521

BIBLIOGRAPHY

You can learn more about the background to the Lifeplan questionnaires, and find advice on how to change aspects of yourself in the following books:

Brown, Paul, and Faulder, Carolyn. *Treat Yourself to Sex: A Guide for Good Loving* (Dent)

Cannon, Geoffrey, and Einzig, Hetty. *Dieting Makes You Fat* (Century)

Cannon, Geoffrey, and Walker, Caroline. *The Food Scandal* (Century)

Carrera, Michael. *Sex, The Facts, The Acts and Your Feelings* (Mitchell Beazley)

Comfort, Alex. *The Joy of Sex* (Mitchell Beazley)

Comfort, Alex. *More Joy of Sex* (Mitchell Beazley)

Cooper, Kenneth. *The Aerobics Way* (Corgi)

Craddock, Dr Denis. *The BMA Slimmer's Guide* (available from Family Doctor Publications, BMA House, Tavistock Square, London WC1H 9JP)

Durkin, Dr Kevin. *Television, Sex Roles and Children* (Open University)

Eysenck, H.J., and Wilson, G. *Know Your Own Personality* (Pelican)

Eysenck, H.J., and Wilson G. *The Psychology of Sex* (Dent)

Freedman, J. *Happy People* (Harcourt Brace Jovanovitch)

Glover, Bob, and Shepherd, Jack. *The Runner's Handbook* (Penguin)

Hanssen, Maurice. *E for Additives* (Thorsons)

Health Education Council. *The Guide to Healthy Eating* (available from P O Box 877, London SE99 6YE)

HMSO. *Manual of Nutrition* (available from HMSO shops)

Home Office. *Violent Crime, Police Advice for Women on How to Reduce the Risks* (available from local police crime prevention officers)

Lucas, M, Wilson, K, and Hart, E. *How to Survive the 9 to 5* (Thames Methuen)

Marks, Isaac. *Living with Fear* (available from McGraw Hill Company, Shoppenhangers Road, Maidenhead, Berks SL6 2QL)

Maryon Davis, Dr Alan, and Thomas, Jane. *Diet 2000* (Pan)

Melville, Joy. *First Aid in Mental Health* (Allen and Unwin) *Phobias and Obsessions* (Allen and Unwin) *The Tranquilliser Trap* (Fontana)

Nelson-Jones, Richard. *Human Relationship Skills* (Cassell)

Nicholson, John. *Men and Women* (Oxford University Press)

Nicholson, John, and Lucas, M. *All in the Mind* (Thames Methuen)

Robertson, I, and Heather, N. *Let's Drink Your Health* (British Psychological Society)

Sharpe, R, and Lewis, D. *The Success Factor* (Souvenir Press)

Zimbardo, P. G. *Shyness* (Pan)

INDEX

Numerals in *italics* refer to illustrations

A

Accidents, in the home, 67
Actors Institute, 93
Adaptability, 13
Addiction(s), 73-75
    alcohol, 73-74
    Research Unit, 75
    smoking, 75
    tranquillizers, 74
Aerobics, 41, 116-17
Aerosol cans, 67
Aeschylus, 78
Age, being your, 26-29
Aggressiveness, 12, 51
Agoraphobia, 72, 73
AIDS, 67, 86, 102
Alcohol, 73-74, 137
Altruism, 24
Ambition, 52, 83
Anxiety, 10, 13, 51, 135
    and learning, 113
Appearance, 13, 30, 34
Arachnophobia, 70-71
Assertiveness, 12, 51
Attitudes, 11, 15, 22-25, 68
    changing, 24-25
    formation of, 24

B

Badminton, 116-17
Baldness, 39
Beeton, Mrs, 58
Behaviour, 11
  therapy, 72
Bigotry, 23
Blake, Peter, *17*, 17
Books, 78-79
Botschinsky, David, *16*, 16
Branson, Richard, *18*, 18
Breakwell, Dr Glynis, 68
British Audience Research Bureau, 81
British Psychological Society, 68
Bronchitis, 66

Building Research Establishment, 67
Building Societies, 61
BUPA, 76
Burgess, Anthony, 79
Burgess, Yvonne, *63*, 63
Burglary, 62-63
Burton, Dr Mike, 68
Butane gas, 67
Byron, 78

C

Cable TV, 82
Calorie counting, 122-23
Car, psychology of the, 48-50
Centre for Personal Construct Psychology, 93
Change, six stages of, *8, 9*, 8-11
Children, 23, 60
    and accidents in the home, 67
    development of, 67
    of smokers, 66
Chilton, Jane, *18*, 19
Cholesterol, 126
Churchill, Randolph, 78
Circuit training, 116-17
Cirrhosis of the liver, 73
Cleese, John, 88
Clegg, Jean, *20*, 20
Co-habitation, 86
Collett, Peter, 82
Communication, 9, 96, 98-100
    non-verbal, 32, 100
    at work, 57
Computers, 68-69
Concentration, 8
Conformist dressing, 33
Connolly, Cyril, 79
Conran, Sir Terence, 46
Conservatism, 14
Contentment, 8
Control of Pollution Act 1974, 67
Coolidge Effect, 105
Cooper, Alan, *72*, 72, *137*, 137
Crawford, Michael, 128, *129*
Credit cards, 60
Cricket, 118
Crime, 25, 64-65
    abductions, 64

    assaults, 64
    burglary, 62-63
    muggings, 64
    prevention, 63
Cycling, 115, 116-17

D

Dale, Caroline, *131*, 131
Dampness in the home, 66
Davies, David, 46
Death, 28
    causes of in winter, 65
Decker, James, *43*, 43
De-humidifiers, 66
Depression, 66-67
Dickens, Charles, 79
Dieting, 120-23, 126
Divorce, 86, 87, 88
Douglas, Carolyn, 92
Dressing, 32-37
    body, *37*, 37
    conformist, *33*, 33
    egalitarian, *35*, 35
    élitist, *35*, 35
    flash, 32, *33*
    hard, *34*, 34
    individual, *33*, 33
    mind, *37*, 37
    respectable, *32*, 32
    soft, *34*, 34
    traditional, *36*, 36
    trendy, *36*, 36
Drinking, 53, 73-74, 83, 135, 137
Drinkwatchers, 74, 137
Driving, 48-50
Dysentery, 67

E

Edwards, Gillian, 93
Eldridge, Jeremy, 46
Electrical wiring, 67
Eliot, George, 86
Emotional versatility, 15, 85, 107
Envy, the chain of, 16-21
Exercise(s), 114, 115, 134
    slow-stretch, 116-17

LIFEPLAN ACKNOWLEDGEMENTS

Lifeplan questionnaires: We are grateful to the following for permission to reproduce text material and for assistance in devising new material: Professor A. Baddeley, C. Mansfield, G. Sik, Professor P. Warr.

Photography by: David Bailey, Clive Barda, J. Allan Cash, Sharon Chazan, Colin Curwood, Ros Drinkwater, Peter Dunne, David Hum, Tom Kidd, David Lavender, Iain McKell, K. McNulty, John Mason, David Montgomery, James Mortimer, Stuart Nicol, Chris Steele Perkins, Miriam Reik, John Rogers, Homer Sykes, John Timbers, The Sunday Times Photographic Library.

Illustrations by: Ed Briant, Michael Davidson, Dolores Fairman, Jeff Fisher, George Hardie.

Dressing the truth: *Respectable:* dress, bag, Jaeger. *Flash:* Clothes, Quasimodo. *Individual:* Leigh Bowery's own designs and make-up. *Conformist:* Marks and Spencer. *Hard:* suit, shirt, Dorothy Perkins; shoes, Next. *Soft:* dress, shoes, Principles; tights, Liberty. *Elitist:* Hackett. *Egalitarian:* Laurence Corner. *Traditional:* dress, Jean Muir; earrings, Butler and Wilson; stockings, Liberty. *Trendy:* Christopher Nemeth, Judy Blame, John Moore at the House of Beauty and Culture. *Mind:* Eat Your Heart Out. *Body:* Johnsons. *Styling:* Sue Odell.

Household Management Chart: compiled by Caroline Davidson.
Personality Growth: Hair by Howard at Vidal Sassoon, Make-up by Laetitia Rix.
Bedroom Politics: Bedlinen, Liberty. Mattress, Furniture Cave.
Sporting Matters Chart: Grundy and Northedge Designers.
Work: Pain or Pleasure? Research by Suzanne O'Farrell.
Height/Weight Chart: The Royal College of Physicians' 1983 Report on Obesity.
Healthy Home: Figures taken from a report by the Building Research Establishment.
Happy Families Cards: Malcolm Taylor Infomercials.

Illustrations supplied by Infomercials taken from *The Sunday Times Lifeplan* video.